TURNING TOWARD HOME

THE AMERICAN RETROSPECTIVE SERIES

TURNING TOWARD HOME

*Reflections
on the Family
from*
HARPER'S MAGAZINE

With an introduction by Verlyn Klinkenborg

NEW YORK

Published by Franklin Square Press, a division of Harper's Magazine,
666 Broadway, New York, N.Y. 10012

First Edition.

First printing 1993.

Library of Congress Cataloging-in-Publication Data

Turning toward home: reflections on the family from Harper's magazine/with
an introduction by Verlyn Klinkenborg; edited by Katharine Whittemore and
Ilena Silverman.—1st ed.
p. cm.—(The American retrospective series; v. 2)
ISBN: 1-879957-09-4: $21.95.
ISBN 1-879957-08-6: $14.95 (pbk.)
1. Family—United States. I.
Whittemore, Katharine. II. Silverman, Ilena. III. Harper's. IV. Series.
HQ536.T8 1993
306.850973—dc20
93-21852CIP

Book design by Deborah Thomas.
Cover design by Louise Fili.

CONTENTS

INTRODUCTION

Verlyn Klinkenborg

DURING HIGH SCHOOL I lived on a street called Bodega Court in Sacramento, California. The court was U-shaped, and its ends adjoined a busy thoroughfare, which grew steadily busier during the years my family lived there, so that we came to feel cut off from the suburban district our street naturally belonged to. To get to Bodega Court from the quiet, winding drives of Arden Park, most of which had improbable Spanish names and were lined with pleasant, ranch-style houses built in the 1950s, you had to enter the main flow of cars hurtling north or south on Watt Avenue. In doing so, the illusion of suburban torpor was soon dispelled. Even on foot you could not cut directly into the sea of houses that lay eastward from us. No one had made a path through the carefully fenced backyards, and in Arden Park there were no sidewalks anyway. To walk in that neighborhood as a teenager was to confess that you had no car or were too young to drive and were, therefore, somehow inadmissible.

There were nearly two dozen houses on Bodega Court in the late 1960s. I felt welcome in two in addition to my own, and I knew kids about my age from six other houses, though I associated with almost none of them. The inhabitants of another half-dozen homes—all on the far side of the court, around the horseshoe from us—I wouldn't have known on sight. But all the houses on Bodega Court had distinctive flavors even when seen from the street, flavors as sharply individual as though each house had been sculpted from a different cheese.

The flavors emanated not from the architecture or the landscaping but from what I imagined of the family life within, the strange adhesions going on behind the juniper foundation-plantings and punctilious camellias, behind the closed doors and picture windows. There was, I knew, a house where the women walked around in their underwear and the TV played all day and night and mayonnaise was a big joke among the men. There was a house spilling over with boys and dogs and fishing rods and bird guns and that had at its heart a wonderfully kind woman who once told me that a paste made from manzanita berries is good for a case of poison oak. The house next to ours had a swimming pool and a bomb shelter in the backyard and a stockpile of American vodka in the garage. There were girls in pancake makeup with uncertain hips and boys with sullen hair, and there was canasta and bridge among the adults. In some houses, it was really the furniture that drove to work or school every morning, and at night, when those neighbors came home, they turned back into their furniture—a recliner, a colonial rocker, and a heart-worn loveseat that was old enough to date but wasn't getting any offers.

When I think back on all those houses and families, I'm struck by a paradox. If I imagine each family on Bodega Court as a set of integers, I can see that there was really very little difference among them. Some sets were larger, some smaller, and one or two were missing a vital member that had once been present. The relationships that bound those integers together were only the familiar ones—spouse to spouse and parent to child—and, as sets of integers go, they were all pretty much of an age. So little variation! But when I imagine those families as humans dwelling in the jungles of their affection and disaffection, burnishing the walls with their shoulders and hips, when I think of the knots they tied and untied in each other, the miasmas they broadcast among themselves, and the objects and memories they accreted over the decades, objects and memories that were steadily losing or gaining significance to their owners, then I know that there was more variation within those apparently ordinary houses than I ever could have guessed at when I still lived among them. Then I remember that you can go no farther from home in this life than across the street from your childhood.

But you can't watch the neighbors for long, swooning at the oddity of their ways, without imagining yourself across the fence, looking back into your own yard. What strangeness have I become habituated to? you would ask if you could see your family as you see your neighbors. When I was much younger, I was a homesick child. Riding in the backseat of my parents' car at dusk through small towns surrounded by cornfields (we lived in Iowa before moving to Sacramento), I looked at the amber lights in the windows of houses along the road and wondered, almost longingly, what it would be like to live in them. But when the friends I knew best invited me to spend the night in their houses, only one or two blocks away from home, something in me would sicken, so much so that I would walk home alone in the darkness. I've thought about this for many years. What sickened me was not the strangeness of the lives my friends led—the unfamiliar smells of the cooking, the unaccustomed brands of toothpaste—but the fact that they saw nothing at all strange in those lives.

In high school, like most teenagers, I acknowledged the essential strangeness of my own family. In spirit I drifted away and looked back from a long distance, or tried not to look back at all. But only once have I seen my family as a collection of strangers essentially unknown to me. I had gone away to college, and near the end of my first quarter at Berkeley I came home to Bodega Court. It was November 1970, and in November Sacramento is often thickly beset with fog and drizzle. The house—3584 Bodega Court—seemed dark and close, almost stifling, not with heat but with the thickness of daily, household time, which had accumulated in the corners and along the baseboards and on the windowsills in the few months since I had left. My brother John had pneumonia and lay under a blanket on the family-room couch. My mother was, I think, just beginning treatment for the leukemia that would kill her not quite ten months later. Entering the house, I felt something much sharper and more durable than homesickness. I felt that somehow I was no longer accountable to these people, not in the old way, at least, and that they were enveloped by something from which I had been loosed. I wanted to run away for good and I wanted to burrow back in. It has taken me a long time to admit what I admit to you now, reader, something you have probably felt yourself: how much I longed to separate myself from my family and how much I have mourned my separateness ever since. Is it just because I'm a writer that I have always wanted to be on both sides at once—outside watching the amber lights burning in those houses of cheese, and inside looking out at the stranger looking in from the street?

It can be hard, as a writer, to understand your impulse toward candor, especially when family is the subject. When you're very young, writing about your family seems like the most natural thing in the world, if only as a means of keeping score. Later, when you begin to sense the power of language and to feel that everything you utter is significant (a bad time for any writer, a time of black shirts and filterless cigarettes), you wonder why anyone would ever waste precious words on something as inevitable, as trite, as irredeemable as family. This can be a hard stage to leave behind, even though as time passes most of us come to reappraise our families and to find an excuse (that is how we often put it) to love them. But writing is by nature an act of separation. You may acknowledge the part your family has played in shaping you as a human being and yet reject out of hand the notion that they had anything to do with your becoming a writer. I think that most writers, no matter how generous they are in forewords and acknowledgments and prefatory remarks and letters home, feel that as writers they have created themselves. They may claim to have been driven to the pen, as to the bottle, by their families, but the credit, they still believe, is uniquely personal to them.

As a writer you have the extraordinary experience of growing up to discover that the internal narrative you sustained as a child now sustains you. True candor comes only when the residual egotisms of the writer and the child have been set aside. But candor is a moral value— an impulse of conscience, if you like—not a literary value. There occurs a moment in a writer's development when you realize that there is at least an analogical connection between any two stories it is possible to tell. And so the stories you tell about your family stop being merely candid personal artifacts, and they become, if only implicitly, attempts to understand the shape of all families. You don't write essays about your family simply to expose its inner workings—for who has ever succeeded at that?—but to sketch the visible boundaries of what can never be known about any family.

Every story that is told obscures the stories that go untold. And yet the family stories that go untold do so not necessarily because they're forbidden or dangerous but because what we know about living in families comes to us not just from the content of our own personal narratives, the dramas and mock dramas we staged in our minds as children, but from the constant household accretion of minute details too numerous, too numbing to convey. What we know in the heart is the geological history of our families—the eons of hourly and daily sedimentation, which are eventually compressed into bedrock. But that history makes a very long story—too long to tell. So we talk about volcanoes and earthquakes and the day the waters rose over the rooftops and carried all the chickens into the next county.

THE HALLMARK OF any television family is its permeability, its openness to the audience. But the hallmark of real families—even happy ones—is precisely the opposite: they are closed to observation from without. Hence the security of family life, hence its danger, and hence, too, the sense of revelation you often have while reading essays like the ones gathered in this volume. Privacy is a construct, but it isn't always an intentional construct, and one of the hardest tasks a writer writing about his family faces is acknowledging what the privacy of family life has concealed even from him. I'm not talking about the subterranean tragedies of family life, like incest or abuse, but about simpler matters. Looking back at yourself as a child, you may—you probably will—detect that you lived a life very much unto yourself, a life full of secrets and privacies you didn't necessarily know you were maintaining. If you imagine family life, à la television, as the shared life of its members, you are likely to forget that family life is also, and perhaps primarily, assembled from what each member chooses to divulge to the others. It is the task of a writer to acknowledge those choices and to try to see what lies behind them.

When I think of the essays gathered in this anthology—essays taken from the pages of *Harper's Magazine*—I think of taking a walk around Bodega Court on a warm summer night, when doors and windows were open and when the block, cut off from the larger suburbs as it was, felt particularly—deceptively—cohesive. Anyone familiar with the word would have called Bodega Court a neighborhood, without reflecting on what an abstraction "neighborhood" really is. To see what I mean, imagine for a moment that each house on Bodega Court, or in the neighborhood where you grew up, truly expressed the individuality of the family within. Not in trivial ways—with an immaculate box hedge, for example, or an MG on blocks in the driveway—but in essential ways, in the very shape of the house, in the complexion of light that gathers under the trees, as if the house itself were a psychological projection of the family that inhabited it. You would quickly see, I think, that a neighborhood is defined more by the homogeneity of its houses, by the magnitude of what they conceal, than by any underlying similarity in the character of life lived within them.

Turning Toward Home is a neighborhood of the imaginary kind. To walk around this block is to marvel at diversity, not sameness. Here every house is a revelation. Here the neighbors hang their linen in the front yard, and here men and women discuss the beauty and the travail of their lives with unparalleled candor. In this neighborhood, the children meet in the boughs of a plane tree to talk over the astonishing things they have seen, to examine their own perspicuity, as it were, and to reflect on the intolerable dominion of adults. It is all done without self-pity. And though time plays like an opera in the background, filling the air with a sense of duration and loss, these are essentially timeless essays, the adult's sense of imminence balanced against the child's sense of eternity.

The themes that emerge in a family's life are largely accidental—a great illness, a bankruptcy, a sudden change of life. But in these essays, the overriding theme is knowledge: knowledge of joy, knowledge of guilt, knowledge of mortality, knowledge of the unintended family conspiracy. They are written as acts of communication, in which the reader is the beneficiary, but they are also written as acts of confirmation, to assure the writer of what he or she knows. And though no writer here explicitly acknowledges it, each of these essays is also "about" the minute volume of memory that an essay—whether it is as long as Richard Ford's "My Mother, in Memory" or as short as David Mamet's "The Rake"—can actually contain. As you begin to write about your family, you can feel the weight of memory pressing upon you, and you discover that each memory, no matter how complete, is a synecdoche for all other memories. But writing is an act of exclusion too, and what remains on the page—precipitated from the past—is knowledge, no matter how tentative it may feel in the writing.

It is the peculiar nature of these essays that the subject of their knowledge is the act of gaining knowledge—of coming to a kind of wisdom about one's father or mother or brother or sister. In almost every one of these works, you can feel a transformation taking place, from the mute understanding of childhood—when you scarcely knew what it was you knew about, say, your mother or father—to the articulate understanding of adulthood. In the transformation, something is lost, of course, for it is the character of explicit understanding, the kind that comes with adulthood, to drive out the intuitions that belong to our early lives. But something is gained in the transformation too. These essays contain many purposes: they memorialize our parents, they honor the intimacy of our homes, they describe the hard limits of a child's world, they acknowledge mortality. But most of all, each of them performs a task we are all engaged in when it comes to our families—turning myth into knowledge, marking terra firma where there was once only terra incognita.

So take a walk around this neighborhood of essays. Some houses here lie deep in repose. Some are aflame. Around some the flood-waters are steadily rising. In some of these houses, a quiet, unremarkable death is taking place, while the survivors reluctantly acknowledge that tragedy means more than dying. In this yard the dog bites, and in this one he licks your hand and rolls his eyes. There are fat ladies and mean men and kind parents all around the block. If you look carefully, you can see that history does impinge upon the families here, though from this street the big world sometimes seems like a distant place. And here is the odd part: in almost every house you pass there is a child, wide-eyed with helplessness—his only defense the swiftness of his perceptions. It is not that he means to write about his family someday—that is not why his memory is so good. But things stick, and what you can't forget you will someday try to put into words, if only to see what else you remember.

MY MOTHER, IN MEMORY

(AUGUST 1987)

Richard Ford

MY MOTHER'S NAME was Edna Akin, and she was born in 1910, in the far northwest corner of the state of Arkansas—Benton County—in a place whose actual location I am not sure of and never have been. Near Decatur or Centerton, or a town no longer a town. Just a rural place. That is near the Oklahoma line there, and in 1910 it was a rough country, with a frontier feel. It had only been ten years since robbers and outlaws were in the landscape. Bat Masterson was still alive and not long gone from Galina.

I remark about this not because of its possible romance, or because I think it qualifies my mother's life in any way I can relate now, but because it seems like such a long time ago and such a far-off and unknowable place. And yet my mother, whom I loved and knew quite well, links me to that foreignness, that other thing that was her life and that I really don't know so much about and never did. This is one quality of our lives with our parents that is often overlooked and, so, devalued. Parents link us—closeted as we are in our lives—to a thing we're not but they are; a separateness, perhaps a mystery—so that even together we are alone.

The act and practice of considering my mother's life is, of course, an act of love. And my incomplete memory of it, my inadequate relation to the facts, should not be thought incomplete love. I loved my mother the way a happy child does, thoughtlessly and without doubts. And when I became an adult and we were adults who knew one another, we regarded each other highly; could say "I love you" when it seemed necessary to clarify our dealings, but without pausing over it. That seems perfect to me now and did then too.

My mother's life I am forced to piece together. We were not a family for whom history had much to offer. This fact must have to do with not being rich, or with being rural, or incompletely educated, or just inadequately aware of many things. For my mother there was simply little to history, no heroics or self-dramatizing—just small business, forgettable residues, some of them mean. The Depression had something to do with it, too. My mother and father were people who lived for each other and for the day. In the Thirties, after they were married, they lived, in essence, on the road. They drank some. They had a good time. They felt they had little to look back on, and didn't look.

My father's family came from Ireland and were Protestants. This was in the 1870s, and an ocean divided things. But about my mother's early life I don't know much. I don't know where her father came from, or if he too was Irish, or Polish. He was a carter, and my mother spoke affectionately about him, if elliptically and without a sense of responsibility to tell anything at all. "Oh," she would say, "my daddy was a good man." And that was it. He died of cancer in the 1930s, I think, but not before my mother had been left by her mother and had lived with him a time. This was before 1920. My sense is that they lived in the country, back near where she was born—rural again—and that to her it had been a good time. As good as any. I don't know what she was enthusiastic for then, what her thoughts were. I cannot hear her voice from that time long ago, though I would like to be able to.

Of her mother there is much to say—a story of a kind. She was from the country, with brothers and sisters. There was Indian blood on that side of the family, though it was never clear what tribe of Indian. I know nothing about her parents, though I have a picture of my great-grandmother and my grandmother with her new, second husband, sitting in an old cartage wagon, and my mother in the back. My great-grandmother is old then, witchy-looking; my grandmother, stern and pretty in a long beaver coat; my mother, young, with piercing dark eyes aimed to the camera.

At some point my grandmother had left her husband and taken up with the younger man in the picture—a boxer and roustabout. A pretty boy. Slim and quick and tricky. "Kid Richard" was his ring name. (I, oddly enough, am *his* namesake.) This was in Fort Smith now. Possibly 1922. My grandmother was older than Kid Richard, whose real name was Bennie Shelley. And to quickly marry him and keep him, she lied about her age, took a smooth eight years off, and began to dislike having her pretty daughter—my mother—around to date her.

And so for a period—everything in her life seemed to happen for a period and never for long—my mother was sent to live at the Convent School of St. Ann's, also in Fort Smith. It must've seemed like a good idea to her father up in the country, because he paid her tuition, and she was taught by nuns. I don't exactly know what her mother—whose name was Essie or Lessie or just Les—did during that time, maybe three years. She was married to Bennie Shelley, who was from Fayetteville and had family there. He worked as a waiter, and then in the dining-car service on the Rock Island. This meant living in El Reno and as far out the line as Tucumcari, New Mexico. He quit boxing, and my grandmother ruled him as strictly as she could because she felt she could go a long way with him. He was her last and best choice for something. A ticket out. To where, I'm not sure.

My mother often told me that she'd liked the sisters at St. Ann's. They were strict. Imperious. Self-certain. Dedicated. Humorous. It was there, I think, as a boarding student, that my mother earned what education she ever did—the ninth grade, where she was an average good student and was liked, though she smoked cigarettes and was punished for it. I think if she had never told me about the nuns, if that stamp on her life hadn't been made, I might never have ordered even this much of things. St. Ann's cast a shadow into later life. In her heart of hearts my mother was a secret Catholic. A forgiver. A respecter of rituals and protocols. Reverent about the trappings of faith; respecter of inner disciplines. All I think about Catholics I think because of her, who was never one at all, but who lived among them at an early age and seemingly liked what she learned and those who taught her. Later in life, when she had married my father and gone to meet his mother, she would always feel she was thought of as a Catholic by them, and that they never truly took her in as they might have another girl.

But when her father, for reasons I know nothing about, stopped her tuition, her mother—now demanding they be known as sisters—took her out of St. Ann's. And that was it for school, forever. She was not a welcome addition to her mother's life, and I have never known why they took her back. It is just one of those inexplicable acts that mean everything.

They moved around. To K.C. To El Reno again. To Davenport and Des Moines—wherever the railroad took Ben Shelley, who was going forward in the dining-car service and turning himself into a go-getter. In time, he would leave the railroad and go to work as a caterer at the Arlington Hotel in Hot Springs. And there he put my mother to work in the cigar shop, where a wider world opened an inch. People from far away were here for the baths, Jews from Chicago and New York. Foreigners. Rich people. She met baseball players, became friends with Dizzy Dean and Leo Durocher. And during that time, sometime when she was seventeen, she must've met my father.

I, of course, know nothing about their courtship except that it took place—mostly in Little Rock, probably in 1927. My father was twenty-three. He worked as a produce stocker for a grocery concern there. I have a picture of him with two other young clerks in a grocery store. He is wearing a clean, white apron and a tie, and is standing beside a bin of cabbages. I don't even know where this is. Little Rock, Hot Springs—one of these. It is just a glimpse. What brought him down from the country to Little Rock I'll never know, nor what he might've had on his mind then. He died in 1960, when I was only sixteen. And I had not by then thought to ask.

But I have thought of them as a young couple. My mother, black-haired, dark-eyed, curvaceous. My father, blue-eyed like me, big, gullible, honest, gentle. I can think a thought of them together. I can sense what they each must've sensed pretty fast—here was a good person, suddenly. My mother knew things. She had worked in hotels, been

12

to boarding school and out. Lived in cities. Traveled some. But my father was a country boy who quit school in the seventh grade. The baby of three children, all raised by their mother—the sheltered son of a suicide. I can believe my mother wanted a better life than working for her ambitious stepfather and contrary mother, at jobs that went no-place; that she may have believed she'd not been treated well, and thought of her life as "rough"; that she was tired of being her mother's sister; that it was a strange life; that she was in danger of losing all expectation; that she was bored. And I can believe my father simply saw my mother and wanted her. Loved her. And that was how that went.

They were married in Morrilton, Arkansas, by a justice of the peace, in 1928, and arrived at my father's home in Atkins the next morning, newlyweds. I have no correct idea what anyone thought or said about any of that. They acted independently, and my mother never felt the need to comment. Though my guess is they heard disapproval.

I THINK IT is safe to say my parents wanted children. How many they wanted or how soon after they were married I do not know. But it was their modest boast that my father had a job throughout the Depression. And I think there was money enough. They lived in Little Rock, and for a while my father worked as a grocer, and then, in 1932, he was fired, and went to work selling starch for a company out of Kansas City. The Faultless Company. Huey Long had worked for them, too. It was a traveling job, and most of the time they just traveled together. New Orleans. Memphis. Texarkana. They lived in hotels, spent their off-hours and off-days back in Little Rock. But mostly they traveled. My father called on groceries, wholesalers, prisons, hospitals, conducted schools for housewives on how to starch clothes without boiling the starch. My mother, typically, never characterized that time except to say he and she had "fun" together—that was her word for it—and had begun to think they couldn't have a child. No children. This time lasted fifteen years. A loose, pick-up-and-go life. Drinking. Cars. Restaurants. Not paying much attention. There were friends they had in New Orleans, Memphis, in Little Rock, and on the road. They made friends of my grandmother and Bennie, who was not much older than my father—four years, at most. I think they were just caught up in their life, a life in the South, in the Thirties, just a kind of swirling thing that didn't really have a place to go. There must've been plenty of lives like that then. It seems a period now to me. A specific time, the Depression. But to them, of course, it was just their life.

Something about that time—to my mother—must've seemed unnarratable. Unworthy of or unnecessary for telling. My father, who was not a teller of stories anyway, never got a chance to recall it. And I, who wasn't trained to want the past filled in—as some boys are—just never asked. It seemed a privacy I shouldn't invade. And I know that my mother's only fleeting references to that time, as if the Thirties were just a long weekend—drinking too much, wildness, rootlessness—gave me the impression something possibly untidy had gone on, some recklessness of spirit and attitude, something that a son would be better off not to think about and be worried with. In essence, it had been *their* time, for their purposes and not mine. And it was over.

But looked at from the time of my birth, 1944, all that life lived childless, unexpectant, must've come to seem an odd time to her; a life encapsulatable, possibly even remembered unclearly, pointless, maybe in comparison to the pointedness of a life *with* a child. Still, an intimacy established between the two of them that they brought forward into more consequential life—a life they had all but abandoned any thought of because no children had come.

All first children, and certainly all only children, date the beginning of their lives as extra-special events. For my parents my arrival came as a surprise and coincident with the end of World War II—the event that finished the Thirties in this country. And it came when my mother had been married to my father fifteen years; when, in essence, their young life was over. He was thirty-nine. She was thirty-three. They, by all accounts, were happy to have me. It may have been an event that made their life together seem conventional for once, that settled them; made them think about matters their friends had thought about years ago. Staying put. The future.

They had never owned a house or a car, although my father's job gave him a company car. They had never had to choose a "home," a place to be in permanently. But now they did. They moved from Little Rock down to Mississippi, to Jackson, which was the geographic center of my father's territory and a place he could return most weekends with ease, since my mother wouldn't be going with him now. There was going to be a baby.

They knew no one in Jackson except the jobbers my father had called on and a salesman or two he knew off the road. I'm not sure, but I think it was not an easy transition. They rented and then bought a brick duplex next to a school. They joined a church. Found a grocery. A bus stop—though you could walk to the main street in Jackson from 736 North Congress. Also to the library and the capitol building. They had neighbors—older citizens, established families hanging on to nicer, older, larger houses in a neighborhood that was itself in transition. This was life now for them. My father went off to work Monday morning and came back Friday night. He had never exactly done that before, but he liked it, I think. One of my earliest memories is of him moving around the sunny house on Monday mornings, whistling a tune.

And so what my beginning life was was this. A life spent with my mother—a shadow in a picture of myself. Days. Afternoons. Nights. Walks. Meals. Dressing. Sidewalks. The movies. Home. Radio. And on the weekend, my father. A nice, large, sweet man who visited us. Happy to come home. Happy to leave.

I don't think my mother longed for a fulfilling career or a more active public life. I don't think my father had other women on the road. I don't think the intrusion of me into their lives was anything they didn't think of as normal and all right. I know from practice that it is my habit to seek the normal in life, to look for reasons to believe this or that is fine. In part, that is because my parents raised me that way and lived lives that portrayed a world, a private existence, that *could be* that way. I do not think even now, in the midst of my own life's concerns, that it is a bad way to see things.

SO THEN, THE part of my life that has to do with my mother.

The first eleven years—the Korean War years, Truman and Eisenhower, television, bicycles, one big snowstorm in 1949—we lived on North Congress Street, down a hill from the state capitol and across from the house where Eudora Welty had been a young girl thirty-five years before. Next door to the Jefferson Davis School. I remember a neighbor stopping me on the sidewalk and asking me who I was; this was a thing that could happen to you. Maybe I was nine or seven then. But when I said my name—Richard Ford—she said, "Oh, yes. Your mother is the cute little black-headed woman up the street." And that affected me and still does. I think this was my first conception of my mother as someone else, as someone whom other people saw and considered: a cute woman, which she was not. Black-haired, which she was. She was, I know, five feet five inches tall. But I never have known if that is tall or short. I think I must have always believed it was normal. I remember this, though, as a signal moment in my life. Small but important. It alerted me to my mother's—what?—public side. To the side that other people saw and dealt with and that was there. I do not think I ever thought of her in any other way after that. As Edna Ford, a person who was my mother and also who was someone else. I do not think I ever addressed her after that except with such a knowledge—the way I would anyone I knew.

It is a good lesson to learn. And we risk never knowing our parents if we ignore it. Cute, black-headed, five five. Some part of her was that, and it didn't harm me to know it. It may have helped, since one of the premier challenges for us all is to know our parents, assuming they survive long enough, are worth knowing, and it is physically possible. This is a part of normal life. And the more we see them fully, as the world sees them, the better all our chances are.

About my mother I do not remember more than pieces up until the time I was sixteen: 1960, a galvanizing year for us both—the year my father woke up gasping on a Saturday morning and died before he could get out of bed; me up on the bed with him, busy trying to find something to help. Shake him. Yell in his sleeping face. Breathe in his soft mouth. Turn him over onto his belly, for some reason. Feeling terror and chill. All this while she stood in the doorway to his bedroom in our new house in the suburbs of Jackson, pushing her knuckles into her temples, becoming hysterical. Eventually she just lost her control for a while.

But before that. Those pieces. They must make a difference or I wouldn't remember them so clearly. A flat tire we all three had, halfway across the Mississippi bridge at Greenville. High, up there, over the river. We stayed in the car while my father fixed it, and my mother held me so tightly to her I could barely breathe. I was six. She always said, "I smothered you when you were little. You were all we had. I'm sorry." And then she'd tell me this story. But I wasn't sorry. It seemed fine then, since we were up there. "Smothering" meant "Here is danger," "Love protects you." They are still lessons I respect. I am not comfortable on bridges now, but my guess is I never would've been.

I remember my mother having a hysterectomy and my grandfather, Ben Shelley, joking about it—to her—about what good "barbers" the nuns at St. Dominic's had been. That made her cry.

I remember once in the front yard on Congress Street something happened, something I said or did—I don't know what—but my mother began running out across the schoolyard next door. Just running away. I remember that scared me and I yelled at her, "No," and halfway across she stopped and came back. I've never known how serious she was about that, but I have understood from it that there might be reasons to run off. Alone, with a small child, knowing no one. That's enough.

There were two fights they had that I was present for. One on St. Louis Street, in the French Quarter in New Orleans. It was in front of Antoine's Restaurant, and I now think they were both drunk, though I didn't know it, or even know what drunk was. One wanted to go in the restaurant and eat. The other didn't and wanted to go back to the hotel around the corner. This was in 1955. I think we had tickets to the Sugar Bowl—Navy vs. Ole Miss. They yelled at each other, and I think my father yanked her arm, and they walked back separately. Later we all got in bed together in the Monteleone and no one stayed mad. In our family no one ever nagged or held grudges or stayed mad, though we could all get mad.

The other fight was worse. I believe it was the same year. They were drinking. My father invited friends over and my mother didn't like it. All the lights were on in the house. She swore. I remember the guests standing in the doorway outside the screen, still on the porch looking in. I remember their white faces and my mother shouting at them to get the hell out, which they did. And then my father held my mother's shoulders up against the wall by the bathroom and yelled at her while she struggled to get free. I remember how harsh the lights were. No one got hit. No one ever did except me when I was whipped. They just yelled and struggled. Fought that way. And then after a while, I remember, we were all in bed again, with me in the middle, and my father cried. "Boo hoo hoo. Boo hoo hoo." Those were the sounds he made, as if he'd read somewhere how to cry.

A long time has passed since then, and I have remembered more than I do now. I have tried to put things into novels. I have written things down and forgotten them. I have told stories. And there was more, a life's more. My mother and I rode with my father summers and sat in his hot cars in the states of Louisiana and Arkansas and Texas and waited while he worked, made his calls. We went to the coast—to Biloxi and Pensacola. To Memphis. To Little Rock almost every holiday. We *went*. That was the motif of things. We lived in Jackson, but he traveled. And every time we could we went with him. Just to be going. The staying part was never stabilized. Only being with them, and mostly being with her. My mother.

And then my father died, which changed everything—many things, it's odd to say, for the better where I was concerned. But not for my mother. Where she was concerned, nothing after that would ever be quite good again. A major part of life ended for her February 20, 1960. He had been everything to her, and all that was naturally implicit became suddenly explicit in her life, and she was neither good at that nor interested in it. And in a way I see now and saw almost as clearly then, she gave up.

NOT THAT SHE gave up where I was concerned. I was sixteen and had lately been in some law scrapes, and she became, I'd say, very aware of the formal features of her life. She was a widow. She was fifty. She had a son who seemed all right, but who could veer off into trouble if she didn't pay attention. And so, in her way, she paid attention.

Not long after the funeral, when I was back in school and the neighbors had stopped calling and bringing over dishes of food—when both grief and real mourning had set in, in other words—she sat me down and told me we were now going to have to be more independent. She would not be able to look after me as she had done. We agreed that I had a future, but I would have to look after me. And as we could, we would do well to look after each other. We were partners now, is what I remember thinking. My father had really never been around that much, and so his actual absence was, for me (though not for her), not felt so strongly. And a partnership seemed like a good arrangement. I was to stay out of jail because she didn't want to get me out. *Wouldn't get me out.* I was to find friends I could rely on instead. I could have a car of my own. I could go away in the summers to find a job in Little Rock with my grandparents. This, it was understood but never exactly stated (we were trying not to state too much then; we didn't want *everything* to have to be explicit, since so much was now and so little ever had been), *this* would give her time to adjust. To think about things. To become whatever she would have to become to get along from there on out.

I don't exactly remember the time scheme to things. This was 1960, '61, '62. I was a tenth-grader and on. But I did not get put in jail. I did live summers with my grandparents, who by now ran a large hotel in Little Rock. I got a black '57 Ford, which got stolen. I got beaten up and then got new friends. I did what I was told, in other words. I started to grow up in a hurry.

I think of that time—the time between my father's death and the time I left for Michigan to go to college—as a time when I didn't see my mother much. Though that is not precisely how it was. She was there. I was there. But I cannot discount my own adjustments to my father's death and absence, to my independence. I think I may have been more dazed than grieved, and it is true my new friends took me up. My mother went to work. She got a job doing something at a company that made school pictures. It required training and she did it. And it was only then, late in 1960, when she was fifty, that she first felt the effects of having quit school in 1924. But she got along,

19

came home tired. I do not think she had trouble. And then she left that. She became a rental agent for a new apartment house, tried afterward to get the job as manager but didn't get it—who knows why? She took another job as night cashier in a hotel, the Robert E. Lee. This job she kept maybe a year. And after that she was the admitting clerk in the emergency room at the University of Mississippi Hospital, a job she liked very much.

And there was at least one boyfriend in all that time. A married man, from Tupelo, named Matt, who lived in the apartment building she worked at. He was a big, bluff man, in the furniture business, who drove a Lincoln and carried a gun strapped to the steering column. I liked him. And I liked it that my mother liked him. It didn't matter that he was married—not to me, and I guess not to my mother. I really have no idea about what was between them, what they did alone. And I don't care about that, either. He took her on drives. Flew her to Memphis in his airplane. Acted respectfully to both of us. She may have told me she was just passing time, getting her mind off her worries, letting someone be nice to her. But I didn't care. And we both knew that nothing she told me about him either did or didn't have to match the truth. I would sometimes think I wished she would marry Matt. And at other times I would be content to have them be lovers, if that's what they were. He had boys near my age, and later I would even meet them and like them. But this was after he and my mother were finished.

What finished them was brought on by me but was not really my doing, I think now. Matt had faded for a time. His business brought him in to Jackson, then out for months. She had quit talking about him, and life had receded to almost a normal level. I was having a hard time in school—getting a D in algebra (I'd already failed once) and having no ideas for how I could improve. My mother was cashiering nights at the Robert E. Lee and coming home by eleven.

But one night for some reason she simply didn't come home. I had a test the next day. Algebra. And I must've been in an agitated state of mind. I called the hotel to hear she had left on time. And for some reason this scared me. I got in my car and drove down to the neighborhood by the hotel, a fringe neighborhood near a black section of town. I rode the streets and found her car, a gray and pink '58 Oldsmobile that had been my father's pride and joy. It was parked under some sycamore trees, across from the apartments where she had worked as a rental agent and where Matt lived. And for some reason I think I panicked. It was not a time to panic but I did anyway. I'm not sure what I thought, but thinking of it now I seem to believe I wanted to ask Matt—if he was there—if he knew where my mother was. This may be right, though it's possible, too, I knew she was there and just wanted to make her leave.

I went in the building—it must've been midnight—and up the elevator and down the hall to his door. I banged on it. Hit it hard with my fists. And then I waited.

Matt himself opened the door, but my mother was there in the room behind him. She had a drink in her hand. The lights were on, and she was standing in the room behind him. It was a nice apartment, and both of them were shocked by me. I don't blame them. I didn't blame them then and was ashamed to be there. But I was, I think, terrified. Not that she was there. Or that I was alone. But just that I didn't know what in the hell. Where was she? What else was I going to have to lose?

I remember being out of breath. I was seventeen years old. And I really can't remember what anybody said or did except me, briefly. "Where have you been?" I said to her. "I didn't know where you were. That's all."

And that *was* all. All of that. Matt said very little. My mother got her coat and we went home in two cars. She acted vaguely annoyed at me, and I *was* mad at her. We talked that night. Eventually she said she was sorry, and I told her I didn't care if she saw Matt, only that she tell me when she would be home late. And to my knowledge she never saw Matt Matthews, or any other man, again as a lover as long as she lived.

Later, years later, when she was dying, I tried to explain it all to her again—my part, what I thought, *had* thought—as if we could still open it and repair that night. All she needed to do was call me or, even years later, say she would've called me. But that was not, of course, what she did or how she saw it. She just looked a little disgusted and shook her head. "Oh, that," she said. "My God. That was just silliness. You had no business coming up there. You were out of your mind. Though I just saw I couldn't be doing things like that. I had a son to raise." And here again she looked disgusted, and at everything, I think. All the cards the fates had dealt her—a no-good childhood, my father's death, me, her own inability to vault over all of this to a better life. It was another proof of something bad, the likes of which she felt, I believe, she'd had plenty.

There are only these—snapshot instances of a time lived indistinctly, a time that whirled by for us but were the last times we would ever really live together as mother and son. We did not fight. We accommodated each other almost as adults would. We grew wry and humorous with each other. Cast glances, gave each other looks. Were never ironic or indirect or crafty with anger. We knew how we were supposed to act and took pleasure in acting that way.

She sold the new house my father had bought, and we moved into a high rise. Magnolia Towers. I did better in school. She was switching jobs. I really didn't register these changes, though based on what I know now about such things they could not have been easy.

I did not and actually do not know about the money, how it was, then. My father had a little insurance. Maybe some was saved in a bank. My grandparents stepped forward with offers. They had made money. But there was no pension from his job; it was not that kind of company. I know the government paid money for me, a dependent child. But I only mean to say I don't know how much she needed to work; how much money needed to come through; if we had debts, creditors. It may have been we didn't, and that she went to work just to thrust herself in the direction life seemed to be taking her—independence. Solitariness. All that that means.

There were memorable moments. When my girlfriend and I had been experimenting in one kind of sexual pleasure and another, quite suddenly my girlfriend—a Texas girl—sensed somehow that she was definitely pregnant and that her life and mine were ruined. Mine, I know certainly, felt ruined. And there was evidence aplenty around of kids marrying at fourteen, having babies, being divorced. This was the South, after all.

But I once again found myself in terror, and on a Sunday afternoon I just unburdened myself to my mother; told her *all* we'd done, all we hadn't. Spoke specifically and methodically in terms of parts and positions, extents and degrees. All I wanted from her was to know if Louise *could* be pregnant, based upon what she knew about those things (how much could that really have been?). These were all matters a boy should take up with his father, of course. Though, really, whoever would? I know I wouldn't have. Such a conversation would've confused and embarrassed my poor father and me. We did not know each other that well at our closest moments. And in any case, he was gone.

But my mother I knew very well. At least I acted that way and she did, too. She was fifty-two. I was eighteen. She was practiced with me, knew the kind of boy I was. We were partners in my messes and hers. I sat on the couch and carefully told her what scared me, told her what I couldn't get worked out right in my thinking, went through it all; used the words "it," "hers," "in." And she, stifling her dread, very carefully assured me that everything was going to be fine. Nobody got pregnant doing what we were doing, and I should forget about it. It was all a young girl's scare fantasies. Not to worry. And so I didn't.

Of course, she was wrong. Couldn't possibly have been wronger. My girlfriend didn't get pregnant, but only because a kind fate intervened. Thousands of people get pregnant doing what we were doing. Thousands more get pregnant doing much less. I guess my mother just didn't know that much, or else understood much more: that what was done was done now, and all the worry and explaining and getting-straight wouldn't matter. I should be more careful in the future if I was to have one. And that was about it. If Louise was pregnant, what anybody thought wouldn't matter. Best just not to worry.

And there is, of course, a lesson in that—one I like and have tried ever since and unsuccessfully to have direct me. Though I have never looked at the world through eyes like hers were then. Not yet. I have never exactly felt how little all you can do can really matter. Full understanding will come to me, and undoubtedly to us all. But my mother showed that to me first, and best, and I think I may have begun to understand it even then.

IN THE SIXTIES after that I went away to college, in Michigan. It was a choice of mine and no one else's, and my mother neither encouraged nor discouraged me. Going to college in Mississippi didn't enter my mind. I wanted, I thought, to be a hotel manager like my grandfather, who had done well at it. I do not, in fact, remember my mother and me ever talking about college. She hadn't been and didn't know much about it. But the assumption was that I was simply going, and it would be my lookout. She was interested, but in a way that was not vital or supervisory. I don't think she thought that I would go away for good, even when it happened that Michigan State took me and I said I was going. I don't know what she thought exactly. She had other things on her mind then. Maybe she thought Michigan wasn't so far from Mississippi, which is true and not true, or that I wouldn't stay and would come home soon. Maybe she thought I would never go. Or maybe she thought nothing, or nothing that was clear; just noticed that I was doing this and that, sending and getting letters, setting dates, and decided she would cross that bridge when the time came.

And it did come.

In September 1962, she and I got on the Illinois Central in Jackson and rode it to Chicago (our first such trip together). We transferred crosstown to the old La Salle Street Station and the Grand Trunk Western, and rode up to Lansing. She wanted to go with me. I think she wanted just to see all that. Michigan. Illinois. Cornfields. White barns. The Middle West. Wanted to see from a train window what went on there, how that was. What it all looked like, possibly to detect how I was going to fit myself among those people, live in their buildings, eat their food, learn their lingo. Why this was where I had chosen to go. Her son. This was how she saw her duty unfolding.

And, too, the ordinary may have been just what she wanted: accompanying her son to college, a send-off; to see herself and me, for a moment in time, fitted into the pattern of what other people were up to, what people in general did. If it could happen to her, to us, that way, then maybe some normal life had reconvened, since she could not have thought of her life as normal then.

So, at the end of that week, late September 1962, when I had enrolled, invaded my room, met my roomies, and she and I had spent days touring and roaming, eating motel dinners together until nothing was left to say, I stood up on a bus-stop bench beside the train tracks, at the old GTW station in Lansing, and held up my arms in the cool, snapping air for her to see me as she pulled away back toward Chicago. And I saw her, her white face recessed behind the tinted window, one palm flat to the glass for me to see. And she was crying. Good-bye, she was saying. And I waved one arm in that cool air and said, "Good-bye. I love you," and watched the train go out of sight through the warp of that bricky old factory town. And at that moment I suppose you could say I started my own life in earnest, and whatever there was left of my childhood ended.

After that the life that would take us to the end began. A fragmented, truncated life of visits long and short. Letters. Phone calls. Telegrams. Meetings in cities away from home. Conversations in cars, in airports, train stations. Efforts to see each other. Leaving dominating everything—my growing older, and hers, observed from varying distances.

She held out alone in Mississippi for a year, moved back into the house on Congress Street. She rented out the other side, worked at the hospital, where for a time, I think, the whole new life she'd been handed worked out, came together. I am speculating, as you can believe, because I was gone. But at least she said she liked her job, liked the young interns at the hospital, liked the drama of the ER, liked working even. It may have started to seem satisfactory enough that I was away. It may have seemed to her that there was a life to lead. That under the circumstances she had done reasonably well with things; could ease up, let events happen without fearing the worst. One bad thing did finally turn into something less bad.

This, at least, is what *I* wanted to think. How a son feels about his widowed mother when he is far away becomes an involved business. But it is not oversimplifying to say that he wants good to come to her.

In all these years, the years of fragmented life with my mother, I was aware (as I have said) that things would never be completely all right with her again. Partly it was a matter of choosing; partly it was a matter just of her own character—of just how she could see her life without my father, with him gone and so much life left to be lived in a not ideal way. Always she was resigned somewhere down deep. I could never plumb her without coming to that stop point—a point where expectation simply ceased. This is not to say she was unhappy after enough time had passed. Or that she never laughed. Or that she didn't see life as life, didn't regain and rejoin herself. All those she did. Only not utterly, not in a way a mother, any mother, could disguise to her only son who loved her. I always saw that. Always felt it. Always felt her—what?—discomfort at life? Her resisting it? Always wished she could relent more than she apparently could; since in most ways my own life seemed to spirit ahead, and I did not like it that hers didn't. From almost the first, I felt that my father's death surrendered to me at least as much as it took away. It gave me my life to live by my own designs, gave me my own decisions. A boy could do worse than to lose his father—a good father, at that—just when the world begins to display itself all around him.

But that is not the way it was with her, even as I can't exactly say how it *was*. I can say that in all the years after my father died, twenty-one years, her life never seemed quite fully engaged. She took trips—to Mexico, to New York, to California, to Banff, to islands. She had friends who loved her and whom she spoke well of. She had an increasingly easy life as her own parents died. She had us—my wife and me—who certainly loved her and included her in all we could. But when I would say to her—and I did say this—"Mother, are you enjoying your life? Are things all right?" she would just look at me impatiently and roll her eyes. "Richard," she'd say. "I'm never going to be ecstatic. It's not in my nature. You concentrate on your life. Leave mine alone. I'll take care of me."

And that, I think, is mostly what she did after his death and my departure, when she was on her own: she maintained herself, made a goal of that. She became brisk, businesslike, more self-insistent. Her deep voice became even deeper, assumed a kind of gravity. She drank in the evenings to get a little drunk, and took up an attitude (particularly toward men, whom she began to see as liabilities). She made her situation be the custom and cornerstone of her character. Would not be taken advantage of by people, though I suspect no one wanted to. A widow had to look out, had to pay attention to all details. No one could help you. A life lived efficiently wouldn't save you, no; but it would prepare you for what you couldn't really be saved from.

Along the way she also maintained me and my wife, at a distance and as we needed it. She maintained her mother, who finally grew ill, then crippled, but never appreciative. She maintained her stepfather—moved, in fact, back to Little Rock. She sold her house, hers and my father's first house, and lived with my grandparents in the hotel, and later—after Ben died—in apartments here and there in the town. She became a daughter again at fifty-five, one who looked after her elderly mother. They had money enough. A good car. A set of friends who were widowed, too—people in their stratum. They accompanied each other. Went to eat in small groups, played canasta afternoons, spoke on the phone, watched TV, planned arguments; grew bored, impatient, furious. Had cocktails. Laughed about men. Stared. Lived a nice and comfortable life of waiting.

Our life during this time—my mother's and mine—consisted of my knowledge of what her life was like. And visits. We lived far away from each other. She in Little Rock. I, and then I and Kristina, in New York, California, Mexico, Chicago, Michigan again, New Jersey, Vermont. To us she arrived on trains and planes and in cars, ready to loan us money and to take us to dinner. To buy us this and that we needed. To have a room painted. To worry about me. To be there for a little while wherever we were and then to go home again.

It must be a feature of anyone's life to believe that particular circumstances such as these are not exactly typical of what the mass of other lives are like. Not better. Not worse. Only peculiar in some way. Our life, my mother's and mine, seemed peculiar. Or possibly it is just imperfect that it seemed. Being away. Her being alone. Our visits and departings. All this consumed twenty years of both our lives—her last twenty, my second, when whatever my life was to be was beginning. It never felt exactly right to me that during all these years I could not see my mother more, that we did not have a day-to-day life. That the repairs we made to things after my father's death could not be shared entirely. I suppose that nowhere in time was there a moment when life for us rejoined itself as it had been before he died. This imperfection underlay everything. And when she left again and again and again, she would cry. And that is what she cried about. That we would never rejoin, that that was gone. This was all there was. Not quite enough. Not a full enough repaying of all that time together lost. She told me once that in an elevator a woman had asked her, "Mrs. Ford, do you have any children?" And she had said, "No." And then thought to herself, "Well, yes, I do. There's Richard."

Our conversations over these years had much to do with television, with movies we had seen and hadn't, with books she was reading, with baseball. The subject of Johnny Bench came up often, for some reason. My wife and I took her to the World Series, where she rooted for the team we didn't like and complained about the seats we'd moved mountains to get—for her, we thought. We took her on the Universal Tour. We took her back to Antoine's. We drove her to California and to Montreal. To Maine. To Vermont. To northern Michigan. To wherever we went that we could take her. We, she and I, observed each other. She observed my wife and my marriage and liked them both. She observed my efforts to be a writer and did not fully understand them. "But when are you going to get a job and get started?" she asked me once. She observed the fact that we had no children and offered no opinion. She observed her life and ours and possibly did not completely see how one gave rise to the other.

I observed that she grew older; saw that life was not entirely to her liking and that she made the most of its surfaces—taking a job once in a while, then finally retiring. I observed that she loved me; would sometimes take me aside early on a morning when we could be alone together as two adults and say: "Richard, are *you* happy?" And when I told her I was, she would warn, "You must be happy. That's so important."

And that is the way life went on. Not quite pointlessly. But not pointedly, either. Maybe this is typical of all our lives with our parents—a feeling that some goal should be reached, then a recognition of what that goal inevitably is, and then returning attention to what's here and present today. To what's only here.

Something, some essence of life, is not coming clear through these words. There are not words enough. There are not events enough. There is not memory enough to give a life back and have it be right, exact. In one way, over these years apart, my mother and I lived toward one another the way people do who like each other and want to see each other more. Like friends. I have not even said about her that she didn't interfere. That she agreed my life with Kristina had retired a part of her motherhood. That she didn't cultivate random judgments. That she saw her visits as welcome, which they were. Indeed, she saw that what we'd made of things—she and I—was the natural result of prior events that were themselves natural. She was now, as before, not a psychologist. Not a quizzer. She played the cards she was dealt. By some strange understanding, we knew that this was life. This is what we would have. We were fatalists, mother and son. And we made the most of it.

IN 1973, MY mother discovered she had breast cancer. It must've been the way with such things, and with people of her background. A time of being aware that something was there. A time of worry and growing certainty. A mention to a friend, who did nothing. Finally a casual mention to me, who saw to it immediately that she visit a doctor, who advised tests and did not seem hopeful.

What I remember of that brief period, which took place in Little Rock, is that following the first doctor visit, when all the tests and contingencies were stated and planned, she and I and my wife took the weekend together. She would "go in" on Monday. But Saturday we drove up to the country, visited my father's family, his cousins whom she liked, his grave. She stated she was "going in for tests," and they—who were all older than she was—put a good face on it. We drove around in her Buick and just spent the time together. It was, we knew somehow, the last of the old time, the last of the period when we were

29

just ourselves, just the selves we had made up and perfected, given all that had gone before. Something in those tests was about to change everything, and we wanted to act out our conviction that, yes, this has been a life, this adroit coming and going, this health, this humor, this affection expressed in fits and starts. This has been a thing. Nothing would change that. We could look back, and it would seem like we were alive enough.

Death starts a long time before it ever ends. And in it, in its very self, there is life that has to be lived out efficiently. There were seven years to go, but we didn't know it. And so we carried on. We went back to being away. To visiting. To insisting on life's being life, in the conviction that it could easily be less. And to me it seems like the time that had gone on before. Not exactly. But mostly. Talking on the phone. Visits, trips, friends, occasions. A more pointed need to know about "how things were," and a will to have them be all right for now.

My mother, I think, made the very best of her bad problems. She had a breast removed. She had some radiation. She had to face going back to her solitary life. And all this she did with a minimum of apparent fear and a great deal of dignity and resignation. It seemed as if her later years had been a training for bad news. For facing down disasters. And I think she appreciated this and was sharply aware of how she was dealing with things.

This was the first time I ever thought seriously that my mother might come to live with me, which was a well-discussed subject all our life, there having been precedent for it and plenty of opportunity to take up a point of view. My mother's attitude was very clear. She was against it. It ruined lives, spoiled things, she thought, and said no in advance. She had lived with her mother, and that had eventuated in years of dry unhappiness. Bickering. Impossibilities. Her mother had resented her, she said, hated being looked after. Turned meaner. Vicious. It was a no-win, and she herself expected nothing like that, wanted me to swear off the idea. Which I did. We laughed about how high and dry I would leave her. How she would be in the poorhouse, and I'd be someplace living it up.

But she was practical. She made arrangements. Someplace called

Presbyterian Village, in Little Rock, would be her home when she was ready, she said. She'd paid money. They'd promised to do their duty. And that was that. "I don't want to have to be at anybody's mercy," she said, and meant it. And my wife and I thought that was a good arrangement all the way around.

So then it was back to regular life, or life as regular as could be. We had moved to New Jersey by then. We had a house. And there were plenty of visits, with my mother doing most of the visiting—walking out in our shady yard, afternoons, talking to our neighbors as if she knew them, digging in the flower beds. She seemed healthy. In high spirits. Illness and the possibility of illness had made her seize her life harder. She wanted to do more, it seemed. Take cruises. Visit Hawaii. Go. She had new friends, younger than she was. Loud, personable Southerners. We heard about them by name. Blanche. Herschel. Mignon. People we never met, who drank and laughed and liked her and were liked by her. I had pictures in my mind.

The year was counted from medical exam to medical exam, always these in the late winter, not long after my birthday. But every year there was good news after worrying. And every year there was a time to celebrate and feel relief. A reprieve.

I do not mean to say that any of our lives then were lived outside the expectation and prism of death. No one, I think, can lose his parent and not live out his life waiting for the other one to drop dead or begin to die. The joy of surviving is tainted by squeamish certainty that you can't survive. And I read my mother's death in almost all of her life during those days. I looked for illness. Listened to her complaints too carefully. Planned her death obscurely, along with my own abhorrence of it—treated myself to it early so that when the time came I would not, myself, go down completely.

At first there were backaches. It is hard to remember exactly when. The spring, 1981—six years since her first operation. She came to New Jersey to visit, and something had gone wrong. She was seventy, but pain had come into her life. She looked worn down, invaded by hurting. She'd seen doctors in Little Rock, but none of this had to do with her cancer, she said they said. It was back trouble. Parts were just wearing out. She went home, but in the summer she hurt more. I would call her and the phone would ring a long time, and then her answering voice would be weak, even barely audible. "I hurt, Richard," she'd tell me, wherever I was. "The doctor is giving me pills. But they don't always work." I'll come down there, I'd say. "No. I'll be fine," she'd say. "Do what you have to do." And the summer managed past that way, and the fall began.

I started a job in Massachusetts, and then one morning the phone rang. It was just at light. I don't know why anyone would call anyone at that hour unless a death was involved; but this wasn't the case. My mother had come to the hospital the night before, in an ambulance. She was in pain. And when she got there her heart had paused, briefly, though it had started again. She was better, a nurse said over the phone from Little Rock. I said I'd come that day, from Massachusetts; find people to teach my classes, drive to the airport in Albany. And that's how I did it.

In Little Rock it was still summer. A friend of my mother's, a man named Ed, met me and drove me in. We went by old buildings, over railroad tracks and across the Arkansas River. He was in a mood to comfort me: this would not turn out well, he said. My mother had been sicker than I knew; had spent days in her apartment without coming out. She had been in bed all summer. It was something I needed to prepare myself for. Her death.

But really it was more than her death. Singular life itself—hers in particular, ours—was moving into a new class of events now. These things could be understood, is what he meant to say to me. And to hold out against them was hopeless and also maybe perverse. This all was becoming a kind of thing that happens. It was inevitable, after all. And it was best to see it that way.

Which, I suppose, is what I then began to do. That ride in the car, across town, to the hospital, was the demarking line for me. A man I hardly knew suggested to me how I should look at things; how I should consider my own mother, my own life. Suggested, in essence, I begin to see *myself* in all this. Stand back. Be him or like him. It was better. And that is what I did.

32

My mother, it turned out, was feeling better. But something very unusual had happened to her. Her heart had stopped. There had been congestion in her lungs, the doctor told me and her. He had already performed some more tests, and the results weren't good. He was a small, curly-headed, bright-eyed young man. He was soft-spoken, and he liked my mother, remembered how she'd looked when she first came to see him. "Healthy," he said, and he was confused now by the course of a disease he supposedly knew about. I do not remember his name now. But he came into her room, sat down in the chair with some papers, and told us bad news. Just the usual bad news. The back pain was cancer, after all. She was going to die, but he didn't know when she would. Sometime in the next year, he imagined. There didn't seem to be any thought of recovering. And I know he was sorry to know it and to say it, and in a way his job may even have been harder than ours was then.

I do not really remember what we said to him. I'm sure we asked very good questions, since we were both good when the chips were down. I do not remember my mother crying. I know I did not cry. We knew, both of us, what class of events *this* was, this message. This was the message that ended one long kind of uncertainty. And I cannot believe we both, in our own ways, did not feel some relief, as if a curiosity had been satisfied and other matters begun. The real question—how serious is this?—can be answered and over with in a hurry. It is actually an odd thing. I wonder if doctors know how odd it is.

But still, in a way, it did not change things. The persuasive powers of normal life are strong, after all. To accept less than life when it is not absolutely necessary is stupid.

I think we had talks. She was getting out of the hospital again, and at least in my memory I stayed around and got out with her before I had to go back to my job. We made plans for a visit. More going. She would come to Massachusetts when she was strong enough. We could still imagine a future, and that was exactly all we asked for.

I went back to teaching, and talked to her most days, though the thought that she was getting worse, that bad things were going on there and I couldn't stop them, made me miss some days. It became an awful time, then, when life felt ruined, futureless, edging toward disappointments.

She stayed out of the hospital during that time, took blood transfusions, which seemed to make her feel better, though they were ominous. I think she went out with her friends. Had company. Lived as if life could go on. And then in early October she came north. I drove down to New York, picked her up, and drove us back to my rented house in Vermont. It was misty, and most of the leaves were down. And in the house it was cold and bleak, and I took her out to dinner in Bennington just to get warm. She said she had had another transfusion for the trip and would stay with me until its benefits wore off and she was weak again.

And that was how we did that. Just another kind of regular life between us. I went to school, did my work, came home nights. She stayed in the big house with my dog. Read. Cooked lunches for herself. Watched the World Series. Watched Sadat be assassinated. Looked out the window. At night we talked. I did my school work, went out not very much. With my wife, who was working in New York and commuting up on weekends, we went on country drives, invited visitors, paid visits, lived together as we had in places far and wide all those years. I don't know what else we were supposed to do, how else that time was meant to pass.

On a sunny day in early November, when she had been with me three weeks and we were, in fact, out of things to do and talk about, she sat down beside me on the couch and said, "Richard, I'm not sure how much longer I can look after myself. I'm sorry. But it's just the truth."

"Does that worry you?" I said.

"Well," my mother said, "yes. I'm not scheduled to go into Presbyterian Village until way next year. And I'm not quite sure what I'm going to be able to do until then."

"What would you like to do?" I said.

"I don't exactly know," she said. And she looked worried then, looked away out the window, down the hill, where the trees were bare and it was foggy.

"Maybe you'll start to feel better," I said.

"Well, yes. I could. I suppose that's not impossible," she said.

"I think it's possible," I said. "I do."

"Well. Okay," my mother said.

"If you don't," I said, "if by Christmas you don't feel you can do everything for yourself, you can move in with us. We're moving back to Princeton. You can live there."

And I saw in my mother's eyes, then, a light. A *kind* of light, anyway. Recognition. Relief. Concession. Willingness.

"Are you sure about that?" she said and looked at me. My mother's eyes were very brown, I remember.

"Yes, I'm sure," I said. "You're my mother. I love you."

"Well," she said and nodded. No tears. "I'll begin to think toward that, then. I'll make some plans about my furniture."

"Well, wait," I said. And this is a sentence I wish, above all sentences in my life, I had never said. Words I wish I'd never heard. "Don't make your plans yet," I said. "You might feel better by then. It might not be necessary to come to Princeton."

"Oh," my mother said. And whatever had suddenly put a light in her eyes suddenly went away then. And her worries resumed. Whatever lay between then and later rose again. "I see," she said. "All right."

I could've not said that. I could've said, "Yes, make the plans. In whatever way all this works out, it'll be just fine. I'll see to that." But that is what I didn't say. I deferred instead to something else, to some other future, and at least in retrospect I know what that future was. And, I think, so did she. Perhaps you could say that in that moment I witnessed her facing death, saw it take her out beyond her limits, and feared it myself, feared all that I knew; and that I clung to life, to the possibility of life and change. Perhaps I feared something more tangible. But the truth is, anything we ever could've done for each other after that passed by then and was gone. And even together we were alone.

WHAT REMAINS CAN be told quickly. In a day or two I drove her to Albany. She was cold, she said, in my house, and couldn't get warm, and would be better at home. That was our story, though there was not heat enough anywhere to get her warm. She looked pale. And when I left her at the airport gate she cried again, stood and watched me go back down the long corridor, waved a hand. I waved. It was the last time I would see her that way. On her feet. In the world. We didn't know that, of course. But we knew something was coming.

And in six weeks she was dead. There is nothing exceptional about that to tell. She never got to Princeton. Whatever was wrong with her just took her over. "My body has betrayed me" is one thing I remember her saying. Another was, "My chances now are slim and none." And that was true. I never saw her dead, didn't care to, simply took the hospital's word about it when they called. Though I saw her face death that month, over and over, and I believe because of it that seeing death faced with dignity and courage does not confer either of those, but only pity and helplessness and fear.

All the rest is just private—moments and messages the world would not be better off to know. She knew I loved her because I told her so enough. I knew she loved me. That is all that matters to me now, all that should ever matter.

And so to end.

Does one ever have a "relationship" with one's mother? No. I think not. The typical only exists in the minds of unwise people. We—my mother and I—were never bound together by guilt or embarrassment, or even by duty. Love sheltered everything. We expected it to be reliable, and it was. We were always careful to say it—"I love you"—as if a time might come, unexpectedly, when she would want to hear that, or I would, or that each of us would want to hear ourselves say it to the other, only for some reason it wouldn't be possible, and our loss would be great—confusion. Not knowing. Life lessened.

My mother and I look alike. Full, high forehead. The same chin, nose. There are pictures to show that. In myself I see her, even hear her laugh. In her life there was no particular brilliance, no celebrity. No heroics. No one crowning achievement to swell the heart. There were bad ones enough: a childhood that did not bear strict remembering; a husband she loved forever and lost; a life to follow that did not require comment. But somehow she made possible for me my truest affections, as an act of great literature would bestow upon its devoted reader. And I have known that moment with her we would all like to know, the moment of saying, "Yes. This is what it is." An act of knowing that certifies love. I have known that. I have known any number of such moments with her, known them even at the instant they occurred. And now. And, I assume, I will know them forever.

FEELING SOMETHING

(JUNE 1990)

Bruce Duffy

IN THE FALL of 1962 I was eleven, still submerged in that murk, or sump, between childhood and puberty. The mind at eleven is raw and mistrustful, forever explaining life to itself, ruthlessly scrutinizing it like something wriggling on the end of a stick. I can still hear that boy's summoning, inward voice crackling like a police radio, trying to unscramble knotted feelings and worries about so many things that to him seemed either unreal or phony, like brownnosing or closing your eyes real tight when you prayed after receiving Communion. Descending from age thirty-eight to the silty deeps of eleven, I can still hear him say, *Come on, how can I cry in front of everybody in public like that? That really stinks!*

How could I cry? I had just lost my mother, and now everybody—my father, my relatives, and the neighbors—was watching me like I was supposed to sob or act some kind of way. But how was I supposed to act—even, say, if I almost *felt* like crying—without also "playacting"? I was stuck. For me, it was the scourged feeling of standing exposed before a wall of urinals in a packed men's room, a feeling of wanting to go real bad but being plugged and powerless to pee. *So everybody quit staring, huh!*

Even now, the intense self-scrutiny and impotence of those days seem like something dreamed. But no, I didn't imagine it. Several years ago, after meeting one of my favorite aunts, my wife playfully asked her what I was like as a boy. "Well, honey," said Aunt Rose coyly, with a darting smile at me. "Wellll, you might say he was one strange kid! One thing I remember. Nobody knew what in the dickens he felt when his poor mom died. He didn't seem to feel a thing."

Felt nothing!? Hearing this old slander, I wanted to fly back, *Christ, Rose, how could you presume that? Are you really that blind or naive?*

But I couldn't fight with my old aunt now. I didn't want to dredge up that old mess. So the matter of what I felt or didn't feel lay undisturbed until last summer, when a young man in a dark suit ushered me into the parlor where my father lay in an open coffin, looking smaller than his six feet three inches and clutching in his hairy, withered hands a black rosary.

His death had been sudden—a massive coronary—and I was his only child. His second wife, my stepmother, was on her way to the viewing, but mercifully for me, I had beaten her there, wanting a few minutes alone so that I might get used, like very deep, cold water, to the feeling of looking down on my father's shellacked face and the buzzing, black whorl inside his ear where the makeup so abruptly ended.

So odd, how we talk to the dead, trailing off, then resuming miles later in the bending force field of memory. Patting my father's immobile shoulder, I was saying squeakily, "Oh, Christ, Pop, why'd this have to happen, huh? Man, you didn't even have a chance to see your first grandchild."

Man. Suddenly, I'm calling him "man": death forces us to take queer liberties, two minds suddenly thrust together, memory to memory. For five minutes I stood there, muttering or half-praying in my head, when out of a kind of desperation to bring him closer, I did something impulsive, something inappropriate, perhaps, but to me intensely natural. This was an old impulse, something I used to do to him as a kid, whether to love or annoy him or both. Lightly, like a wing, I skipped my open palm like a Hellcat fighter plane over his bushy gray flattop, humming, *NYYYYeeeerrroowwwWWW*—

That's what got me. That dumb kid's love prank was what finally broke loose those jammed feelings—back to when his hair was bristly dark and tipped with light, back to 1958 and the summer in Maine, when, both wearing white bucks, really snazzy, we twanged two sprunged-out tennis rackets and wiggle-waggled our knees singing Elvis's "Hound Dog" and Mom got the hiccups, and it was such a riot—back when life was a given, and happiness ever youthful, the goodness surging in like a cold Maine tide.

NYYYYeeeerrroowwwWWW, and I was too much feeling something. Lurching off to the men's room, I turned on the spigots, washing my face of this blackness because people were coming and I still didn't understand a goddamned thing.

THE ODD THING was, for months before this I'd had this peculiar, gathering sense of my life as something fated. Slowly, my past seemed to be rolling toward me, heaving down hard, then rushing back with the heavy, dark purgings of ocean waves.

But why this prickly, fated feeling? I wondered. Maybe it was the imminent birth of our first child after two miscarriages that made me feel so dangerously lucky. On the other hand, maybe it was the two good friends who had just lost parents that made me feel this dark breath on my neck. Then again, if I was seeing the emergence of a certain curious shape to my life, that was also because I was actively *seeking* it. I was nearing thirty-eight, the age my mother was when she died. I guess I had always imagined that at thirty-eight we would converge, my mother and I. Catching her in age after twenty-seven years of pursuit, I thought at last I might better understand her life and what she felt when she left: I awaited that day when we would be not just mother and son but simply Joan and Bruce, as if we'd met at some raucous party of the memory.

But all the while my mother had been changing. After dying once, she had been slowly dying out of me as I grew into adulthood, dying twice and a dozen times, never leaving for good or remaining what she was but receding ever further, growing ever more the mocking dream. When I look back through my youth, I see my mother vanish repeatedly, only to return like a comet, here darker and more obscure, there more brilliant, and yet always returning in the bending bow of memory. And me always struggling, either to evade or deny her, like a man confronting an old lover, insisting that I'm strong and independent, hardened and now immune to her sting. We don't know our own hearts. After a time, once the spell of grief is broken, the truth is, we don't *want* the dead to return, that's our dark secret and the bitter root of our confusion. Oh, Mother, so many years I've spent running and never catching up, cursing you because I could neither catch you nor kill you as a memory, powerless ever to get free. Or so it has been until now, when the light shifts and suddenly I see I've surpassed you— when I must endure the cruel irony of growing older, perhaps even wiser, while remaining forever a captive child, ever subject to your fickle will.

But I wasn't just struggling with my mother all that time. For years after her death my father and I also fought, and fought bitterly. From my teens through my late twenties, my father and I were sucked through the undertow of a bitterness so progressive and consuming that I don't think either of us understood it, in either its unholy force or its prolonged and insidious effects. My chief consolation now is that when he died our days of warring were miraculously over—so resoundingly over that at times I still found it stunning that we could actually be friends, at times almost buddies. But this doesn't account for our former estrangement, those jumbled, tormented feelings of love, awe, contempt, and even hatred that I had for him when I was younger.

A premature death is never quite forgiven: after someone dies too messily, early, or pointlessly, someone else always gets blamed. I had, and still have, my mother's long nose and dark eyes, her small, insistent chin and bratty mouth. Maybe I was too much like her for him then, too flamboyant and playful, too cunning and desirous to put on airs and live, as she had, beyond our class and modest means. He was such a straight arrow, really. Maybe that's what he had found so alluring about her, the way she had so blithely lived the risky life he couldn't quite allow himself and certainly couldn't afford then—not when his business partner, taking advantage of his distraction, had screwed him and her hospital bills had all but wiped us out.

But what most irked him then was my "unfeelingness," as he put it. He hated the fact that her death seemed to have passed clean through me, leaving precious little grief that he could see and only my wild, obnoxious propensity to laugh at inappropriate times. I saw his pain. Yet why couldn't I give in, if only to ease his distress at watching our life unravel? I saw his red and silent face at supper, a glowering, slapped face that my hot ears could hear sneering, *Eat your food, you miserable little prick. Feel something.* And me in my willfulness, just staring him down in a so-go-cut-my-tongue-out way, hiding my true feelings while feeling such perverse contempt for him, that he shouldn't somehow have divined my obviously profound and courageous grief. And anyway, who was *he,* forcing me, like a criminal, to express remorse for a crime I didn't commit? He didn't know what I felt . . . *that was the point!*

Then, in a way, I guess, I irrationally blamed him for his failure to save her after the progressive botchings of a supposedly routine appendectomy. He always said he could have sued the hospital for malpractice, but as a matter of honor he said he wouldn't use the damaging information the doctors had given him against them in court. "Well, come on," he said, with that dour, mumps look he would take on when he felt beaten and intimidated by life. "Whatever else, the doctors acted in good faith." But hearing this intended note of reassurance, I only felt more frantic, outraged by his complacency and cowardice. "What do you mean, *'Good faith'*?" I stood there goggling at him. "They *killed* her, for Christ's sake!"

I thought he was a chump for swallowing that shit, for resolutely playing the gentleman while his partner bilked him and the doctors lost his wife. As a culprit I craved culprits, yet even so, the kid partly knew it was just a plain humiliation to see his proud father crippled with grief and the bills so punctiliously submitted by the very idiots he said had killed her.

My father was a complex mixture of power and passivity, a tall, commanding presence, with his bushy dark flattop. A former Eagle Scout and Navy lieutenant, he was an intense, compulsively active man, a mechanical engineer by profession and a man of intimidating prowess in the physical world—able to build a house or tear down an engine. In contrast to this powerful builder was the defeated man who emotionally would retreat, like a crab, into the ritual order of his workshop when life got too upsetting. This was the irascible man, the hopeless gumhand who, it seemed to me, could fix anything in the world but our life, the man who periodically would lash out at me as he did once about a year after she died: "What's wrong with you, you stupid kid! You never cried. Not one miserable tear for your mother. You faced me like a snowman—still do! Oh, sure, go on! Just gape at me with that sneaking, idiot grin smeared all across your face!"

EIGHT YEARS LATER—a century later, the chasm between 1962 and 1970—things between us were only worse. He couldn't stand me growing my hair and wasting his money studying English in college—this to him was "basket weaving," as deluded and impractical as my grandiose, gigolo plans of becoming a writer. ("Oh, sure! A big shot! Another way to run your mouth!") At nineteen, the day after I got my draft number (351, no chance of being drafted), I drove home from college and told him I wouldn't cut my hair, which was tantamount to saying I was leaving. But this familiar struggle wasn't merely about hair or values. For me, I think, it was about freedom from the past, one final expectoration of that swillish death-taste tinged with vileness and failure.

Yet was I really so ready to leave? I remember gently stopping him at the precipice, as he pulled the screen door shut, hopelessly asking if we might sit outside on the stoop and maybe *talk* for a while.

But it was way too late to talk. Mostly through sick silences we talked, the words sticking like fish bones in our throats, until I climbed into my faded blue VW and left. God, what a waste that was, the young, raw, pissed-off one driving away in stubbornness and the older one standing in stubbornness as if his feet were cast in cement.

For more than a year there was total silence, a contest, mano a mano, to see who could hold his breath longer. Then came years of brief, awkward reunions and holiday thaws engineered by my stepmother. In his stiff, resentful way he tried during these truces. In my sullen, arrogant way I suppose I tried, too, but it was still terrible. One way or another we always parted gored and heartbroken. After a curt, embarrassed hug I would walk into the cool darkness, feeling absolutely scalded before his all-too-evident bitterness about the waste and folly of my life, about the women who inevitably left me, and about my pigheaded delusions of eventually being published.

By the time I was twenty-six—a promising unpublished writer/security guard—there was still too much bitterness and mistrust between us to sustain much more than a punishing twice-yearly visit. Pride dies slowly. Only years later, when I was well past thirty and happily married, could he admit how during our warring years he would sit out back on the patio under the big maple. "Yeah," he said, gritting his teeth in that way he did when about to hook a fish, "on Friday nights I'd sit out there, half-bombed, just crying my damned eyes out, asking myself what I'd ever done to deserve you dumping me like that."

We both had tears in our eyes. Squeezing his shoulder, I said, "So why couldn't you ever pick up the phone? Do you think I ever would have wanted to put you through that? Do you, even for a second? I can't stand to think of you in pain, I can't. But how was I to know? With me you always acted like you were made of fucking stone."

Nothing is sadder for me than to think of him under that smothering tree, with the tears streaming down his stiff, red face. And, of course, he was deeply emotional. You can see this clearly in one unforgettable picture of him in our wedding album. There he is, sitting in the front row of the pine grove where my wife and I were married, his eyes wet, staring off into the trees, utterly oblivious to the camera and the people around him. It was my party-crashing mother, so long absent, who had visited him that day. Closing an ellipse of nineteen years, she returned to him as the ceremony was about to begin, intensely visible in the way that dust is illuminated by the spokes of noon, no ghost but rather a memory summoned by a power of memory. Later that evening, by the bar, he told my friend Steve, "You know, it's strange—I mean, to be with one wife while thinking about the old one. It's like getting stuck in a revolving door."

According to Steve, my father said only a few words more before he took his drink and drifted outside, out into the evening wind, under the rushing locust trees. Between two wives he stood: two selves and two pasts at the great white confluence where rivers marry the drowned to the living. So trapped he must have felt, so swamped between times, to have one wife inside, in that flushed warmth where everyone was dancing, while this other, younger one still abided in his mind, ageless and impervious in those rushing branches where the wind still stirred.

I think it's fair to say that three years ago, when I published my first novel, he was deeply shocked. Truly, he was strangely tickled that at last my thrashings and confusions had panned out. By then he had semi-retired from his heating and air-conditioning business. He'd had a mild heart attack, a good whiff of mortality, but he was still going hard, working part-time, testing an invention he was patenting, bicycling for miles, and traveling, first to the Mideast, then to Australia, then the next summer to Ireland.

I remember him as being more relaxed then, happier than he'd been in years, actually. I could say, with a child's condescension, that he had mellowed, but the truth is, we both had. Over the last two summers, my wife and I had an annual weekend with him down at the beach. My dad and I also talked regularly and—unusual for us—had several long lunches together. Unmistakable resemblance, the tall, graying older man with the perennial flattop and the tall, short-haired ex-hippie in the suit, the two of them gabbing and laughing, then rather fastidiously eating dribbling bay oysters, two platters, followed by gamy shad roe and bacon washed down with schooners of beer.

In his quiet way he was especially excited about becoming a grandfather. Just two days before he died, he and my stepmother came to our house with gifts—baby clothes, bedding, and a new stroller. What hurts now is remembering him sitting in the freshly painted baby's room, rocking in the maple glider chair, peering around the room, just smiling and luxuriating in the sheer, uncanny idea of it, a granddaughter.

TWO DAYS LATER I was up in New York, deciding on a new publisher. For three hours that day I'd talked with editors in two different publishing houses about a new novel—one about, among other things, the queer, continuing relationship between a child and a dead parent. But, God, the timing was rotten. Why dig all this up now, especially when my father was still alive? For months I fought it like a seasickness, feeling guilty yet mindful that the book couldn't be deferred or avoided.

But at last I'd made my decision to publish, and as I boarded the train for Washington, I was excited by a suggestion my new editor had just made. No sooner did I find my seat on the train home than I began to write the scene of the father picking up his son at school, then evasively explaining, in those fumbling conditional tenses we use for death, how the boy's mother might possibly die. Ordinarily, I never write on trains, yet now I wrote steadily, propulsively. Over the next two hours I covered nearly six pages in my notebook, describing that mysterious feeling of coincidence that accompanies death—that whammy feeling that out of millions of possible targets death should strike you. Describing the boy's inner thoughts, I wrote: *But still it could happen. It could happen like a ball whizzing straight for your head.*

For more than two weeks the kid's mother has been in the hospital, worsening to the point that for days the boy hasn't seen her. Shunted from family to family, the boy has hardly seen his father either, what with him being all the time at the hospital, mixed up in some kind of conspiracy with the doctors. But then one morning the boy is called up to the principal's office. Singled out! All the other kids aghast, watching him as he rushes out, his head engulfed in flames. But, hey, what's his dad doing at the principal's? "I thought we'd go home for a while," he says evasively, quickly ushering the boy out. Yet once outside, as they're getting into the car, the father says, "You know, we've gotta be prepared. I hope I'm wrong, but your mother could die, she really might. It's real close and, to tell the truth—well, things don't look too good."

The boy nods, but he can't fathom this any more than he can understand why, when they have such a short way to go, his father should keep fiddling with the radio dial like he can't find the proper, slithery frequency or words for this. But then, as his father fumbles, the boy hears his decoding head explain:

Even so, it could happen for real, you know. It could happen like a ball whizzing straight for your head.

Suddenly, the boy can see it. He's thinking of how he once watched a walloping line drive—*kapow*, right off the bat, screwing straight for his forehead. *Woof.* Powerless to move, he stupidly watches that widening white ball, knowing no matter which way he ducks it's gonna bean him for sure. And then, as he and his dad open the door to the house—the phone rings, and his dad looks at him scared, because, of course, now he sees it, too. That ball's burning for them both, and the kid just stands there, stunned in the doorway, wondering how he should act. Act surprised? Act upset and run wailing into his dad's arms? Act no way because his ears are ringing and he doesn't know how to act yet? But it's too late, because he knows, sure as sin, that whatever he does he'll be wrong—he'll be impure and phony because he wondered. He'll be wrong because he thought and didn't just act.

But, in truth, that ball was heading straight for me as I scribbled down this scene. After twenty-seven years, it was burning in again as my train arrived in Washington and my wife pulled up in our red Toyota.

"Boy, what a marathon day—" I swung my briefcase into the backseat. "Well, how are you?"

There were tears in her eyes. "I feel so bad," she wheezed. "Honey, your father died this afternoon. A heart attack. Your stepmother came home and found him dead on the bathroom floor."

I didn't cry then. I couldn't move. For the next hour, as I spoke to my stepmother on the phone, I fell into that same old ear-buzzing stupor, waiting for the pain to bloom and burn through—waiting in the transfixed way the boy used to hold a slow-burning match in his fingers, seeing how long he could stand it before flicking it away with a teary wince.

But this gray, dumbstruck phase passed soon enough. Once my wife and I got into bed, I cried all right. This time I felt none of the shame and prudishness the boy had felt before his father's red, exposed grief. Up in bed then, in my wife's arms, pressed against her pregnant belly, I learned again how to cry. Like an old song I learned it, with that same witless, eye-burning helplessness the kid had felt late at night, blurting into his pillow with the ends wrapped around his ears so his old man would never know.

In my memory the man asleep in the next room was no longer just affable old "Pop," not the "old man," "Dad," or that more forbidding word, "Father"; in my regressive state of mind he was not even remotely so well formed or sophisticated a concept. Rather, my mind reverted to the primitive squall of "Daddy," back to the point where you remember only the least and deepest, most lost and buried childish things: back to the "once" of that little creek by your house and him squatting beside you, when his hair was dark and life was still a wondrous, sunny, after-rain thing. Once his upturned shoes in the squishy, and once the echoes you two made in the darkness under the loud bridge, both bombing the water with rocks and whanging your little cap gun because, as you both knew, this was absolutely the wildest, most funnest thing ever.

That sublime coincidence of life was once him and you—actually, it was the both of you, and your mother, once. It was all of you, but the truly astounding thing is to lapse into that deep amnesia of childhood, that glimmering primordial lake when to you "Daddy," like "Mama," meant all in the world that was good. With that, it doesn't matter that you once fought with your father, or that once there were times when you seriously imagined hating him. You see, none of that matters now, because for some time you can't rationally speak of any of this, just as you can't, for the life of you, remember even a single thing bad about him.

Bound Upon a Wheel of Fire

(January 1990)

Sallie Tisdale

EVERY WINTER NIGHT of my childhood my father built a fire. Every element of the evening's fire was treated with care—with the caress of the careful man. The wood, the wood box, the grate, the coal-black poker and shovel: he touched these more often than he touched me. I would hold back, watching, and when the fire was lit plant myself before it and fall into a gentle dream. No idea was too strange or remote before the fire, no fantasy of shadow and light too bizarre.

But for all the long hours I spent before his fires, for all the honey-colored vapors that rose like smoke from that hearth, these aren't the fires of memory. They aren't my father's fires. When I remember fire, I remember houses burning, scorched and flooded with flame, and mills burning, towers of fire leaping through the night to the lumber nearby like so much kindling, and cars burning, stinking and black and waiting to blow. I loved those fires with a hot horror, always daring myself to step closer, feel their heat, touch.

My father is a fireman. My submission to fire is lamentably obvious. But there is more than love here, more than jealousy—more than Electra's unwilling need. It is a fundamental lure, a seduction of my roots and not my limbs. I am propelled toward fire, and the dual draw of fascination and fear, the urge to walk into and at the same time conquer fire, is like the twin poles of the hermaphrodite. I wanted to be a fireman before, and after, I wanted to be anything else.

Firemen are big, brawny, young, and smiling creatures. They sit in the fire hall with its high ceilings and cold concrete floors and dim corners, waiting, ready. Firemen have a perfume of readiness. They wash their shiny trucks and hang the long white hoses from rods to dangle and dry. And when the alarm rings, firemen turn into hurrying bodies that know where to step and what to do, each with a place and duty, without excess motion. Firemen wear heavy coats and big black boots and hard helmets. They can part crowds. They are calescent and virile like the fire, proud, reticent, and most content when moving; firemen have their own rules, and they break glass, make messes, climb heights, and drive big loud trucks very fast.

Forgive me; I am trying to show the breadth of this fable. I wanted to be a fireman so much that it didn't occur to me for a long time that they might not let me. Fires marked me; I got too close. The hearth fire was my first and best therapist, the fire-dreams were happy dreams of destruction and ruin. The andiron was the ground, the logs our house, and each black space between the logs a window filled with helpless people, my father and mother and siblings. The fire was the world and I was outside and above, listening to their calls for rescue from the darting blaze, and sometimes I would allow them to escape and sometimes not, never stirring from my meditative pose. If I felt uncharitable, I could watch the cinders crumble from the oak and cedar like bodies falling to the ground below and the fire turn to ashes while I, the fire fighter, sat back safe and clear and cool.

At odd times—during dinner, late at night—the alarm would sound, and my father would leap up, knocking dogs and small children aside as he ran from the house. I grew up used to surprise. He was a bulky man, and his pounding steps were heavy and important in flight; I slipped aside when he passed by.

The fire department was volunteer, and every fireman something else as well. My father was a teacher. We had a private radio set in the house, and we heard alarms before the town at large did. It was part of the privilege of fire. Before the siren blew on the station two blocks away, the radio in the hallway sang its high-pitched plea. He was up and gone in seconds, a sentence chopped off in mid-word, a bite of food dropped to the plate. Squeal, halt, go: I was used to the series; it was part of our routine.

Then my mother would stop what she was doing and turn down the squeal and listen to the dispatcher on the radio. His voice, without face or name, was one of the most familiar voices in my home, crowned with static and interruptions. My mother knew my father's truck code and could follow his progress in a jumble of terse male voices, one-word questions, first names, numbers, and sometimes hasty questions and querulous shouts. She stood in the hallway with one hand on the volume and her head cocked to listen; she shushed us with a stern tension. She would not betray herself, though I knew and didn't care; in the harsh wilderness of childhood, my father's death in a fire would have been a great and terrible thing. It would have been an honor.

The town siren was a broad foghorn call that rose and fell in a long ululation, like the call of a bird. We could hear it anywhere in town, everyone could, and if I was away from our house I would run to the station. (I had to race the cars and pickups of other volunteer firemen, other teachers, and the butcher, the undertaker, an editor from the local newspaper, grinding out of parking lots and driveways all over town in a hail of pebbles.) If I was quick enough and lucky enough, I could stand to one side and watch the flat doors fly up, the trucks pull out one after the other covered with clinging men, and see my father driving by. He drove a short, stout pumper, and I waved and called to him high above my head. He never noticed I was there, not once; it was as though he ceased to be my father when he became a fireman. The whistle of the siren was the whistle of another life, and he would disappear around a corner, face pursed with concentration, and be gone.

Oh, for a fire at night in the winter, the cold nocturnal sky, the pairing of flame and ice. It stripped life bare. I shared a room with my sister, a corner room on the second floor with two windows looking in their turn on the intersection a house away. The fire station was around that corner and two blocks east, a tall white block barely visible through the barren trees. Only the distant squeal of the alarm downstairs woke us, that and the thud of his feet and the slam of the back door; before we could open the curtains and windows for a gulp of frigid air, we'd hear the whine of his pickup and the crunch of its tires on the crust of snow. The night was clear and brittle and raw, and the tocsin called my father to come out. Come out, come out to play, it sang, before my mother turned the sound off. He rushed to join the hot and hurried race to flames. We knelt at the windows under the proximate, twinkling stars, in light pajamas, shivering, and following the spin of lights on each truck—red, blue, red, blue, red—flashing across houses, cars, faces. We could follow the colored spin and figure out where the fire must be and how bad and wonder out loud if he'd come back.

There were times when he didn't return till morning. I would come downstairs and find him still missing, my mother sleepy-eyed and making toast, and then he would trudge in. Ashen and weary, my father, beat, his old flannel pajamas dusted with the soot that crept through the big buckles of his turnout coat, and smelling of damp, sour smoke.

I SHOULD BE a fire setter. I should be that peculiar kind of addict, hooked on stolen matches and the sudden conflagration in mother's underwear and father's shoes. There are plenty of them, many children, thieving flame and setting its anarchic soul free in unexpected places. But I lack that incendiary urge; my Electra is more subtle, the knotty recesses of my own desires cunning even to me.

"What we first learn about fire is that we must not touch it," Gaston Bachelard writes in his book *The Psychoanalysis of Fire,* in the course of explaining the "Prometheus Complex" that the prohibition against fire creates. I talk about my father infrequently, always with hunger and anger; I build fires almost every winter night. But I've never built a wrong fire, and I worry over flammables like a mother hen. I'm scared of being burned and of all of fire's searing lesions. I class it with the other primitive, deadly joys: the sea deeps and flying—the runaway edge of control.

I fear one particular fire. My father was also an electrician, a tinker of small appliances. I am wary of outlets and wires of all kinds, which seem tiny and potent and unpredictable; the occult and silent river of electrical fire racing behind the walls can keep me awake nights. Electricity is just another flame, but flame refined. (In this way it is like alcohol: literally distilled.) Not long ago I put a pot of water to boil on my stove, and a little sloshed over; suddenly a roaring arc of electricity shot from beneath the pot and curved back upon itself. The kitchen air filled with the acrid smoke of burning insulation and the crackling, sputtering sound of short circuits, and I didn't have the slightest idea what to do. I wanted my father to put it out, and he was three hundred miles away. It seemed the most untenable betrayal, my stove lunging out at me in such a capricious way. It seemed *mean;* that arc of blue-white current burned down my adulthood.

Prometheus stole more than fire; he stole the *knowledge* of fire, the hard data of combustion. I wanted all my father's subtle art. I wanted the mystery of firewood and the burning, animated chain saw, the tree's long fall, the puzzle of splitting hardwood with a wedge and maul placed just so in the log's curving grain. I wanted to know the differences of quality in smoke, where to lay the ax on the steaming roof, how the kindling held up the heavy logs. What makes creosote ignite? How to know the best moment to flood a fire? What were the differences between oak and cedar, between asphalt and shake? And most of all I wanted to know how to go in to the fire, what virtue was used when he set his face and pulled the rim of his helmet down and ran inside the burning house. It was arcane, obscure, and unaccountably male, this fire business. He built his fires piece by piece, lit each with a single match, and once the match was lit I was privileged to watch, hands holding chin and elbows propped on knees, in the posture Bachelard calls essential to the "physics of reverie" delivered by fire.

I build fires now. I like the satisfying scritch-scratch of the little broom clearing ash. I find it curious that I don't build very good fires; I'm hasty and I don't want to be taught. But at last, with poorly seasoned wood and too much paper, I make the fire go, and then the force it exerts is exactly the same. That's something about fire: all fire is the same, every ribbon of flame the same thing, whatever that thing may be. There is that fundamental quality, fire as an irreducible element at large; fire is fire is fire no matter what or when or where. The burning house is just the hearth freed. And the fire-trance stays the same, too. I still sit cross-legged and dreaming, watching the hovering flies of light that float before me in a cloud, as fireflies do.

How I wanted to be a fireman when I grew up. I wanted this for a long time. To become a volunteer fireman was expected of a certain type of man—the town's steady, able-bodied men, men we could depend on. As I write this I feel such a tender pity for that little wide-eyed girl, a free-roaming tomboy wandering a little country town and friend to all the firemen. I really did expect them to save me a place.

Every spring we had a spring parade. I had friends lucky enough to ride horses, others only lucky enough to ride bikes. But I rode the pumper and my father drove slowly, running the lights and siren at every intersection and splitting our ears with the noise. We the firemen's children perched on the hoses neatly laid in pleated rows, bathed in sunlight, tossing candy to the spectators as though, at parade's end, we wouldn't have to get down and leave the truck alone again.

He would take me to the station. I saw forbidden things, firemen's lives.

On the first floor was the garage with its row of trucks. Everything shivered with attention, ripe for work: the grunt of a pumper, the old truck, antique and polished new. And the Snorkel. When I was very small, a building burned because it was too high for the trucks to reach a fire on its roof; within a year the town bought the Snorkel, a basher of a truck, long, white, sleek, with a folded hydraulic ladder. The ladder opened and lifted like a praying mantis rising from a twig, higher and higher.

Above the garage was the real station, a single room with a golden floor and a wall of windows spilling light. The dispatcher lived there, and the unmarried volunteers could bunk there if they liked; along one wall was a row of beds. No excess there, no redundancy, only a cooler of soda, a refrigerator full of beer, a shiny bar, a card table, a television. I guess I held my father's hand while he chatted with one of the men. In the corner I saw a hole, a hole in the floor, and in the center of the hole the pole plunging down; I peeked over the edge and followed the light along the length of the shining silver pole diving to the floor below.

I remember one singular Fourth of July. It was pitch dark on the fairgrounds, in a dirt field far from the exhibition buildings and the midway. Far from anything. It was the middle of nothing and nowhere out there on a moonless night, strands of dry grass tickling my legs, bare below my shorts. There was no light at all but a flashlight in one man's hand, no sound but the murmurs of the men talking to one another in the dark, moving heavy boxes with mumbles and grunts, laughing very quietly with easy laughs. My father was a silhouette among many, tall and black against a near-black sky. Then I saw a sparkle and heard the fuse whisper up its length and strained to see the shape of it, the distance. And I heard the whump of the shell exploding and the high whistle of its flight; and when it blew, its empyreal flower filled the sky. They flung one rocket after another, two and four at once, boom! flash! One shell blew too low and showered us with sparks, no one scared but smiling at the glowworms wiggling through the night as though the night were earth and we the sky and they were rising with the rain.

ONLY RECENTLY HAVE I seen how much more occurred, hidden beneath the surface of his life. I presumed too much, the way all children do. It wasn't only lack of sleep that peeled my father's face bald in a fire's dousing. He hates fire. Hates burning mills; they last all night and the next day like balefires signaling a battle. He hated every falling beam that shot arrows of flame and the sheets of fire that curtain rooms. And bodies: I heard only snatches of stories, words drifting up the stairs in the middle of the night after a fire as he talked to my mother in the living room in the dark. Pieces of bodies stuck to bedsprings like steaks to a grill, and, once, the ruin of dynamite. When my mother died I asked about cremation, and he flung it away with a meaty hand and chose a solid, airtight coffin. He sees the stake in fire. He suffered the fear of going in.

I was visiting my father last year, at Christmastime. There are always fires at Christmastime, mostly trees turning to torches and chimneys flaring like Roman candles. And sure enough, the alarm sounded early in the evening, the same bright squeal from the same radio, for a flue fire. There have been a thousand flue fires in his life. (Each one is different, he tells me.)

As it happened, this time it was our neighbor's flue, across the street, on Christmas Eve, and I put shoes on the kids and we dashed across to watch the circus, so fortunately near. The trucks maneuvered their length in the narrow street, bouncing over curbs and closing in, and before the trucks stopped the men were off and running, each with a job, snicking open panels, slipping levers, turning valves. We crept inside the lines and knelt beside the big wheels of the pumper, unnoticed. The world was a bustle of men with terse voices, the red and blue lights spinning round, the snaking hose erect with pressure. The men were hepped up, snappy with the brisk demands. And the house—the neighbor's house I'd seen so many times before—had gone strange, a bud blooming fire, a ribbon of light behind a dark window. Men went in, faces down.

My father doesn't go in anymore. He's gotten too old, and the rules have changed; young men arrive, old men watch and wait. He still drives the truck. He lives for it, for the history and the books, his models, the stories, meetings, card games. But he's like a rooster plucked; I have a girlish song for Daddy, but I sing it too far away for him to hear.

I wanted to feel the hot dry cheeks of fever and roast with the rest of them. I wanted to go in, and I kept on wanting to long after my father and the others told me I couldn't be a fireman because I wasn't a man. I wanted to be the defender, to have the chance to do something inarguably good, pit myself against the blaze. I wanted it long after I grew up and became something else altogether, and I want it still.

"That which has been licked by fire has a different taste in the mouths of men," writes Bachelard. He means food, but when I read that I thought of men, firemen, and how men licked by fire have a different taste to me.

I live in a city now, and the fire fighters aren't volunteers. They're college graduates in Fire Science, and a few are women, smaller than the men but just as tough, women who took the steps I wouldn't—or couldn't—take. Still, I imagine big, brawny men sitting at too-small desks in little rooms lit with fluorescent lights, earnestly taking notes. They hear lectures on the chemistry of burning insulation, exponential curves of heat expansion, the codes of blueprint. They make good notes in small handwriting on lined, white paper, the pens little in their solid hands.

Too much muscle and nerve in these men and women both, these firemen; they need alarms, demands, heavy loads to carry up steep stairs. They need fires; the school desks are trembling, puny things, where they listen to men like my father, weary with the work of it, describing the secrets of going in.

Between Father and Daughter

(April 1992)

Reginald Gibbons

BUCKLED INTO THE cramped backseat, she sings to herself as I drive toward her school through the town streets. Straining upward to see out her window, she watches the things that go by, the ones she sees—I know only that some of them are the houses we sometimes say we wish were ours. But today as we pass them we only think it; or I do, while she's singing—the big yellow one with a roofed portico for cars never there, the pink stucco one with red shutters that's her favorite. Most of what she sings rhymes as it unwinds in the direction she goes with it. Half the way to school she sings, and then she stops, the song becomes a secret she'd rather keep to herself, the underground sweet-water stream through the tiny continent of her, on which her high oboe voice floats through forests softly, the calling of a hidden pensive bird—this is the way I strain my grasp to imagine what it's like for her to be thinking of things, to herself, to be feeling her happiness or fear.

After I leave her inside the school, which was converted from an old house in whose kitchen you can almost still smell the fruit being cooked down for canning, she waves good-bye from a window, and I can make her cover her mouth with one hand and laugh and roll her eyes at a small classmate if I cavort a little down the walk.

In some of her paintings, the sun's red and has teeth but the houses are cheerful, and fat flying birds with almost human faces and long

61

noses for beaks sail downward toward the earth, where her giant bright flowers overshadow like trees the people she draws.

At the end of the day, her naked delight in the bath is delight in a lake of still pleasures, a straight unhurried sailing in a good breeze, and a luxurious trust that there will always be this calm warm weather, and someone's hand to steer and steady the skiff of her. Ashore, orchards are blooming.

Before I get into bed with her mother at night, in our house, I look in on her and watch her sleeping hands come near her face to sweep away what's bothering her dreaming eyes. I ease my hand under her back and lift her from the edge of the bed to the center. I can almost catch the whole span of her shoulders in one hand—five pears or peaches, it might be, dreaming in a delicate basket—till they tip with their own live weight and slip from my grasp.

SOMETHING NEEDS TO be done—like dragging a big black plastic sack through the upstairs rooms, emptying into it each wastebasket, the trash of three lives for a week or so. I am careful and slow about it, so that this little chore will banish the big ones. But I leave the bag lying on the floor and I go into my daughter's bedroom, into the north morning light from her windows, and while this minute she is at school counting or spelling a first useful word I sit down on her unmade bed and I look out the windows at nothing for a while, the unmoving buildings—houses and a church—in the cold street.

Across it a dark young man is coming slowly down the white sidewalk with a snow shovel over his shoulder. He's wearing only a light coat, there's a plastic shower cap under his navy-blue knit hat, and at a house where the walk hasn't been cleared he climbs the steps and rings the doorbell and stands waiting, squinting sideways at the wind. Then he says a few words I can't hear to the storm door that doesn't open, and he nods his head with the kindly farewell that is a habit he wears as disguise, and he goes back down the steps and on to the next house. All of this in pantomime, the way I see it through windows closed against winter and the faint sounds of winter.

My daughter's cross-eyed piggy bank is also staring out blankly, and in its belly are four dollar bills that came one at a time from her grand-mother and which tomorrow she will pull out of the corked mouth-hole. (It's not like the piggy banks you have to fill before you empty them because to empty them you have to smash them.) Tomorrow she will buy a perfect piece of small furniture for her warm well-lit doll-house where no one is tired or weak and the wind can't get in.

Sitting on her bed, looking out, I didn't see the lame neighbor child, bundled up and out of school and even turned out of the house for a while, or the blind woman with burns or the sick veteran—people who might have walked past, stoop-shouldered with what's happened and will keep happening to them. So much limping is not from physical pain—the pain is gone now, but the leg's still crooked. The piggy bank and I see only the able young man whose straight back nobody needs.

When he finally gets past where I can see him, it feels as if a kind of music has stopped, and it's more completely quiet than it was, an emptiness more than a stillness, and I get up from the rumpled bed and smooth the covers, slowly and carefully, and look around the room for something to pick up or straighten, and take a wadded dol-lar bill from my pocket and put it into the pig, and walk out.

AFTER SHE HAD been in her first school for months already, one afternoon at home she was crying because of something a friend had done or maybe only said to her, and I was trying to offer some solace, some distraction, when she nearly shouted all of a sudden, "You and Mommy left without even saying good-bye to me!" I said—shocked to have caused a wound so lingering that other pain must inevitably lead back to it—"When?"

"The first day of kindergarten," she said, and she really began to wail, looking up at the ceiling, tears pouring from her, her face crumpling.

"But you wanted us to leave! You were lined up with the other kids to go into class behind the teacher. I thought you were happy to go in!"

"But the other parents were still there! And you left without even saying good-bye!" she said. The way rain can arrive with a violent flur-ry of pouring and thunder but then settles into a steady fall that is the real rain, that will after a while flood gutters and basements and streets and fields and rivers till there's damage it will take time to repair—so she settled wearily and deeply into her crying.

However a wound was caused, it is already there, it can't be undone, it needs to be healed.

My child is standing before me on the steps down to the back door, her eyes level with mine as I sit on a higher step holding both her hands, and she is crying as if she will never stop, and the friend's slight is forgotten, the first day of kindergarten is forgotten, there is deeper sorrow than that, incomprehensible and punishing, and for now I am pouring over her the unslakable longing and helpless protective presentiment that bind me irremediably to her in love, and I understand again what I must do as long as she and I live, and how much I want to do this, to love her, and need to, and how, too, it is not enough. It is in the way of things, and no blame on anyone for it, that it is not enough.

A WOMAN'S WORK

(MAY 1993)

Louise Erdrich

WE CONCEIVE OUR children in deepest night, in blazing sun, out-doors, in barns and alleys and minivans. We have no rules, no cere-monies; we don't even need a driver's license. Conception is often something of a by-product of sex, a candle in a one-room studio, pure brute chance, a wonder. To make love with the desire for a child between two people is to move the act out of its singularity, to make the need of the moment an eternal wish. But of all passing notions, that of a human being for a child is perhaps the purest in the abstract, and the most complicated in reality. Growing, bearing, mothering or fathering, supporting, and at last letting go of an infant are powerful and mun-dane creative acts that rapturously suck up whole chunks of life.

Other parents—one New Hampshire's first female judge, another my own midwife, yet another a perpetually overwhelmed movie researcher and television producer, and our neighbor, who baby-sits to make a difficult living—seem surprised at their own helplessness in the face of the passion they feel for their children. We live and work with a divided consciousness. It is a beautiful enough shock to fall in love with another adult, to feel the possibility of unbearable sorrow at the loss of that other, essential personality, expressed just so, that par-ticular touch. But love of an infant is of a different order. It is twinned love, all-absorbing, a blur of boundaries and messages. It is uncomfortably close to self-erasure, and in the face of it one's fat ambitions, desperations, private icons, and urges fall away into a dreamlike *before* that haunts and forces itself into the present with tough persistence.

The self will not be forced under, nor will the baby's needs gracefully retreat. The world tips away when we look into our children's faces. The days flood by. Time with children runs through our fingers like water as we lift our hands, try to hold, to capture, to fix moments in a lens, a magic circle of images or words. We snap photos, videotape, memorialize while we experience a fast forward in which there is no replay of even a single instant.

One such year, all I can do is take notes. We have a baby: our sixth child, our third birth. During that year, our older adopted children hit adolescence like runaway trucks. Dear grandparents weaken and die. My husband, Michael, and I both work full-time. He rises at four in the morning, hardly seems to sleep at all, juggles schedules, his own work, and day-care trips. To keep the door to the other self, the writing self, open, I scratch messages on the envelopes of letters I can't answer, in the margins of books I'm too tired to review. On pharmacy prescription bags, dime-store notebooks, children's construction paper, I keep writing. The fragments accumulate, the jotted scraps become a journal.

OCTOBER. FIRST SNOW AND SECOND TRIMESTER

The small gray house where I work is across the road from the old, red renovated farmhouse where we live. My office was built in the hope of feeding snowmobilers. Twenty years ago, a rough trail was carved out of the New Hampshire timberland a hundred yards from the door. Buzzing down from the trailhead—hidden now by a thick growth of pine and maple—bundled riders were supposed to stop here for hot chocolate, hot dogs, doughnuts drizzled with maple syrup. But the plan fell through before it could be tested, and all this long winter I will hear no more than a dozen snowmobilers pass by, though the snowfall is deep. The oddly shaped door in my back room opens where the counter was supposed to be, but instead of a stove and deep fryer, books line the walls.

In its first years this place was rented out to a series of people who believed themselves handy with tools, and as a result it is a strange house: constantly improved, but still missing fixtures, light-socket covers, cupboard doors. The man who drove a Pepsi delivery truck for a living fit together a wall of bricks behind the small, black wood stove. One renter cultivated a marijuana patch at a secluded edge of our land, put down a carpet, and punched round fist holes into the Sheetrock one night in a jealous fit. Those who've lived in this house haunt it, and their dogs do too. The brown Doberman, the harlequin Great Dane, and the two willful breedless dogs with wide muzzles, short hair, and horrifying growls have laid out invisible and maybe eternal territories of scent—lines our gentle dog still won't cross.

There was also, in this house's short life, a suicide. I don't know much about him except that he was young, lived alone, rode a motorcycle to work. I don't know where in the house he was when he shot himself. I do not want to know, except I do know. There is only one place. It is here, where I sit, before the window, looking out into the dark shapes of trees.

Perhaps it is odd to contemplate a subject as grim as suicide while anticipating a child so new she'll have a navel tassel and smell of nothing but her purest self. But beginnings suggest endings, and I can't help thinking about the continuum, the span, the afters, and the befores.

I come here every day to work, starting while invisibly pregnant. I imagine myself somewhere else, into another skin, another person, another time. Yet simultaneously my body is constructing its own character. It requires no thought at all for me to form and fix a whole other person. First she is nothing, then she is growing and dividing at such a rate I think I'll drop. I come here in ecstasy and afraid of labor, all at once, for this is the heart of the matter. No matter what else I do, when it comes to pregnancy I am my physical self first, as are all of us women. We can pump gas, lift weights, head a corporation, tune pianos. Still, our bodies are rounded vases of skin and bones and blood that seem impossibly engineered for birth. I look down at my smooth, huge lap, feel my baby twist, and I can't figure out how I'll ever stretch wide enough. I fear I've made a ship inside a bottle. I'll have to break. I'm not myself. I feel myself becoming less a person than a place, inhabited, a foreign land. I will experience pain, lose physical control, or know the uncertainty of anesthetic. I fear these things, but vaguely, for my brain buzzes in the merciful wash of endorphins that preclude any thought from occupying it too long. Most of all, I worry over what I hold. I want perfection. Each day I pray another perfect cell to form. A million of them. I fear that my tears, my moods, my wrenched weeping will imprint on the baby's psyche. I fear that repression, a stoic face shown to the world, will cause our child to hide emotions. I make too much of myself, expect too many favors, or not enough. I rock and rock and stare out the window into my life.

BLUEJAYS

I come to this little house morning-sick, then heavier, wearing a path through snow, carrying an orange plastic sand pail full of bird-seed. I come here hoping to find a couple of words to rub together. I cast my bread on the waters and feed the ravens, the woodpeckers, the handsome black-and-yellow evening grosbeaks who land in flocks, and the bluejays.

Nuisance birds, the jays are all screeching greed and hungry jeers. Over the years we've lived here their numbers have grown from the scruffy two who fed off spilled cat food and nested near the back door to nearly a sleek dozen. I think of them as a bomb squad, a gang, a small platoon. As soon as I've put down the seed, before I've even gone into the little house and closed the door, the jays appear, kamikaze-diving from the low branches of the poplars. They feed voraciously, filling their crops without pausing to remove shells. They zip off to cache their seeds and return with a desperation of intent that would be comical if it weren't for the way they threaten the miniature chickadees, the shy and solitary nuthatches, the purple finches, state birds of New Hampshire, which look exactly like sparrows held by the feet and dipped into raspberry juice.

ADVICE

Most of the instruction given to pregnant women is as chirpy and condescending as the usual run of maternity clothes—the wide tops with droopy bows slung beneath the neck, the T-shirts with arrows pointing to what can't be missed, the childish sailor collars, puffed sleeves, and pastels. It is cute advice: what to pack in the hospital bag (don't forget a toothbrush, deodorant, comb, or hair dryer). Or it's worse: pseudo-spiritual, misleading, silly, and even cruel. In giving birth to my daughters, I have found it impossible to eliminate pain through breathing, by focusing on a soothing photograph. It is true *pain* one is attempting to endure in drugless labor, not discomfort, and the way to deal with pain is not to call it something else but to increase in strength, to prepare the will. Women are strong, strong, terribly strong. We don't know how strong we are until we're pushing out our babies. We are too often treated like babies having babies when we should be in training, like acolytes, novices to high priestess-hood, like serious applicants for the space program.

WINTER. BIRTH AND BABYHOOD

When we make love in the darkness of anticipation, we are inviting accident and order, the careful lining up of genes. Unlocking the components of another person, we are safecrackers—setting the combinations, unconsciously twirling dials. Shadow brothers, sisters, potential unfused others cease. We grow into existence particularized, yet random. At last, with the birth of each daughter, Michael and I experience a certainty of apprehension, a sensation so profound that I feel foggy-brained attempting to describe it. The *actual being* of a new person appears in the first moment after birth. We read our baby's essential mystery. The three of us are soul to soul.

I know from the first that the babyhood of our youngest will be surprising. She is acutely sensitive, a mine of emotions, an easily saturated sponge for the most minute sensations. She is a cloud of sweeping sadness bunched around a germ of a purely focused will. Her roots into this life are dartlike, fine hairs. She isn't sure that she wants to be here. Unlike her older sisters, who always seemed absolutely positive, she is still making up her mind. We had planned with this baby to share infant care, for Michael was teaching full-time when the other girls were small, as well as parenting and shepherding our older children through school, and we felt that he'd missed out. We count on combining our experience, but circumstances don't cooperate. We find that we have a smart, touchy, wakeful, breast-fixated baby. At the same time our life together becomes too big, too unwieldy, too fast. One of us has to manage the shifting complications, the other of us gets our baby.

I confess that, in deep love, I want her, I choose her, I fight Michael for her constant care even though to write this paragraph requires long preparation. I have never been able to leave our children to their weeping, to let them cry themselves to sleep, as some experts suggest. In order to write I have to plan: last night, at 11:00 P.M., I begin with a late feeding in the hope of getting a night of sleep for all of us. Then at three and at six, more feedings, Michael rising to rock and soothe her. At 9:00 A.M. I put her into her bunting and cart her across the road to this little house.

One reason there is not a great deal written about what it is like to be the mother of a new infant is that there is rarely a moment to think of anything else besides that infant's needs. Endless time with a small baby is spent asking, *What do you want? What do you want?* The sounds of her unhappiness range from mild yodeling to extended bawls. *What do you want?* Our baby's cries are not monotonous. They seem quite purposeful, though hard to describe. They are a language that changes every week, one that is so primal that the meaning I gather is physical. I do what she "tells" me to do—feed, burp, change, amuse, distract, hold, look at, help to sleep, reassure—without consciously choosing to do it. I take her instructions without translating her meaning into words but simply bypassing straight to action. Until I've satisfied her need, my brain is a white blur. I lose track of what I've been doing, where I've been, who I am.

Walking. Walking. Walking. Rocking her while her cries fill me. They rise like water. A part of me has been formed and released and set upon the earth to wail. Her cries are painful to me, physically hard to take. Her cries hurt my temples, my breasts. I often cry along if I cannot comfort her. What else is there to do? This morning she falls asleep, finally, as I rock her. Sucking her favorite three fingers, she drifts. All of the tension leaves her small, round, tender body. She goes heavy against me. In this old chair, woven of tough bent willow, I keep rocking her. My chance to work has come, but I hate to put her down.

Watching her tiny, unconscious, tender face, I wonder if my mission to relocate her in this universe, to satisfy her every need, to comfort every trouble, to seduce her into loving life isn't all just so much rationalizing claptrap.

Maybe, I think, watching her breast deepen, feeling her body go limp at last in bliss, *maybe she's just a crank!*

MARCH. LATE-WINTER STORMS. RAVENS AND WILD TURKEYS

She is a winter baby, and all day there is just her, me, snow, and the birds outside. Every morning I dump pans of sunflower seeds, old bread, lumpy oatmeal on a stump in the yard. For the omnivorous ravens, I add a cup of cat food, and for the wild turkeys and the deer, should they ever come near, cracked corn. Of course, the deer are far off in their winter yards, or long frozen in a hunter's deep freeze. But three wild turkey hens visit the bird feeder twice a day, at around eleven o'clock and again at three. I am always surprised to see them, sensing before they appear at the edge of the woods their great dark shapes—bundles of rags on stilts. They walk purposefully, elegantly and quickly, toward the apple tree and corn I've tossed beneath. Sometimes they approach the house. This morning, they pick their way in formation up to the door.

Inside, I have put baby down to sleep, still wearing her bright red snowsuit, and she has woken. She is making small dove noises that attract the three hens, who crane their sinuous necks, shake their angry scarred red faces, and stare raptly in at her. We're all caught in fascination, regarding one another. Then the smallest of the hens, who nevertheless is huge, whirls around, takes four long galloping strides, and reaches the edge of the yard. The others watch her with disapproval and annoyance, then lift their three-toed feet delicately and stalk off—rich, dark, iridescent, leaving shit like rolled cigar ash.

Each morning too, as we approach the house and riffle of woods, the ravens harshly gossip down at us from a favorite branch in the lightning-cleft white pine, where they have established a nest. Last spring the oldest two hatched five young, and sometime last summer, as Michael and I sat idly in the yard tossing sticks for the dog, seven ravens, two full-grown and five smaller, ragged teenagers, flew overhead, making a commotion. It was easy to see that the parents were giving a flying lesson. There was no mistaking the yells of encouragement, the cries of fear and delight from the fledglings.

I sit at the window watching seven huge and handsome black ravens as the snow begins to fall through the windless morning air in chains, endless chains. Only three feed at one time. The others sit in the branches, keeping watch or playing fair, according to raven etiquette. Occasionally they descend, their beaks balled with new snow. The light is brilliant, the snow fluffy and half a foot deep. Hunched and sleek, the largest raven runs the fresh snow up and down the shaft of each feather, then dives once, twice, straight into a drift, body-surfing into a motionless wave. One thing is clear: I am not the only watcher in the woods. Sometimes, as I'm taking notes before the window, in easy view, I feel eyes upon me and slowly look up to see that on the nearest branch a raven sits, watching my pen move across the page.

MAY NIGHTS, WARM DAYS IN JUNE. DESIRE

She hates the playpen and prefers to be in the thick of things, not apart from us even with the cleverest toys. She hates her car seat. She tolerates her baby carrier only in short bursts. Help, help, help. I spread toys in a hazard-free trajectory across the carpet laid by the marijuana grower. As I write, I hear her dogged progress. This will last fifteen minutes, until she explores the last toy, a musical bluebird with an orange beak and great black cartoon eyes. She has learned how to prop herself, how to swivel on her stomach, but she can't crawl, not yet. Instead, she lunges. She props herself on her arms and pushes with her knees, lands with a solid thump, pushes up and throws herself again and again toward the toy. It is a paradigm of something, I think, idly, pausing to study her absolute striving concentration, but what? Turning back to this page, I know. It is what I am doing now. My face is hers. Unyielding eagerness. That is her work, just as this page is my play, just as all this is our life. It is what we do, afraid and avid, full of desire, hurling ourselves again and again toward the musical object.

My days here have become sensuous, suffused with the particular, which is not to say that they aren't difficult, or that I get much done. With each pregnancy, I have been thrown into a joy of the body that is religious, that seizes me so thoroughly that the life of the imagination sometimes seems a spare place. But the physical pleasures of nursing, touching, smelling the exquisite fragrance of our baby—a yellow-pink fragrance of sun-heated cotton and tepid cream—all are tempered by sleep deprivation. We know why prisoners break more easily without sleep. *I give up, I'll tell you anything,* I want to say to her, nearly weeping. I'm an instinctive mother, not a book-read one, and my feeling is that our baby must be weaned slowly from its other body—mine. At night I keep her close, sleep with her curled tight.

Spring dusk. It is the blue of a smoking engine out there, and now, from the pond, the rippling sexual sobs of wood frogs, bullfrogs, the full-throated breathing of the deep night, begin. It is a song so powerful I lie upon the bed pressed into the waves. The air throbs, filled and running over. This is the night in its entirety—leaves, grass, quaking air. The sound inhabits me, as if the dark passes into me, thrilling and complete. Sometimes I walk out at midnight to stand within the tension as the moon shows, gleaming and porous, through the stanchions of pine.

Black stalls housing black horses, black grass, black trees, whir of black wings at the back of my head. Waking in the deep blackness, nursing a baby is the most sensuous of animal tasks. All night I wake, feed our baby, sleep, wake again to the tiny body curled to me in the depth of that seething music.

JUNE, JULY, AND AUGUST

Some days it seems that I have not put her down for weeks. I am her existence after all, the way she gets what she wants, the outlet, the method, the tool of her need. Sometimes I hold my child in one arm, nursing her, and write with the other hand. With no separation of thought and physical being, there are times I live within a perfect circle.

Then there are the other times. Months go by, and with the end of summer the dim realization surfaces—I cannot concentrate on one thought, one idea. Our baby is a catnapper, sleeping for irregular, short periods, and because of this I've found that allowing the mind to solve a task is not so much a luxury as a mental necessity, like dreaming. The primary parent of a new infant loses the ability to focus, and that in turn saws on the emotions, wears away the fragile strings of nerves.

Hormones, milk, heaviness, no sleep, internal joy all fuse in the first few months after a baby is born, so that I experience a state of tragic confusion. Most days I can't get enough distance on myself to define what I am feeling. I walk through a tunnel from one house to the other. It is dark, scraped out of the emotional mess of life, as gray and ridged as an esophagus. I'm being swallowed alive. On those days suicide is an idea too persistent for comfort. *There isn't a self to kill,* I think, filled with melodramatic pity for who I used to be. That person is gone. Yet once I've established that I have no personal self, killing whatever remains seems hardly worth the effort. For those dark and stupid days I have developed a mantra to ward off the radical lack of perspective that is also called depression. The chant, absurdly, goes something like this:

I don't have to wear panty hose to work. I don't have to wear high heels. This job is easier than any other job I've done—easier than rising at five to catch the truck at six and hoe sugar beets, shedding clothes as the sun arches to its severe height. More rewarding than selling popcorn at the movie theater and cleaning the butter machine with pink soap after the last feature. Easier than baby-sitting other people's children, than lifeguarding, than picking cucumbers for local farmers. More fulfilling than selling Kentucky Fried Chicken or working the night shift at an all-night family diner. Preferable to reshelving library books and flipping eggs and pancakes on the morning shift as a short-order cook.

This job is more interesting than explaining the history of Sacher torte for the millionth time to a customer at the pastry shop in Brattle Square. It is more varied than hauling gravel and weighing dump trucks and tying steel. I'm more capable of doing this than of standing hunched over a light table and making up ad copy, or writing grants, or developing photographs. This job is certainly easier than the jobs of other women who also care for their babies while they work. It is less emotionally taxing than the job I had one long year that required putting on rubber-soled white shoes and a white polyester uniform, then walking over to the locked ward of the state mental hospital to start the day by stripping the night-soiled beds of insane women.

FALL RAINS

I have no profound reason to be depressed and have always hated and despised depression, fought it with every argument I possess, tried my best to walk it off, run it off, drink it out, crush it with leaves and solitude in the accepting Northeastern woods. But the deaths of three of my grandparents, within months of one another, seem to trigger a downward trend I cannot stave off even with a baby in my arms. Somehow, over all these miles, I must have been sustained by my grandparents because the silence in their wake roars over me, their absences shake me, and it seems as though something within me were pulled deeply under, into the earth, as though I still follow after them, stumbling, unable to say good-bye.

My maternal grandfather—tribal chairman, powwow dancer, a man of subtle humor and intelligence—dies after years of wandering in a dark place. His illness was cruel and took nearly two decades to destroy him. He disappears cell by cell, losing his sense of time and place slowly, and then weakening still further, so there is no clear moment of obvious loss—only the tiny and incremental lacks, the odd habits becoming the completely irrational, then frightening. At last, he was a paralyzed vacuity nursed with tenderness and patience by my grandmother. She gave to him the vigor of her old age, as she had given herself at age fourteen: completely and with some unknown and rocklike composition of will.

FEBRUARY THAW. OUTWALKING DEATH

We pass out of this world as grasshoppers, the prophet Esdras complained to God, and our life is astonishment and fear. The snow is covered with a heavy crust of ice; the world seems lifeless, monotonous.

The air is the gray color of the ground. Four months after my grand-father's death, my paternal grandmother is dying in a faraway Minnesota hospital. Tomorrow I'll be on a plane. She has come back from the brink of death twice before and survived falls, widowhood, disease, disappointment. She has seemed so strong-willed that nothing could kill her, but this is congestive failure of the heart.

As the old go walking into the night, we lose our sense of time, we lose our witnesses, our living memories. We lose them, and we lose the farthest reach of ourselves. To walk off the panic I feel at our impending loss, I put baby in her blue backpack and take to the snowmobile trails on a Sunday afternoon. My boots are a windfall from a friend long disappeared into the catering business. They were too big for her, just right for me. I've worn them for fifteen years. Hiking boots are light and tough now, but I prefer these heavy ones. Our dog usually grows tense with happiness when I lace these boots, but not today. This is a desperation walk, and he senses a dark motive.

We begin. Our legs carry us and carry us. Just behind the house perhaps a mile uphill the trail begins, packed for us by a snowmobiler. We pass through mixed hardwood and small pine, then a beautiful section of young gray birch. The snow on the ground is clean, melted smooth. The birch bark is seamlessly beautiful, set on regular poles that go on as far as we can see. We come to some old growth, white pines of perhaps a hundred years, a hundred feet tall, the favorite resting places of wild turkeys. We keep going.

The silence is so intense that we stop from time to time to listen to a branch scraping on another branch, a woodpecker drumming dead-wood, far down the hill a motor revving. We've progressed to the place I usually turn around. Here the trail goes straight up, a narrowing alley of green-black, ferny hemlock. We climb. There is nothing to think. Nothing to do but step and step. The trees shut behind me. I walk beside the trail, punching toeholds, ascending, trying to outwalk death. With each step, the baby on my back grows. She's bigger, surely heavier, so heavy I don't think that I can move—except I do move. Maybe this is some strange and painful test of motherhood, or just brute macha. Near the top we finally rest on a moss-cushioned boulder.

Our baby is almost a year old, and down to one or two breast feedings a day. If we miss one, she begins to suck my collar cuffs, makes cloth nipples between her fists and wet marks on my shirt. I soothe myself with her need too, for I hate to wean her. Michael has promised to divert her tenderly while I am gone, with a set of colored pacifiers. In the shelter of my parka she nurses for the last time for days, then takes a graham cracker. I share a sandwich with our dog, and together we smell the dusty piles of leaves glowing rust-red through the melt. I think of snowmobilers going straight down, their brakes burning, flying off the side of the trail, wrapping their machines around these old trees. My life is like that—I don't stop myself from going into the feeling, the emotion that pulls like gravity. Surely there are gentler courses, switchbacks, but for some reason I can't bring myself to take them. My grandmother's death comes at me straight on.

Death is the least civilized rite of passage. The way we handle it, even with our loved ones, our old ones, seems wild and strange, kitsch- and cliché-ridden, shocking. Nearly half of us die in hospitals, usually with no family present. The other half kick off anywhere—in streets, on planes, in our kitchens, at our writing desks. My grandmother, who fought death with cleverness and consistency and lots of brewer's yeast, would rather have died in her own backyard than in a hospital bed. She would have preferred to go while looking into the brilliant cups of her prize seven-foot-high hollyhocks, with a dog at her feet, birds pecking the slabs of suet she nailed to the bark of an old box elder just outside her door.

LEAP DAY

As I write this, my left hand rests lightly on our baby's back. With two fingers I stroke the hair above her aching ear. If I take the fingers away, she wakes, she wails, as if my hand served a medicinal purpose. My arm below the elbow feels enormous, throbs with blood, seems almost to hum with electricity. It's a toss-up which will first lose consciousness: my arm or her head. At her inoculation last week, she shrieked in surprise at the sudden pain of the needle. Then, to take the hurt away, she put the sting against my bare arm, held our skin together. Her tears stopped. My flesh still had magic. I could absorb her pain by touch.

WALKING

To pull herself upright, to strain upward, to climb, has been baby's obsession for the past three months, and now, on her first birthday, it is that urge I celebrate and fear. She has pulled herself erect by the strings of her sister's hair, by using my clothes, hands, earrings, by the edges and the rungs and the unstable handles of the low drawers. She has yanked herself up, stepped, and it is clear from her grand excitement that walking is one of the most important things we ever do. It is raw power to go forward, to lunge, catching at important arms and hands, to take control of the body, tell it what to do, to leave behind the immobility of babyhood. With each step she swells, her breath goes ragged, and her eyes darken in a shine of happiness. A glaze of physical joy covers her, moves through her, more intense than the banged forehead, bumped chin, the bruises and knocks and losses, even than the breathtaking falls and solid thumps, joy more powerful than good sense.

It would seem she has everything she could want—she is fed, she is carried, she is rocked, put to sleep. But no, *walking* is the thing, the consuming urge to seize control. She has to walk to gain entrance to the world. From now on she will get from here to there more and more under her own will. As she goes, she will notice worn grass, shops or snow or the shapes of trees. She will walk for reasons other than to get somewhere in particular. She'll walk to think or not to think, to leave the body, which is often the same as becoming at one with it. She will walk to ward off anger in its many forms. For pleasure, purpose, or to grieve. She'll walk until the world slows down, until her brain lets go of everything behind, and until her eyes see only the next step. She'll walk until her feet hurt, her muscles tremble, until her eyes are numb with looking. She'll walk until her sense of balance is the one thing left and the rest of the world is balanced too, and eventually, if we all do the growing up right, she will walk away from us.

THE ZERO

She sits on my lap and looks at snow. It is not like her to be so still. Perhaps she watches my pen as it moves, a black shape, or my hand, shadowing the page. She watches the wind turn silver, the snowflakes blown backward, the sight of pure falling. We sit in the willow rocker before the window. This is a house of ardor and affection, the house of a writer, of a woman and a child—the unborn baby stirring, the newborn nursing herself to sleep, the infant running a plump and capable small hand through the new six-month hair, the longer nine-month hair, and now the year's growth, so fine and brown. It is a house where a child wakes and pushes herself up to glare through the mesh of her bed at her mother, and then, piecing together the scraps of vision through the squares, she bursts into a smile of astonished recognition.

I assemble the pieces to form her too. Our children come from the house of the unborn, from the biological zero. I sit here pondering this very ordinary mystery. We do not ask for life. Our gift is our burden, and our burden is our freedom. We are free at any time to lay it down, to return to the zero, as the man who once sat in this little house did, choosing his way over what he must have seen in front of him: this view of stilled trees.

THE BLUEJAY'S DANCE

The hawk sweeps over, light shining through her rust-red tail. She makes an immaculate cross in flight, her shadow running along the ground behind her as I'm walking below. Our shadows join momentarily and then separate, both to our appointed rounds. Always she hunts flying into the cast of the sun, making a pass east to west. Once inside I settle baby, resettle baby, settle and resettle myself, and have just lowered my head into my hands to proofread a page when a blur outside my vision causes me to look up.

The hawk drops headfirst out of a cloud. She folds her wings hard against her and plunges into the low branches of the apple tree, moving at such dazzling speed I can barely follow. She strikes at one of seven bluejays who make up the raucous gang, and it tumbles before her, head over feet, end over end. She plunges after it from the branches, flops in the sun. They both light on the ground and square off, about a foot apart in the snow.

The struck jay thrusts out its head, screams, raises its wings, and dances *toward* the gray hawk. The plain of snow must seem endless, an arena without shelter, and the bird gets no help from the other six jays except loud encouragement at a safe distance. I hardly breathe. The hawk, on the ground, its wings clattering against the packed crust, is so much larger than its shadow, which has long brushed in and out of mine. It screams back, eyes filled with yellow light. Its hooked beak opens and it feints with its neck. Yet the jay, ridiculous, continues to dance, hopping forward, hornpiping up and down with tiny leaps, all of its feathers on end to increase its size. Its crest is sharp, its beak open in a continual shriek, its eye-mask fierce. It pedals its feet in the air. The hawk steps backward. She seems confused, cocks her head, and does not snap the bluejay's neck. She watches. Although I know nothing of the hawk and cannot imagine what moves her, it does seem to me that she is fascinated, that she puzzles at the absurd display before she raises her wings and lifts off.

Past the gray moralizing and the fierce Roman Catholic embrace of suffering and fate that so often cloud the subject of suicide there is the bluejay's dance. Beyond the impossible corners, stark cliffs, dark wells of trapped longing, there is that manic, successful jig—cocky, exuberant, entirely a bluff, a joke. That dance makes me clench down hard on life. But it is also a dance that in other circumstances might lead me, you, anyone, to choose a voluntary death. I see in that small bird's crazy courage some of what it took for my grandparents to live out the tough times. I peer around me, stroke my own skin, look into this baby's eyes that register me as a blurred self-extension, as a function of her will. I have made a pact with life: if I were to die now it would be a form of suicide for her. Since the two of us are still in the process of differentiating, since my acts are hers and I do not even think, yet, where I stop for her or where her needs, exactly, begin, I must dance for her. I must be the one to dip and twirl in the cold glare, and I must teach her, as she grows, the unlikely step.

WHO WON THE WEST?

(APRIL 1988)

William Kittredge

AFTER A HALF mile in soft rain on the slick hayfield stubble, I would crouch behind the levee and listen to the gentle clatter of the water birds, and surprise them into flight—maybe a half-dozen mallard hens and three green-headed drakes lifting in silhouetted loveliness against the November twilight, hanging only yards from the end of my shotgun. This was called jump shooting or meat hunting, and it almost always worked. But I wish someone had told me reasons you should not necessarily kill the birds every time. I wish I'd been told to kill ducks maybe only once or twice a winter, for a fine meal with children and friends, and that nine times out of ten I was going to be happier if I let the goddamned birds fly away.

In 1959, on the MC Ranch, in the high desert country of southeastern Oregon, an agricultural property my family owned, I was twenty-seven, prideful with a young man's ambition, and happy as such a creature can be, centered in the world of my upbringing, king of my mountain, and certain I was deep into the management of perfection. It was my responsibility to run a ranch-hand cookhouse and supervise the labors of from ten to twenty-five workingmen. Or, to put it most crudely, as was often done, "hire and fire and work the winos."

Think of it as a skill, learnable as any other. In any profession there are rules, the most basic being enlightened self-interest. Take care of your men and they will take care of you.

And understand their frailties, because you are the one responsible for taking care. Will they fall sick to death in the bunkhouse, and is there someone you can call to administer mercy if they do? What attention will you give them as they die?

Some thirty-six miles west of our valley, over the Warner Mountains in the small lumbering and ranching town of Lakeview, a workingman's hotel functioned as a sort of hiring hall. There was a rule of thumb about the men you would find there. The best of them wore a good pair of boots laced up tight over wool socks; this meant they were looking for a laboring job. The most hapless would be wearing low-cut city shoes, no socks, no laces. They were looking for a place to hide, and never to be hired. It was a rule that worked.

ON BRIGHT AFTERNOONS when my people were scrambling to survive in the Great Depression, my mother was young and fresh as she led me on walks along the crumbling small-town streets of Malin, Oregon, in the Klamath Basin just north of the California border. This was before we moved to the MC Ranch; I was three years old and understood the world as concentric circles of diminishing glory centered on the sun of her smile. Outside our tight circle was my father, an energetic stranger who came home at night and, before he touched anything, even me or my mother, rolled up his sleeves over his white forearms and scrubbed his hands in the kitchen sink with coarse lava soap. Out beyond him were the turkey herders, and beyond them lay the vast agricultural world, on the fringes of the Tule Lake Reclamation District, where they worked.

What the herders did in the turkey business, as it was run by my father, was haul crates full of turkeys around on old flatbed trucks. When they got to the backside of some farm property where nobody was likely to notice, they parked and opened the doors on those crates and turned the turkeys out to roam and feed on grasshoppers. Sometimes they had permission, sometimes my father had paid a fee; and some of the time it was theft, grazing the turkeys for free.

Sometimes they got caught, and my father paid the fee then. And once in a while they had to reload the turkeys into their crates and move on while some farmer watched them with a shotgun.

The barnyard turkey, you have to understand, is a captive, bitter creature. (Some part of our alienation, when we are most isolated, is ecological. We are lonely and long to share in what we regard as the dignity of wild animals—this is the phantom so many of us pursue as we hunt, complicating the actual killing into a double-bind sort of triumph.) My upbringing taught me to consider the domesticated turkey a rapacious creature, eyes dull with the opaque gleam of pure selfishness, without soul. I had never heard of a wild one. The most recent time I had occasion to confront turkeys up close was in the fall of 1987, driving red scoria roads in the North Dakota badlands. I came across farmstead turkeys, and, true or not, I took that as a sign we were where agriculture meant subsistence. No doubt my horror of turkeys had much to do with my fear of the men who herded them.

From the windows of our single-bedroom apartment on the second floor of the only brick building in Malin, where I slept on a little bed in the living room, we could look south across the rich irrigated potato- and barley-raising country of the Tule Lake basin and see to California and the lava-field badlands where the Modoc Indians had hidden out from the U.S. Army in the long-ago days of their rebellion. I wonder if my mother told me stories of those natives in their caves, and doubt it, but not because she didn't believe in the arts of make-believe. It's just that my mother would have told me other stories. She grew up loving opera. My grandfather, as I will always understand him, even though we were not connected by blood, earned the money for her music lessons as a blacksmith for the California/Oregon Power Company in Klamath Falls—sharpening steel, as he put it. So it is unlikely my mother was fond of stories about desperate natives and hold-out killings and the eventual hanging of Captain Jack, the Modoc war chief, at Fort Klamath. That was just the sort of nastiness she was interested in escaping; and besides, we were holding to defensive actions of our own.

After all, my father was raising turkeys for a living in a most haphazard fashion. So my mother told me stories about Christmas as perfection realized: candied apples glowing in the light of an intricately decorated tree, and little toy railroads that tooted and circled the room as if the room were the world.

But we live in a place more complex than paradise, some would say richer, and I want to tell a story about my terror on Christmas Eve, and the way we were happy anyhow. The trouble began on a sunny afternoon with a little snow on the ground, when my mother took me for my first barbershop haircut, a step into manhood as she defined it. I was enjoying the notion of such ceremony, and even the snipping of the barber's gentle shears as I sat elevated to manly height by the board across the arms of his chair—until Santa Claus came in, jerked off his cap and the fringe of snowy hair and his equally snowy beard, and stood revealed as an unshaven man in a Santa Claus suit who looked like he could stand a drink from the way his hands were shaking.

The man leered at my kindly barber and muttered something. I suppose he wanted to know how long he would have to wait for a shave. Maybe he had been waiting all day for a barbershop shave. A fine, brave, hung-over sort of waiting, all the while entombed in that Santa Claus suit. I screamed. I like to think I was screaming against chaos, in defense of my mother and notions of a proper Christmas, and maybe because our Santa Claus who was not a Santa, with his corded, unshaven neck, even looked remotely like a turkey as this story turns edgy and nightmarish.

My father's turkeys had been slaughtered the week before Thanksgiving in a couple of boxcars pulled onto a siding in Tule Lake, and shipped to markets in the East. Everyone was at liberty and making ready to ride out winter on whatever he had managed to accumulate. So the party my parents threw on the night before Christmas had ancient ceremonial resonances. The harvest was done, the turkeys were slaughtered, and the dead season of cold winds was at hand. It was a time of release into meditation and winter, to await rebirth.

But it was not a children's party. It is difficult to imagine my father at a children's party. As I recall from this distance, it was a party for the turkey herders, those men who had helped my father conspire his way through that humiliating summer with those terrible creatures. At least the faces I see in my dream of that yellow kitchen are the faces of those men. Never again, my mother said, and my father agreed; better times were coming and everybody got drunk.

I had been put down to sleep on the big bed in my parents' bedroom, which was quite a privilege in itself, and it was only late in the night that I woke to a sense of something gone wrong. The sacred place where I lived with my mother had been invaded by loud laughter and hoedown harmonica music and people dancing and stomping. As I stood in the doorway looking into the kitchen in my pajamas, nobody saw me for a long moment—until I began my hysterical momma's-boy shrieking.

The harmonica playing stopped, and my mother looked shamefaced toward me from the middle of the room, where she had been dancing with my father while everyone watched. All those faces of people who are now mostly dead turned to me, and it was as if I had gotten up and come out of the bedroom into the actuality of a leering nightmare, vivid light and whiskey bottles on the table and those faces glazed with grotesque intentions.

Someone saved it, one of the men, maybe even my father, by picking me up and ignoring my wailing as the harmonica music started again, and then I was in my mother's arms as she danced, whirling around the kitchen table and the center of all attention in a world where everything was possible and good, while the turkey herders watched and smiled and thought their private thoughts, and it was Christmas at last in my mother's arms, as I have understood it ever since.

For years the faces of the turkey herders in their otherness, in that bright kitchen, were part of a dream I dreaded as I tried to go to sleep. In struggling against the otherness of the turkey herders I made a start toward indifference to the disenfranchised. I was learning to inhabit distance, from myself and people I should have cared for.

A COUPLE OF years later my family moved the hundred miles east to the MC Ranch. My grandfather got the place when he was sixty-two years old, pledging everything he had worked for all his life, unable to resist owning such a kingdom. The move represented an enormous change in our fortunes.

Warner Valley is that place which is sacred to me as the main staging ground for my imagination. I see it as an inhabited landscape where the names of people remind me of places, and the places remind me of what happened there—a thicket of stories to catch the mind if it might be falling.

It was during the Second World War that wildlife biologists from up at the college in Corvallis told my father the sandhill cranes migrating through Warner were rare and vanishing creatures, to be cherished with the same intensity as the ring-necked Manchurian pheasants, which had been imported from the hinterlands of China. The nests of sandhill cranes, with their large off-white speckled eggs, were to be regarded as absolutely precious. "No matter what," I heard my father say, "you don't break those eggs."

My father was talking to a tall, gray-faced man named Clyde Bolton, who was stuck with a day of riding a drag made of heavy timbers across Thompson Field, breaking up cow shit in the early spring before the irrigating started so the chips wouldn't plug up the John Deere mowing machines come summer and haying. Clyde was married to Ada Bolton, the indispensable woman who cooked and kept house for us, and he had a damaged heart, which kept him from heavy work. He milked the three or four cows my father kept, and tended the chickens and the house garden, and took naps in the afternoon. He hadn't hired out for field work, and he was unhappy.

But help was scarce during those years when so many of the able-bodied were gone to the war, and there he was, take it or leave it. And anyway, riding that drag wouldn't hurt even a man with a damaged heart. Clyde was a little spoiled—that's what we used to say. Go easy on the hired help long enough and they will sour on you. A man, we would say, needs to get out in the open air and sweat and blow off the stink.

This was a Saturday morning in April after the frost had gone out, and I was a boy learning the methodologies of field work. The cranes' nests my father was talking about were hidden down along unmowed margins—in the yellow remnants of knee-high meadow grass from the summer before, along the willow-lined sloughs through the home fields. "The ones the coons don't get," my father said.

I can see my father's gray-eyed good humor and his stockman's fedora pushed back on his head as he studied Clyde, and hear the ironic rasp in his voice. At that time my father was more than ten years younger than I am now, a man recently come to the center of his world. And I can see Clyde Bolton hitching his suspenders and snorting over the idea of keeping an eye out for the nest of some sandhill crane. I can see his disdain.

This going out with Clyde was as close to any formal initiation as I ever got on the ranch. There really wasn't much of anything for me to do, but it was important I get used to the idea of working on days when I was not in school. It wouldn't hurt a damned bit. A boy should learn to help out where he can, and I knew it, so I was struggling to harness the old team of matched bay geldings, Dick and Dan, and my father and Clyde were not offering to help because a boy would never make a man if you helped him all the time.

"You see what you think out there," my father said, and he spoke to Clyde seriously, man to man, ignoring me. They were deeply serious all at once and absorbed into what I understood as the secret lives of men. It was important to watch them for clues.

My father acted like he was just beginning to detail Clyde's real assignment. You might have thought we faced a mindless day spent riding that drag behind a farting old team. But no, it seemed Clyde's real mission involved a survey of conditions and experienced judgment.

"Them swales been coming to swamp grass," my father said. "We been drowning them out." He went on to talk about the low manure dams which spread irrigation water across the swales. Clyde would have the day to study those dams, and figure where they should be relocated.

Once we believed work done well would see us through. But it was not true. Once it seemed the rewards of labor would be naturally rationed out with at least a rough kind of justice. But we were unlettered and uninstructed in the true nature of our ultimate values. Our deep willingness to trust in our native goodness was not enough.

But we tried. This is what I am writing of here, that trying and also about learning to practice hardening of the heart. Even back then I might have suspected my father wasn't much worried about swamp grass in the swales, and that Clyde Bolton knew he wasn't, and that it wasn't the point of their negotiations. My father was concerned about dignity, however fragile, as an ultimate value.

"Your father was the damnedest son of a bitch," one of the ranch hands once told me. "He'd get you started on one thing, and make you think you were doing another thing which was more important, and then he would go off and you wouldn't see him for days, and pretty soon it was like you were working on your own place."

It was not until I was a man in the job my father perfected that I learned the sandhill cranes were not endangered at all. It didn't matter. Those birds were exotic and lovely as they danced their mating dances in our meadows, each circling the other with gawky tall-bird elegance, balanced by their extended fluttering wings as they seized the impulse and looped across the meadows with their long necks extended to the sky and their beaks open to whatever ecstasy birds can know. I think my father was simply trying to teach me and everyone else on the property that certain vulnerabilities should be cherished and protected at whatever inconvenience.

I have to wish there had been more such instruction, and that it had been closer to explicit in a philosophical sense. Most of all I wish my father had passed along some detailed notion of how to be boss. It was a thing he seemed to do naturally. I wish he had made clear to me the dangers of posturing in front of people who are in some degree dependent on your whims, posturing until you have got yourself deep into the fraud of maintaining distance and mystery in place of authenticity.

A man once told me to smoke cigars. "They see you peel that cellophane," he said, "and they know you don't live like they do."

MY FATHER SET up the Grain Camp on a sagebrush hill slope, beneath a natural spring on the west side of Warner Valley. And it was an encampment, short on every amenity except running water in the early days—a double row of one-room shacks, eight in all, trucked in from a nearby logging camp abandoned in the late 1930s. There were also two shacks tacked across one another in a T shape to make a cookhouse, one cabin for the cooking and another for the long table where everyone ate.

The men, who lived two to a cabin in the busy seasons, sweltering on that unshaded hill slope in the summers and waking in the night to the stink of drying work clothes as they fed split wood to their little stoves in the winter, were a mix of transients and what we called homesteaders, men who stayed with us for more than an occasional season, often years in the same cabin, which became known as theirs. Those men have my heart as I write this, men who were my friends and my mentors, some of whom died at the Grain Camp and have been inconspicuously dead for many years. Louie Hanson, Vance Beebe, Jake O'Rourke, Lee Mallard, so many others. I would like the saying of their names to be an act of pure celebration.

When I came home from the Air Force in the fall of 1957, I was twenty-five years old and back to beginnings after most of eight years away, a woeful figure from American mythology, the boss's kid and heir to the property, soon to inherit, who didn't know anything. Then in the spring of 1958, the myth came directly home to roost. I found myself boss at the Grain Camp.

There was no choice but to plead ignorance and insinuate myself into the sympathies of the old hands. Ceremony demanded that I show up twice a day to sit at the head of the long table for meals, breakfast and noon, and in the course of those appearances negotiate my way through the intricacies of managing 8,000 acres of irrigated land. For a long time I was bluffing, playing a hand I didn't understand, risking disgrace and reaping it plenty enough. The man who saved my bacon mostly was an old alcoholic Swede in filthy coveralls named Louie Hanson, who sat at my right hand at the table.

About five-thirty on a routine morning, after a hot shower and instant coffee, I would drive the three or so miles from the house to the Grain Camp. The best cabin, walls filled with sawdust for insulation, belonged to Louie. He had worked for my father since our beginnings in Warner, hiring out in 1937 to build dikes with a secondhand Caterpillar RD-6, the first tracklayer my father bought, and made his way up to Cat mechanic, and into privileges, one of which was occasional drinking. Theoretically, we didn't allow any drinking. Period. Again, there were rules. You need to drink, go to town. Maybe your job will be waiting when you get back. Unless you were one of the old hands. Then your job was secure. But nobody was secure if he got to drinking on the job or around camp.

Except for Louie. Every morning in winter he would go down to the Cat shop to build his fire before breakfast, and dig a couple of beers from one of the bolt-rack cubbyholes, pop the tops, and set the bottles on the stove to heat. When they were steaming he would take them off, drink the beer in a few long drafts, and be set to seize the day.

So it would not be an entirely sober man I greeted when I came early to get him for breakfast and knocked on the door to his cabin. Louie would be resting back on the greasy tarp that covered his bed, squinting through the smoke from another Camel, sipping coffee from a filthy cup, and looking up to grin. "Hell, you own the place," he would say, "you're in."

Louie would blink his eyes. "Chee-rist. You got enough water in Dodson Lake?" He was talking about one of the huge grain fields we flooded every spring. And I wouldn't know. Did I have enough water in Dodson Lake? Louie would look at me directly. "Get a south wind and you are going to lose some dikes." I knew what that meant: eroded levee banks, washouts, catastrophe, 450 acres of flooded alfalfa.

Up at the breakfast table, while Louie reached for the pounded round steak, I would detail a couple of men to start drawing down the water in Dodson Lake, a process involving the opening of huge valves, pulling headgate boards, running the eighteen-inch pump. All of which would have been unnecessary if I had known what I was doing in the first place. Which everybody knew and nobody mentioned. All in all a cheap mistake, easily covered—wages for the men and electricity to run the pump, wasted time and a little money, maybe a couple hundred bucks. Without Louie's intercession, maybe twenty thousand.

THE DEEPLY FEARFUL are driven to righteousness, as we know, and they are the most fearsome fools we have. This is a story I have told as a tavern-table anecdote, in which I call our man the Murderer, since I have no memory of his real name. Call the story "The Day I Fired the Murderer." It is designed, as told in taverns, to make me appear winsome and ironic, liberated, guilty no more. Which of course implies there was guilt. And there was, in a way that cornered me into thinking it was anger that drove me, and that my anger was mostly justifiable.

I had been boss at the Grain Camp for four or five years, and I had come to understand myself as a young man doing good work, employing the otherwise unemployable (which was kind of true), and also as someone whose efforts were continually confounded by the incompetence of the men who worked for me. We were farming twenty-four hours a day through early May while the Canada honkers hatched their downy young and the tulips pushed up through the crusted flower beds and the Lombardy poplars broke their buds and the forsythia bloomed lurid yellow against the cookhouse wall. But I don't think of such glories when I remember those spring mornings. I remember the odor of dank peat turning up behind those disc Cats as we went on farming twenty-four hours a day, and how much I loved breaking ground.

Before sunrise on those mornings I would come awake and go piss, then stand in my undershorts on the screened-in veranda attached to the house where I lived with my wife and young children. I would shiver with chill and happiness as I smelled the world coming awake. Far out across our valley the lights on our D-7 disc Cats would flicker as lights do when seen through a screen, moving almost imperceptibly. I would take my binoculars and open the screen door and gaze out to those lights as if I might catch one of my night-shift Catskinners at some dog-fuckery, but really all I wanted to see was the machinery moving. Those Cats would clank along at two or three miles an hour all through the hours of darkness, turning a thirty-six-foot swath—a hundred acres every night and another hundred acres on the day shift. The upturned soil would mellow in the air for a day, and then we would harrow it and seal it with dust and drill it to barley. In ten days or so the seedlings would break earth, and those orderly drill-rows undulating over the tilled ground toward the sundown light were softly yellow-green and something alive I had seen to completion.

It came to a couple hundred acres of barley every day for fifteen days, three-thousand-some-odd acres in all. By the end of harvest in late September, at roughly a ton per acre, that came to 3,000 tons of barley at $50 a ton, or $150,000, real money in the early 1960s in our end of the world.

We drained the wetlands and thought that made them ours. We believed the world was made to be useful; we ditched and named the intersections of our ditches: Four Corners, Big Pump, Center Bridge, Beatty Bridge. We thought such naming made the valley ours.

And we thought the people were ours.

The man I call the Murderer was one of those men who rode the disc Cats, circling toward the sunrise. My involvement with him that spring had started the previous fall, when someone from the Oregon Board of Parole called and asked if we would participate in what they called their Custody Release Program. They would send us a parolee if we would guarantee a job; in return we got an employee who was forbidden to drink or quit, on penalty of being sent back to prison. If there was "anything," we could call and the state police would come take him away. It seemed like a correct idea; it had been twenty-some years since the Murderer killed his wife in an act of drunken bewilderment he couldn't recall.

Frail and dark-eyed in a stiff new evergreen-colored workshirt, with the sleeves rolled to expose thin white arms, pensive and bruised and looking incapable of much beyond remorse, the Murderer spent the winter feeding bales to the drag at our feed mill, a cold, filthy job, and as monotonous an enterprise as it is possible to imagine this side of automation. So when it came time to go farming in the spring, I sat him up at the controls of a D-7, taught him to pull frictions and grease the rollers, and called him a Catskinner, which is to say, gave him some power. The Murderer responded by starting to talk. Bright, misinformed chatter at the breakfast table.

All I remember is annoyance. Then it rained, and we couldn't work. My crew went off to town for a couple of days with my blessing, and the Murderer went with them. That was against our rules, his and mine. And he came back drunk, and I fired him on the spot. He came up to breakfast drunk, terribly frightened and unable to be sober, lowering himself into my mercies, which did not exist.

Only in the imagination can we share another person's specific experiences. I was the ice queen, which means no stories, please, there is no forgiveness for you and never will be, just roll your goddamned bed and be gone. If I fired him, he would go back to prison. I knew that. I am sure I imagined some version of his future—isolation again in the wrecked recognition that in this life he was not to be forgiven.

Stories bind us by reminding us that our lives all participate in the same fragilities, and this should soften us so that we stay humane. But I didn't want to be humane; I wanted to be correct. If I had not ignored his devastation as I no doubt saw it, imagined it, I might have found a way to honor common sense and taken him riding around with me that day as he sobered up, and listened to his inane chatter. But I sent him down the road, and thought I was doing the right thing. There were rules. As I tell the story I mean to say, See, I am not like that anymore. See. But we know this is only another strategy.

I FIRED A lot of men, and Louie Hanson more than once, after on-the-job binges. But Louie wouldn't go away; he understood the true nature of our contract. I needed his assurances exactly as he needed his life at the Grain Camp. After a few days Louie would sober up, and one morning he would be at the breakfast table like nothing had happened. In fact, he was fired the day he died.

He was too drunk to make sense by three in the afternoon, feeding shots of whiskey to the chore man, which meant I had to take some action. So I told him to clear out. What he did was go off to visit an old woman he had known years before in a small town just down into California.

"A fancy woman," Louie said after drawing himself up to fine old-man lewdness. "Screw you, I am going to see a woman I should have been seeing." He was seventy-seven years old and unkillable so far as I

93

knew as he drove away in his old Plymouth, squinting through his cracked eyeglasses.

A stranger in a pickup truck hauled him home late in the night, and Louie, having wrecked the Plymouth, was ruined, a cut over one eye, hallucinating as he lay curled into himself like an old knot, reeking with vomit, sick on the floor, unwilling to even open his eyes, complaining that his eyeglasses were lost. This descent into nowhere had happened before. Let him lie. And he did, facing the wall for three days.

By then it was clear something extraordinary and terrible was afoot, but Louie refused to hear of the hospital in Lakeview. They'll kill you, he said. Around the time of World War I, in the Imperial Valley of California near Calexico, his back had been broken when a bridge caved in under the weight of a steel-wheeled steam tractor. The doctors got him on morphine for the pain, and then fed him alcohol to get him off morphine, and that was it for the rest of his life, he said. Booze.

They just left me there, he would say, half-drunk and grinning like it was a fine joke. Maybe he felt the doctors had already killed him. I called his son in Napa, California, who came overnight in an old car and talked Louie onto his feet, as I should have done, and into a trip over the Warner Mountains to the hospital.

All that should have been my responsibility. Days before, I should have ignored his wounded objections. The doctors wouldn't kill him, and I knew it. He would have lived some more, not for long maybe, but some more. But such obligations were a bit beyond my job description, and I fell back on excuses.

Louie Hanson died in the automobile, slumped sideways against his son—dead with a broken rib through one lung, which would have been fixable a day or so earlier. I went to the funeral but wouldn't look in the coffin. There was nothing I wanted to know about the look of things in coffins.

There had been an afternoon when I stood on a ditch bank with a dented bucket of carrot slices marinated in strychnine, poisoning badgers and dreading every moment I could foresee, all things equally unreal, my hand in the rubber glove, holding the slice of carrot, which was almost luminous, clouds over Bidwell Mountain, the sound of my breathing. I would have to move soon if I was ever going to get home. I was numb with dread and sorrowed for myself because I felt nothing but terror, and I had to know this was craziness. There is no metaphor for that condition; it is precisely like nothing.

By craziness I mean nearly catatonic fearfulness generated by the conviction that nothing you do connects to any other particular thing inside your daily life. Mine was never real craziness, although some fracturing of ice seemed to lie just around the corner of each moment. It was easy to imagine vanishing into complete disorientation. My trouble could be called "paralyzed before existential realities," a condition I could name, having read Camus like any boy of my time. But such insight was useless. Nothing was valuable unless it helped toward keeping the lid on my own disease.

THE FEE POINT reaches into the old tule beds on the east side of Warner. A homesteader shack out there was my father's first Grain Camp cookhouse, in 1938. I see my mother at the Fee in a soft summery wind, a yellow cotton dress, a young woman on a summer day, gazing out to plow-ground fields being cut from the swamps.

Close to thirty years later my Catskinners crushed that shack into a pile of weathered gray jack lumber, dumped on the diesel, and burned it. It was January and we all warmed our hands on the flames, then drank steaming coffee and ate cold roast-beef sandwiches sent out from another cookhouse.

In Latin *familia* means residence and family, which I take to mean community, an interconnection of stories. As I lie down to sleep I can stand out at the Fee Point and see my mother and those Catskinners and the old shack burning, although I have not lived on the ranch in Warner Valley for twenty years. It's a fact of no more than sentimental interest except as an example of the ways we are inhabited by stories, and the ways they connect.

Water birds were a metaphor for abundance beyond measure in my childhood. A story about water birds: On a dour November afternoon, my father sat on a wooden case of shotgun shells in the deep tules by Pelican Lake like a crown prince of shotgunning, and dropped 123 ducks for an Elks Club feed. The birds were coming north to water from the grain fields and fighting a stiff head wind. They flared and started to settle, just over him, and they would not stop coming into the long red flame from his shotgun as darkness came down from the east. The dead birds fell collapsed to the water and washed back to shore in the wind. Eventually it was too dark to shoot, and the dead birds were heaped in the back of his pickup and he hauled them to town; he dumped them off to the woman he had hired to do the picking and went on to a good clear-hearted night at the poker table, having discharged a civic duty.

When someone had killed too many birds, their necks would be strung together with baling twine, and they would be hung from spikes in an old crab-apple tree back of our house, to freeze and be given away to anyone who might come visiting. When time came to leave, we would throw in three or four Canada honkers as a leave-taking gift, frozen and stiff as cordwood, and give you the name of the lady in town who did the picking.

What is the crime here?

It is not my father's. In later years men came to me and told me he was the finest man they ever worked for, and I envy that fineness, by which, I think, they meant fair and convivial—and just, in terms of an implied contract. From an old hand who had worked for room and board and no wages through the Great Depression, that was a kind of ultimate praise. They knew he hadn't broken any promises, and he had sense enough to know that finally you can't really help anybody die, no matter how much you owe him.

But there was an obvious string of crimes. Maybe we should have known the world wasn't made for our purposes, to be remodeled into our idea of an agricultural paradise, and that Warner Valley wasn't there to have us come along and drain the swamps, and level the peat ground into alfalfa land. No doubt we should have known the water birds would quit coming. But we had been given to understand that places we owned were to be used as we saw fit. The birds were part of all that.

96

What went wrong? Rules of commerce or cowardice or what? Bad thinking? Failure to identify what was sacred? All of the above? Did such failures lead me to treat men as if they were tools, to be used?

Probably. But that is no excuse for participating in the kind of cold-heartedness we see everywhere, the crime we commit while we all claim innocence.

One night in Lakeview I was dancing with a woman we all knew as the Crop Duster's Wife. She came to the taverns every night, and she was beautiful in an over-bruised sort of way, but she wouldn't go find a bed with any of us. She was, she claimed, married forever to a man who was off in Arkansas dusting cotton from an old Steerman biplane. She said she just hoped he didn't wreck that Steerman into some Arkansas church. We sat at the bar and I was drunk and started telling her about Louie Hanson and how he died, eager to confess my craziness. Maybe I thought a woman who waited for a man who flew crop-dusting aircraft would understand. Maybe I thought she would fall for a crazy man.

"There is nothing to dislike but the meanness," she said, picking at her words. "You ought to be glad you ever knew those old farts."

Failures of the sympathy, she was saying, if I read her right, originate in failures of the imagination, which is a betrayal of self. Like so many young men, I could only see myself in the mirror of a woman. Offering the utility of that reflection, and solace, was understood to be the work of women, their old job, inhabit the house and forgive, at least until they got tired of it.

In those days a woman who wanted to be done with such duties might do something like buy herself a wedding ring and make up a story about a faraway romantic husband who flew his Steerman every morning to support her. This woman might say people like me were no cure for her loneliness. But she might excuse my self-centered sorrowing. She might say we don't have any choice, it's the creature we are. Or she might tell me to wise up and understand that sympathy can be useful only if it moves us to quit that coldness of the heart.

It is possible to imagine a story in which the Murderer does not return to prison but lives on at the Grain Camp for years and years, until he has forgiven himself and is healed—a humorous old man you could turn to for sensible advice. In the end all of us would be able to forgive and care for ourselves. We would have learned to mostly let the birds fly away, because it is not necessarily meat we are hunting.

Under the Influence

(NOVEMBER 1989)

Scott Russell Sanders

MY FATHER DRANK. He drank as a gut-punched boxer gasps for breath, as a starving dog gobbles food—compulsively, secretly, in pain and trembling. I use the past tense not because he ever quit drinking but because he quit living. That is how the story ends for my father, age sixty-four, heart bursting, body cooling, slumped and forsaken on the linoleum of my brother's trailer. The story continues for my brother, my sister, my mother, and me, and will continue as long as memory holds.

In the perennial present of memory, I slip into the garage or barn to see my father tipping back the flat green bottles of wine, the brown cylinders of whiskey, the cans of beer disguised in paper bags. His Adam's apple bobs, the liquid gurgles, he wipes the sandy-haired back of a hand over his lips, and then, his bloodshot gaze bumping into me, he stashes the bottle or can inside his jacket, under the workbench, between two bales of hay, and we both pretend the moment has not occurred.

"What's up, buddy?" he says, thick-tongued and edgy.

"Sky's up," I answer, playing along.

"And don't forget prices," he grumbles. "Prices are always up. And taxes."

In memory, his white 1951 Pontiac with the stripes down the hood

99

and the Indian head on the snout lurches to a stop in the driveway; or it is the 1956 Ford station wagon, or the 1963 Rambler shaped like a toad, or the sleek 1969 Bonneville that will do 120 miles per hour on straightaways; or it is the robin's-egg-blue pickup, new in 1980, battered in 1981, the year of his death. He climbs out, grinning dangerously, unsteady on his legs, and we children interrupt our game of catch, our building of snow forts, our picking of plums, to watch in silence as he weaves past us into the house, where he drops into his overstuffed chair and falls asleep. Shaking her head, our mother stubs out a cigarette he had left smoldering in the ashtray. All evening, until our bedtimes, we tiptoe past him, as past a snoring dragon. Then we curl fearfully in our sheets, listening. Eventually he wakes with a grunt, Mother slings accusations at him, he snarls back, she yells, he growls, their voices clashing. Before long, she retreats to their bedroom, sobbing—not from the blows of fists, for he never strikes her, but from the force of his words.

Left alone, our father prowls the house, thumping into furniture, rummaging in the kitchen, slamming doors, turning the pages of the newspaper with a savage crackle, muttering back at the late-night drivel from television. The roof might fly off, the walls might buckle from the pressure of his rage. Whatever my brother and sister and mother may be thinking on their own rumpled pillows, I lie there hating him, loving him, fearing him, knowing I have failed him. I tell myself he drinks to ease the ache that gnaws at his belly, an ache I must have caused by disappointing him somehow, a murderous ache I should be able to relieve by doing all my chores, earning A's in school, winning baseball games, fixing the broken washer and the burst pipes, bringing in the money to fill his empty wallet. He would not hide the green bottles in his toolbox, would not sneak off to the barn with a lump under his coat, would not fall asleep in the daylight, would not roar and fume, would not drink himself to death, if only I were perfect.

I am forty-four, and I know full well now that my father was an alcoholic, a man consumed by disease rather than by disappointment. What had seemed to me a private grief is in fact, of course, a public scourge. In the United States alone, some ten or fifteen million people

100

share his ailment, and behind the doors they slam in fury or disgrace, countless other children tremble. I comfort myself with such knowledge, holding it against the throb of memory like an ice pack against a bruise. Other people have keener sources of grief: poverty, racism, rape, war. I do not wish to compete to determine who has suffered most. I am only trying to understand the corrosive mixture of helplessness, responsibility, and shame that I learned to feel as the son of an alcoholic. I realize now that I did not cause my father's illness, nor could I have cured it. Yet for all this grown-up knowledge, I am still ten years old, my own son's age, and as that boy I struggle in guilt and confusion to save my father from pain.

CONSIDER A FEW of our synonyms for "drunk": tipsy, tight, pickled, soused, and plowed; stoned and stewed, lubricated and inebriated, juiced and sluiced; three sheets to the wind, in your cups, out of your mind, under the table; lit up, tanked up, wiped out; besotted, blotto, bombed, and buzzed; plastered, polluted, putrefied; loaded or looped, boozy, woozy, fuddled, or smashed; crocked and shit-faced, corked and pissed, snockered and sloshed.

It is a mostly humorous lexicon, as the lore that deals with drunks—in jokes and cartoons, in plays, films, and television skits—is largely comic. Aunt Matilda nips elderberry wine from the sideboard and burps politely during supper. Uncle Fred slouches to the table glassy-eyed, wearing a lampshade for a hat and murmuring, "Candy is dandy, but liquor is quicker." Inspired by cocktails, Mrs. Somebody recounts the events of her day in a fuzzy dialect, while Mr. Somebody nibbles her ear and croons a bawdy song. On the sofa with Boyfriend, Daughter Somebody giggles, licking gin from her lips, and loosens the bows in her hair. Junior knocks back some brews with his chums at the Leopard Lounge and stumbles home to the wrong house, wonders foggily why he cannot locate his pajamas, and crawls naked into bed with the ugliest girl in school. The family dog slurps from a neglected martini and wobbles to the nursery, where he vomits in Baby's shoe.

It is all great fun. But if in the audience you notice a few laughing faces turn grim when the drunk lurches onstage, don't be surprised, for these are the children of alcoholics. Over the grinning mask of Dionysus, the leering face of Bacchus, these children cannot help seeing the bloated features of their own parents. Instead of laughing, they wince, they mourn. Instead of celebrating the drunk as one freed from constraints, they pity him as one enslaved. They refuse to believe *in vino veritas*, having seen their befuddled parents skid away from truth toward folly and oblivion. And so these children bite their lips until the lush staggers into the wings.

My father, when drunk, was neither funny nor honest; he was pathetic, frightening, deceitful. There seemed to be a leak in him somewhere, and he poured in booze to keep from draining dry. Like a torture victim who refuses to squeal, he would never admit that he had touched a drop, not even in his last year, when he seemed to be dissolving in alcohol before our very eyes. I never knew him to lie about anything, ever, except about this one ruinous fact. Drowsy, clumsy, unable to fix a bicycle tire, balance a grocery sack, or walk across a room, he was stripped of his true self by drink. In a matter of minutes, the contents of a bottle could transform a brave man into a coward, a buddy into a bully, a gifted athlete and skilled carpenter and shrewd businessman into a bumbler. No dictionary of synonyms for "drunk" would soften the anguish of watching our prince turn into a frog.

Father's drinking became the family secret. While growing up, we children never breathed a word of it beyond the four walls of our house. To this day, my brother and sister rarely mention it, and then only when I press them. I did not confess the ugly, bewildering fact to my wife until his wavering and slurred speech forced me to. Recently, on the seventh anniversary of my father's death, I asked my mother if she ever spoke of his drinking to friends. "No, no, never," she replied hastily. "I couldn't bear for anyone to know."

The secret bores under the skin, gets in the blood, into the bone, and stays there. Long after you have supposedly been cured of malaria, the fever can flare up, the tremors can shake you. So it is with the fevers of shame. You swallow the bitter quinine of knowledge, and you learn to feel pity and compassion toward the drinker. Yet the shame lingers and, because of it, anger.

FOR A LONG stretch of my childhood we lived on a military reservation in Ohio, an arsenal where bombs were stored underground in bunkers and vintage airplanes burst into flames and unstable artillery shells boomed nightly at the dump. We had the feeling, as children, that we played within a minefield, where a heedless footfall could trigger an explosion. When Father was drinking, the house, too, became a minefield. The least bump could set off either parent.

The more he drank, the more obsessed Mother became with stopping him. She hunted for bottles, counted the cash in his wallet, sniffed at his breath. Without meaning to snoop, we children blundered left and right into damning evidence. On afternoons when he came home from work sober, we flung ourselves at him for hugs and felt against our ribs the telltale lump in his coat. In the barn we tumbled on the hay and heard beneath our sneakers the crunch of broken glass. We tugged open a drawer in his workbench, looking for screwdrivers or crescent wrenches, and spied a gleaming six-pack among the tools. Playing tag, we darted around the house just in time to see him sway on the rear stoop and heave a finished bottle into the woods. In his good-night kiss we smelled the cloying sweetness of Clorets, the mints he chewed to camouflage his dragon's breath.

I can summon up that kiss right now by recalling Theodore Roethke's lines about his own father:

> The whiskey on your breath
> Could make a small boy dizzy;
> But I hung on like death:
> Such waltzing was not easy.

Such waltzing was hard, terribly hard, for with a boy's scrawny arms I was trying to hold my tipsy father upright.

For years, the chief source of those incriminating bottles and cans was a grimy store a mile from us, a cinderblock place called Sly's, with two gas pumps outside and a mangy dog asleep in the window. Inside, on rusty metal shelves or in wheezing coolers, you could find pop and Popsicles, cigarettes, potato chips, canned soup, raunchy postcards, fishing gear, Twinkies, wine, and beer. When Father drove anywhere on errands, Mother would send us along as guards, warning us not to let him out of our sight. And so with one or more of us on board, Father would cruise up to Sly's, pump a dollar's worth of gas or plump the tires with air, and then, telling us to wait in the car, he would head for the doorway.

Dutiful and panicky, we cried, "Let us go with you!"

"No," he answered. "I'll be back in two shakes."

"Please!"

"No!" he roared. "Don't you budge or I'll jerk a knot in your tails!"

So we stayed put, kicking the seats, while he ducked inside. Often, when he had parked the car at a careless angle, we gazed in through the window and saw Mr. Sly fetching down from the shelf behind the cash register two green pints of Gallo wine. Father swigged one of them right there at the counter, stuffed the other in his pocket, and then out he came, a bulge in his coat, a flustered look on his reddened face.

Because the mom and pop who ran the dump were neighbors of ours, living just down the tar-blistered road, I hated them all the more for poisoning my father. I wanted to sneak in their store and smash the bottles and set fire to the place. I also hated the Gallo brothers, Ernest and Julio, whose jovial faces beamed from the labels of their wine, labels I would find, torn and curled, when I burned the trash. I noted the Gallo brothers' address in California and studied the road atlas to see how far that was from Ohio, because I meant to go out there and tell Ernest and Julio what they were doing to my father, and then, if they showed no mercy, I would kill them.

WHILE GROWING UP on the back roads and in the country schools and cramped Methodist churches of Ohio and Tennessee, I never heard the word "alcoholic," never happened across it in books or magazines. In the nearby towns, there were no addiction-treatment programs, no community mental-health centers, no Alcoholics Anonymous chapters, no therapists. Left alone with our grievous secret, we had no way of understanding Father's drinking except as an act of will, a deliberate folly or cruelty, a moral weakness, a sin. He drank because he chose to, pure and simple. Why our father, so playful and competent and kind when sober, would choose to ruin himself and punish his family we could not fathom.

Our neighborhood was high on the Bible, and the Bible was hard on drunkards. "Woe to those who are heroes at drinking wine and valiant men in mixing strong drink," wrote Isaiah. "The priest and the prophet reel with strong drink, they are confused with wine, they err in vision, they stumble in giving judgment. For all tables are full of vomit, no place is without filthiness." We children had seen those fouled tables at the local truck stop where the notorious boozers hung out, our father occasionally among them. "Wine and new wine take away the understanding," declared the prophet Hosea. We had also seen evidence of that in our father, who could multiply seven-digit numbers in his head when sober but when drunk could not help us with fourth-grade math. Proverbs warned: "Do not look at wine when it is red, when it sparkles in the cup and goes down smoothly. At the last it bites like a serpent and stings like an adder. Your eyes will see strange things, and your mind utter perverse things." Woe, woe.

Dismayingly often, these biblical drunkards stirred up trouble for their own kids. Noah made fresh wine after the flood, drank too much of it, fell asleep without any clothes on, and was glimpsed in the buff by his son Ham, whom Noah promptly cursed. In one passage—it was so shocking we had to read it under our blankets with flashlights—the patriarch Lot fell down drunk and slept with his daughters. The sins of the fathers set their children's teeth on edge.

Our ministers were fond of quoting St. Paul's pronouncement that drunkards would not inherit the kingdom of God. These grave preachers assured us that the wine referred to in the Last Supper was in fact grape juice. Bible and sermons and hymns combined to give us the impression that Moses should have brought down from the mountain another stone tablet, bearing the Eleventh Commandment: Thou shalt not drink.

The scariest and most illuminating Bible story apropos of drunkards was the one about the lunatic and the swine. We knew it by heart: When Jesus climbed out of his boat one day, this lunatic came charging up from the graveyard, stark naked and filthy, frothing at the mouth, so violent that he broke the strongest chains. Nobody would go near him. Night and day for years, this madman had been wailing among the tombs and bruising himself with stones. Jesus took one look at him and said, "Come out of the man, you unclean spirits!" for he could see that the lunatic was possessed by demons. Meanwhile, some hogs were conveniently rooting nearby. "If we have to come out," begged the demons, "at least let us go into those swine." Jesus agreed, the unclean spirits entered the hogs, and the hogs raced straight off a cliff and plunged into a lake. Hearing the story in Sunday school, my friends thought mainly of the pigs. (How big a splash did they make? Who paid for the lost pork?) But I thought of the redeemed lunatic, who bathed himself and put on clothes and calmly sat at the feet of Jesus, restored—so the Bible said—to "his right mind."

When drunk, our father was clearly in his wrong mind. He became a stranger, as fearful to us as any graveyard lunatic, not quite frothing at the mouth but fierce enough, quick-tempered, explosive; or else he grew maudlin and weepy, which frightened us nearly as much. In my boyhood despair, I reasoned that maybe he wasn't to blame for turning into an ogre: maybe, like the lunatic, he was possessed by demons.

If my father was indeed possessed, who would exorcise him? If he was a sinner, who would save him? If he was ill, who would cure him? If he suffered, who would ease his pain? Not ministers or doctors, for we could not bring ourselves to confide in them; not the neighbors, for we pretended they had never seen him drunk; not Mother, who fussed and pleaded but could not budge him; not my brother and sister, who were only kids. That left me. It did not matter that I, too, was only a child, and a bewildered one at that. I could not excuse myself.

ON FIRST READING a description of delirium tremens—in a book on alcoholism I smuggled from a university library—I thought immediately of the frothing lunatic and the frenzied swine. When I read stories or watched films about grisly metamorphoses—Dr. Jekyll becoming Mr. Hyde, the mild husband changing into a werewolf, the kindly neighbor inhabited by a brutal alien—I could not help but see my own father's mutation from sober to drunk. Even today, knowing better, I am attracted by the demonic theory of drink, for when I recall my father's transformation, the emergence of his ugly second self, I find it easy to believe in being possessed by unclean spirits. We never knew which version of Father would come home from work, the true or the tainted, nor could we guess how far down the slope toward cruelty he would slide.

How far a man *could* slide we gauged by observing our back-road neighbors—the out-of-work miners who had dragged their families to our corner of Ohio from the desolate hollows of Appalachia, the tight-fisted farmers, the surly mechanics, the balked and broken men. There was, for example, whiskey-soaked Mr. Jenkins, who beat his wife and kids so hard we could hear their screams from the road. There was Mr. Lavo the wino, who fell asleep smoking time and again, until one night his disgusted wife bundled up the children and went outside and left him in his easy chair to burn; he awoke on his own, staggered out coughing into the yard, and pounded her flat while the children looked on and the shack turned to ash. There was the truck driver, Mr. Sampson, who tripped over his son's tricycle one night while drunk and got mad, jumped into his semi, and drove away, shifting through the dozen gears, and never came back. We saw the bruised children of these fathers clump onto our school bus, we saw the abandoned children huddle in the pews at church, we saw the stunned and battered mothers begging for help at our doors.

Our own father never beat us, and I don't think he beat Mother, but he threatened often. The Old Testament Yahweh was not more terrible in His rage. Eyes blazing, voice booming, Father would pull out his belt and swear to give us a whipping, but he never followed through, never needed to, because we could imagine it so vividly. He shoved us, pawed us with the back of his hand, not to injure, just to clear a space. I can see him grabbing Mother by the hair as she cowers on a chair during a nightly quarrel. He twists her neck back until she gapes up at him, and then he lifts over her skull a glass quart bottle of milk, the milk spilling down his forearm, and he yells at her, "Say just one more word, one goddamn word, and I'll shut you up!" I fear she will prick him with her sharp tongue, but she is terrified into silence, and so am I, and the leaking bottle quivers in the air, and milk seeps through the red hair of my father's uplifted arm, and the entire scene is there to this moment, the head jerked back, the club raised.

When the drink made him weepy, Father would pack, kiss each of us children on the head, and announce from the front door that he was moving out. "Where to?" we demanded, fearful each time that he would leave for good, as Mr. Sampson had roared away for good in his diesel truck. "Someplace where I won't get hounded every minute," Father would answer, his jaw quivering. He stabbed a look at Mother, who might say, "Don't run into the ditch before you get there," or "Good riddance," and then he would slink away. Mother watched him go with arms crossed over her chest, her face closed like the lid on a box of snakes. We children bawled. Where could he go? To the truck stop, that den of iniquity? To one of those dark, ratty flophouses in town? Would he wind up sleeping under a railroad bridge or on a park bench or in a cardboard box, mummied in rags like the bums we had seen on our trips to Cleveland and Chicago? We bawled and bawled, wondering if he would ever come back.

He always did come back, a day or a week later, but each time there was a sliver less of him.

IN KAFKA'S *METAMORPHOSIS*, which opens famously with Gregor Samsa waking up from uneasy dreams to find himself transformed into an insect, Gregor's family keep reassuring themselves that things will be just fine again "when he comes back to us." Each time alcohol transformed our father we held out the same hope, that he would really and truly come back to us, our authentic father, the tender and playful and competent man, and then all things would be fine. We had grounds for such hope. After his tearful departures and chapfallen returns, he would sometimes go weeks, even months, without drinking. Those were glad times. Every day without the furtive glint of bottles, every meal without a fight, every bedtime without sobs encouraged us to believe that such bliss might go on forever.

Mother was fooled by such a hope all during the forty-odd years she knew Greeley Ray Sanders. Soon after she met him in a Chicago deli-catessen on the eve of World War II and fell for his butter-melting Mississippi drawl and his wavy red hair, she learned that he drank heavi-ly. But then so did a lot of men. She would soon coax or scold him into breaking the nasty habit. She would point out to him how ugly and foolish it was, this bleary drinking, and then he would quit. He refused to quit during their engagement, however, still refused during the first years of marriage, refused until my older sister came along in 1942. The shock of fatherhood sobered him, and he remained sober through my birth at the end of the war and right on through until we moved in 1951 to the Ohio arsenal. The arsenal had more than its share of alco-holics, drug addicts, and other varieties of escape artists. There I turned six and started school and woke into a child's flickering awareness, just in time to see my father begin sneaking swigs in the garage.

He sobered up again for most of a year at the height of the Korean War, to celebrate the birth of my brother. But aside from that dry spell, his only breaks from drinking before my senior year in high school were just long enough to raise and then dash our hopes. Then during the fall of that year—the time of the Cuban Missile Crisis, when it seemed that the nightly explosions at the munitions dump and the nightly rages in our household might spread to engulf the globe—Father collapsed. His liver, kidneys, and heart all conked out. The doctors saved him, but only by a hair. He stayed in the hospital for weeks, going through a withdrawal so terrible that Mother would not let us visit him. If he wanted to kill himself, the doctors solemnly warned him, all he had to do was hit the bottle again. One binge would finish him.

Father must have believed them, for he stayed dry the next fifteen years. It was an answer to prayer, Mother said, it was a miracle. I believe it was a reflex of fear, which he sustained over the years through courage and pride. He knew a man could die from drink, for his brother Roscoe had. We children never laid eyes on doomed Uncle Roscoe, but in the stories Mother told us he became a fairy-tale figure, like a boy who took the wrong turn in the woods and was gobbled up by the wolf.

The fifteen-year dry spell came to an end with Father's retirement in the spring of 1978. Like many men, he gave up his identity along with his job. One day he was a boss at the factory, with a brass plate on his door and a reputation to uphold; the next day he was a nobody at home. He and Mother were leaving Ontario, the last of the many places to which his job had carried them, and they were moving to a new house in Mississippi, his childhood stomping ground. As a boy in Mississippi, Father sold Coca-Cola during dances while the moonshiners peddled their brew in the parking lot; as a young blade, he fought in bars and in the ring, winning a state Golden Gloves championship; he gambled at poker, hunted pheasant, raced motorcycles and cars, played semiprofessional baseball, and, along with all his buddies—in the Black Cat Saloon, behind the cotton gin, in the woods—he drank hard. It was a perilous youth to dream of recovering.

After his final day of work, Mother drove on ahead with a car full of begonias and violets, while Father stayed behind to oversee the packing. When the van was loaded, the sweaty movers broke open a six-pack and offered him a beer.

"Let's drink to retirement!" they crowed. "Let's drink to freedom! to fishing! hunting! loafing! Let's drink to a guy who's going home!"

At least I imagine some such words, for that is all I can do, imagine, and I see Father's hand trembling in midair as he thinks about the fifteen sober years and about the doctors' warning, and he tells himself, *Goddamnit, I am a free man,* and *Why can't a free man drink one beer after a lifetime of hard work?* and I see his arm reaching, his fingers closing, the can tilting to his lips. I even supply a label for the beer, a swaggering brand that promises on television to deliver the essence of life. I watch the amber liquid pour down his throat, the alcohol steal into his blood, the key turn in his brain.

SOON AFTER MY parents moved back to Father's treacherous stomping ground, my wife and I visited them in Mississippi with our four-year-old daughter. Mother had been too distraught to warn me about the return of the demons. So when I climbed out of the car that bright July morning and saw my father napping in the hammock, I felt uneasy, and when he lurched upright and blinked his bloodshot eyes and greeted us in a syrupy voice, I was hurled back into childhood.

"What's the matter with Papaw?" our daughter asked.

"Nothing," I said. "Nothing!"

Like a child again, I pretended not to see him in his stupor, and behind my phony smile I grieved. On that visit and on the few that remained before his death, once again I found bottles in the workbench, bottles in the woods. Again his hands shook too much for him to run a saw, to make his precious miniature furniture, to drive straight down back roads. Again he wound up in the ditch, in the hospital, in jail, in the treatment center. Again he shouted and wept. Again he lied. "I never touched a drop," he swore. "Your mother's making it up."

I no longer fancied I could reason with the men whose names I found on the bottles—Jim Beam, Jack Daniel—but I was able now to recall the cold statistics about alcoholism: ten million victims, fifteen million, twenty. And yet, in spite of my age, I reacted in the same blind way as I had in childhood, by vainly seeking to erase through my efforts whatever drove him to drink. I worked on their place twelve and sixteen hours a day, in the swelter of Mississippi summers, digging ditches, running electrical wires, planting trees, mowing grass, building sheds, as though what nagged at him was some list of chores, as though by taking his worries upon my shoulders I could redeem him. I was flung back into boyhood, acting as though my father would not drink himself to death if only I were perfect.

I failed of perfection; he succeeded in dying. To the end, he considered himself not sick but sinful. "Do you want to kill yourself?" I asked him. "Why not?" he answered. "Why the hell not? What's there to save?" To the end, he would not speak about his feelings, would not or could not give a name to the beast that was devouring him.

In silence, he went rushing off the cliff. Unlike the biblical swine, however, he left behind a few of the demons to haunt his children. Life with him and the loss of him twisted us into shapes that will be familiar to other sons and daughters of alcoholics. My brother became a rebel, my sister retreated into shyness, I played the stalwart and dutiful son who would hold the family together. If my father was unstable,

I would be a rock. If he squandered money on drink, I would pinch every penny. If he wept when drunk—and only when drunk—I would not let myself weep at all. If he roared at the Little League umpire for calling my pitches balls, I would throw nothing but strikes. Watching him flounder and rage, I came to dread the loss of control. I would go through life without making anyone mad. I vowed never to put in my mouth or veins any chemical that would banish my everyday self. I would never make a scene, never lash out at the ones I loved, never hurt a soul. Through hard work, relentless work, I would achieve something dazzling—in the classroom, on the basketball court, in the science lab, in the pages of books—and my achievement would distract the world's eyes from his humiliation. I would become a worthy sacrifice, and the smoke of my burning would please God.

It is far easier to recognize these twists in my character than to undo them. Work has become an addiction for me, as drink was an addiction for my father. Knowing this, my daughter gave me a placard for the wall: WORKAHOLIC. The labor is endless and futile, for I can no more redeem myself through work than I could redeem my father. I still panic in the face of other people's anger, because his drunken temper was so terrible. I shrink from causing sadness or disappointment even to strangers, as though I were still concealing the family shame. I still notice every twitch of emotion in those faces around me, having learned as a child to read the weather in faces, and I blame myself for their least pang of unhappiness or anger. In certain moods I blame myself for everything. Guilt burns like acid in my veins.

I AM MOVED to write these pages now because my own son, at the age of ten, is taking on himself the griefs of the world, and in particular the griefs of his father. He tells me that when I am gripped by sadness, he feels responsible; he feels there must be something he can do to spring me from depression, to fix my life. And that crushing sense of responsibility is exactly what I felt at the age of ten in the face of my father's drinking. My son wonders if I, too, am possessed. I write, therefore, to drag into the light what eats at me—the fear, the guilt, the shame—so that my own children may be spared.

I still shy away from nightclubs, from bars, from parties where the solvent is alcohol. My friends puzzle over this, but it is no more peculiar than for a man to shy away from the lions' den after seeing his father torn apart. I took my own first drink at the age of twenty-one, half a glass of burgundy. I knew the odds of my becoming an alcoholic were four times higher than for the children of nonalcoholic fathers. So I sipped warily.

I still do—once a week, perhaps, a glass of wine, a can of beer, nothing stronger, nothing more. I listen for the turning of a key in my brain.

ABSENCES

(JUNE 1991)

James Conaway

I HAD BEEN going home to Memphis for twenty-five years when I first noticed that my father was losing his mind. I say first noticed, but the signs had for a long time stretched across the sheets of graph paper on which he occasionally wrote letters—he was an engineer but would not have used formal stationery in any case—in a hand so crabbed that the letters grew increasingly brief and finally ceased. I should have asked why; I should have put aside the concerns of my own life and formally recognized the little routine absences that were leading, inexorably, to an absence of life.

In truth, I knew little about my father's ailment, not enough to admit that "it" even existed beyond the natural mental perambulations of an independent old man who had lived within the bounds of propriety, disappointment, and some hardship. There were other signs: a hesitancy on the telephone, an awkwardness with numbers—for years it had been his business to calculate how much refrigerated air a Memphis skyscraper needed to remain habitable—and a slight stammer. I attributed that to bourbon and learned too late it had little to do with that recreational beverage. What it had to do with has a name, but the name is irrelevant, even harmful, since the naming doesn't alleviate the pain and relegates the victim, as it relegated my father, to the role of an incurable in an age of medical self-congratulation.

It was late autumn—monsoon season—and the ragged skies rolling out of Arkansas would have dropped tornadoes on a city less blessed than Memphis. I had flown in from Knoxville in a polished steel tube, owned by a bank in east Tennessee, that was filled to capacity with successful dealers in estates, real and imagined. One of them would soon be indicted and sent to prison, but for the moment they were happily chasing deals around the South, and I was to write about them for the *Washington Post,* my employer at the time. Dad met me on the street where the bankers' limousine left me, at the wheel of his small car; I knew immediately something was wrong. The face beneath the snap-brim hat seemed diminished, the eyes full of misgiving. The neighborhood should have been familiar territory, but he regarded it as alien. "Hello, sonny boy," he said when I got in; I kissed him and felt the stubble and smelled the remnants of my own childhood, not tobacco now, not whiskey, but the enfeebled suggestions of black coffee, Noxzema, and the dead leaves he moved ceaselessly from lawn to street.

He drove without talking, concentrating on the task at hand, running a stop sign, turning a corner without regard for the oblique stream of oncoming traffic or horn blasts, passing a pedestrian who wisely decided not to challenge our passage because otherwise he would have been killed, probably not by the violence of the initial blow but by the car's dogged persistence in running him over. Dad did not intend to stop until he had returned to the shelter of the carport, attached to a house that had been sleek and modern in the Sixties, set back among the trees and shrubs that render east Memphis botanical anarchy in the spring and that now, in November, enfolded the low eaves in near-tropical profusion.

My mother met us at the door in bathrobe and slippers—the uniform. Looking after my father had become a full-time endeavor. Together we got him out of his hat and raincoat and seated on the low couch, where he watched the evening news without interest. When Mom and I were alone, I said savagely, "He shouldn't be driving," and she said, "It's all he's got left."

HE WAS KNOWN as Connie, and he decided to go fight the

Japanese when I was a baby. I shouldn't be able to remember that day but I do: hot metal stairs leading up to a railway platform in midtown, my father's smooth cheeks and shining summer dress uniform, the hat emblazoned with a gold eagle as he leans out the door of the departing train, an immaculate white wedge, smiling unhappily, one hand raised as if testing the wind. Connie didn't have to enlist in the Navy, being too old for the draft and not skilled enough to be crucial; my mother never forgave him. As a Seabee he fought alongside the Marines on Guam and Peleliu and came back to Memphis full of stories of air raids and a sun hotter than the one at home, of tropical birds that flew backward, of an enemy that holed up in caves or floated facedown, dead, in mountain pools, or appeared at dawn, naked, uniforms neatly bundled and placed on rocks, to surrender. At least some of the stories were buttressed by hardware: a knife made from the wreckage of a Japanese aircraft, glass balls that had held afloat the fishing nets of other yellow people on that far ocean. Nothing reinforced the exotic quality of Connie's war more than those smooth, green globes, the smoky glass full of bubbles and strange imperfections.

My mother's resentment was poured out in letters. She kept his replies wrapped in ribbon in a box on the closet floor. He joined us in the house of his mother-in-law and her new husband, a house where, for him, work became the closest thing to having fun, a bulwark against a future that stretched before him, unavoidably. He built and painted fences, and installed a huge attic fan that sucked moths flat against the screens, and put in a bathroom upstairs. I was pressed into helping whenever my older brother managed to escape. "Jimbo, would you like to bring me that hammer?" Dad would say. "Jimbo, would you like to run over there and get me that board?" "Jimbo, would you like to crawl up under there and see if you can find that goddamn roll of electrical tape?" In the process I learned journeyman carpentry and glimpsed in the intentness of Dad's gaze and the alacrity of his muscular hands, heard in his murmured, monumental impatience, the unease that lay behind his domestic complicity. I didn't know then that other men were out playing golf, shooting ducks, trolling for smallmouth bass, drinking in comfortable chairs, doing the things men did on weekends.

117

Dad spent those years moving his file cabinets and battered desk from one building to another, taking advantage of developers' offers as Memphis shifted ever eastward. He made a modest living selling cooling devices to building contractors. Even I was aware of some irony in that: his family predated my mother's in Memphis. His mother's forebear, a fierce, one-legged Confederate veteran, had once owned a sizable piece of what became Overton Park; his descendants qualified as burghers.

As the younger brother of the bluff, funny Edwin, my father grew up believing in the successful enterprise. I remember a certain windiness when Uncle Edwin entered a room. He had introduced ice to the mid-South, and that had made him rich. Edwin Conaway's ice houses—barns with sweaty oak doors opening into the murk, hung with sides of beef and ham haunches and stacked blue-green slabs of ice giving off fog in layers that crept along floors and spilled over thresholds—were money machines. He used them to build a fortune in stocks.

My father, sixteen years younger than Edwin, had seemed destined to get rich through ice, too. First he went off to Washington and Lee; Edwin had offered to pay his way. But while in Lexington he received word that Edwin and his ice houses were in trouble—the '29 crash had caught him—and his life now took another turn. Dad left W & L to take up something more practical; he enrolled in engineering school at a state university. Years later, Edwin, driving at night along a two-lane highway, far from Memphis, met on the downward slope of a hill the opposite and equal force of his own headlight-flashing sedan (the other car was driven by a drunk on the wrong side of the road) and died of it.

THE PROCESS OF recognizing my father's predicament, if that is the right word, must be common to other families: discomfort, denial, acquiescence, grief, anger. The doctors were particularly inept, ranging from the affable family physician, who assured us that all old people lose their memories and functions, to a tactless psychiatrist whose specialty was assisting the aged; he wore a heavy gold ID bracelet and demanded that my father count backward from one hundred and, in the midst of Dad's struggling to do so, proudly proclaimed dementia.

Money was a problem. Though the disease had a name, it had no cure, and so my father could not be committed to the hospital. For this reason the government could not be induced to help pay. It fell to my mother, also in her seventies, to care for an invalid who increasingly failed to remember names, hid the mail, shuffled and sometimes stumbled, defied the most potent pharmacopoeia to keep her awake, dribbled his food, railed at her for the loss of his right to drive and other frustrations, and eventually threatened violence if the increasingly phantasmagoric landscape would not hold still. Yet she refused to entomb him in a nursing home. They owned the house but could not afford both it and a nurse, and buying a smaller place was a subject that could not be discussed calmly. Mom talked instead of nonexistent equity, including stock in a moviemaking company that supposedly had Goldie Hawn in tow, sold to my mother by another specialist in assisting the aged. Those lucre-driven arguments released a rancor in me that I will always regret.

During visits to Memphis my brothers and I shot pool with Dad, always the best. We watched him clean the table with displays of his beautiful follow-through as he disregarded color and numbers on the balls, sinking the cue ball off the eight and the eight off the eleven and so on until he lost interest and we started the game all over again.

Once, when I announced I was going to take a shower, Dad said, "Don't forget a spoon."

He fell in love with women on sight and offered, in a friendly way, to knock me down if I didn't stop talking to the female director of the Alzheimer's clinic to whom he was suddenly attracted. He never lost his appetite while still at home, demolishing roast beef, sweet potatoes, tacos, grits, biscuits, and lemon meringue pie without discrimination or regard for the manners that had once been important, but somehow he kept growing smaller.

As it happened, my mother succumbed first, to an aneurysm—a ballooning of a blood vessel—in the right side of the brain. Fortunately, by then they had hired a man to work around the house, since Dad was no longer able to rake leaves; it was he who found my mother in time. From the hospital, Dad somehow managed to telephone me in Washington; like a child, he asked, "Where is everybody?"

Mom survived the surgery but not as the person we knew, and so she was the first to be institutionalized. My brothers and I found another nursing home for Dad just blocks from the corner where he met me that wet November. The night before we moved him we all got a little drunk—I, my brothers, Frank and Dan, my nephew, Danny, and of course Dad.

Too much has been written about whiskey in the South. It was often talked about when I was growing up and utilized at odd moments. Frank once heard our uncle, in the alcoholic blush of Christmas Eve, cradling fifths of his two favorite bourbons, proclaim to all present, "These are the standards!" The idea was that good things followed if you knew what and how to drink, and kept in practice. Dad would travel with a quart of sour mash, and he kept one in the desk drawer at his office and another in the cabinet above the refrigerator. I often saw him extract and uncork it on a tedious afternoon, an act that required neither apology nor explanation. Boys going off for the first time to Ole Miss or U.T. or Chapel Hill took with them an intimate knowledge of the mysteries of drink and were known for it.

This time alcohol undeniably served a purpose beyond the reach of sentiment or drugs. Dad's drinking had been severely curtailed, and now, as we sat around the kitchen table and he sipped some wine, an amazing thing happened: he shed, however briefly, the lost look of the terminally deranged and put on the old, sweet insouciance of the perennial party boy. He no longer knew our names but he did know that he belonged to us, and he teased, and cussed a bit, and even threw—gingerly—a piece of cutlery. Boys, even three generations of them together, were supposed to be cutups, a bit dangerous but adorable. He had been viewed that way as a child, and by my mother too, despite their differences; and in this brief, boozy epiphany I glimpsed all that had been bundled down to me and my brothers and our children, and wondered what place on the planet could possibly replicate such a curious blend of love and delusion.

We hung my mother's oils on the wall of his room at Bright Glade. One painting was of the house outside Tucson where my parents had spent a glorious year in the Thirties, but Dad was not happy with his new digs. The day after we left him we received a call from the director, saying that Dad had attempted to walk out and, when detained, threatened to strike the attendant. I inferred that he had also used the racial epithet once so common in Memphis, and I went out and lectured Dad, who listened in perplexity, sitting in the stuffed chair we had hauled over from the house. I feared the staff would lose patience and neglect him, but I was wrong. In my fumbling attempt to apologize for my father I must have lost my composure, and I remember a large black woman taking my hand sympathetically, as if I were the patient and all this discord was transitory and ultimately insignificant.

I saw him only a few times after that, sitting in the foyer of the nursing home, where America's actuarial bias lay starkly exposed. Except for Dad and one other man, the many patients were women, in wheelchairs, facing the door like a school of steelhead watching for the river to rise. Dad almost always slept. First they fed him with a spoon and then with a big plastic syringe. He continued to shrink. When awake, his eyes danced desperately. Pushing him along the outdoor walkway, I saw him attempt to follow the flight of a jay and imagined him living with a relentless mental strobe, each flickering image bearing no relation to what preceded or followed it. He died a year after he went in, Dan holding a hand grown thin and dry as cardboard.

HIS WILL WAS an old one, scribbled on graph paper. Dad had requested cremation and the spreading of his ashes on the surface of the Mississippi River, at a point of our choosing. We were told by the Coast Guard that this was not permissible but decided to do it anyway; one bleak spring day the three of us boarded a houseboat piloted by my brother's neighbor and set out from the marina on Mud Island, at the foot of the city, with a small metal can that had a snap-on plastic lid. Dad's name was typed on a piece of paper taped to the lid. What he'd hoped for, I think, was accord among the three of us, and maybe even some festivity. I had bought a half-pint of Jim Beam but left it under the car seat.

We headed upstream. In another month the river would rise above the levee on the Arkansas bank and spread away like an inland, caramel-colored sea. A strong current rode up the stone buttresses beneath new, arching spans; we felt the tug of that dark water.

Our pilot said, "Be sure the wind's behind you."

We removed the lid and sprinkled ashes in turn, starting with my older brother. Dan sank the tin; I tossed the lid, which floated my father's name briefly beneath the eye of the world before slipping under.

A month later I dreamed of a man walking with assurance along an empty airport corridor carrying a hanging bag. It was Dad, thirty years younger, his hair thick on the sides, deep chestnut in color; his lean, muscular arms protruded from the rolled sleeves of his shirt with the old-fashioned wing-tip collars. I was surprised to see him there because he did not like to fly—flying is expensive and tends to take you to places where you would just as soon not be—and yet he was off, waving, through a dim, untended portal.

A year later I dreamed of a distant city I wanted to leave, to get to a place where I had left something of significance. My inquiries, made to a faceless person behind a cash register, elicited no response. Across the street sat a station wagon, red in the streaking rain; a clipboard on the seat suggested scheduling, imminent departure. A man sat in the passenger seat. "Dad," I said, and he turned and smiled, the polished rims of his spectacles gathering the light. His gray beard was trimmed to fit the squarish contours of his jaw, and he wore the tan raincoat I knew so well. He said, "Get in, son," with the friendly authority of a man who knows where he, where *we*, are going and is happy to provide deliverance and good company.

SLEEPYTOWN

(JULY 1992)

Donna Tartt

I REMEMBER MY great-grandfather—who was born fourteen years before the end of Queen Victoria's reign, and who was therefore Victorian not only by temperament but by statute as well—once saying that Thomas De Quincey was the greatest prose stylist in the English language. He was given to proclamations like that, usually announced loudly in the midst of some entirely unrelated conversation: the greatest Natural Wonder of the World, say, or the greatest book in the Bible. These recipients of his favor happened to change as the mood struck him; Dickens, for instance, and James Fenimore Cooper being on other occasions bestowed the prose stylist's laurel. I was ten at the time, and aware of both Dickens and Cooper (it was hard, in our household, not to be aware of Dickens, as my great-grandfather spoke of Dickens frequently and in a manner that led one to believe he had been personally acquainted with him), but De Quincey was a mystery. Though there were plenty of books in our house, there were none by him. I supposed that they had been lost, along with other lamented articles, either in one of my great-grandparents' moves or in the big fire at the old house, an event that occurred thirty years before my birth and that had assumed, in my imagination, the importance of the burning of the library at Alexandria.

Three years later I happened to run across a copy of *Confessions of an English Opium-Eater,* in the college apartment of one of my older cousin's hippie friends. It was the end of term; I had come along with my aunt and uncle to fetch my cousin from school, and my cousin, who was seven years older than me and took a perverse and active interest in my corruption, had invited me to come inside with him, ostensibly to say good-bye to the hippie friend but actually to smoke pot, while Aunt and Uncle waited trustfully in the car.

Though I was more than willing to be corrupted—and would have been heartbroken if my cousin, whom I idolized, had left me outside with his parents—I was both unused to pot and shy around the friend, who had a beard and scared me. Another guy was there, whom I didn't know, and a couple of girls. Wretchedly stoned after three or four awkward puffs, I left them all sitting on the living-room floor—chatting, still passing the reefer around, apparently unaffected—and wandered speechlessly around the apartment. I found myself in a room that was empty except for a stack of books and some record albums. The records were predictable (*Abbey Road, Are You Experienced?*) and so were the books, except for the Thomas De Quincey. I sat down on the floor and looked at it. It was, to me, pretty much incomprehensible. But there were pictures, black-and-white engravings—of Chinese dragons screaming through the London skies and enormous bat wings spread over the sooty roof of St. Paul's—which struck a dim, sweet chord in my imagination. Overtly sinister, they were also oddly soothing, like the certain nightmare from childhood which had grown so familiar that—when I found myself standing on the windswept dream-hillside where it invariably began—I was somehow strangely comforted, because I always knew exactly what was going to happen. I looked at the pictures for a long time. Then my cousin came to find me and dragged me out to the car, where I sat very still on the drive home and tried not to act weird, as my unsuspecting aunt and uncle talked loudly in the paranoid, vibrating silence.

"O JUST, SUBTILE, and mighty opium!" says De Quincey, ". . . thou buildest upon the bosom of darkness, out of the fantastic imagery of the brain, cities and temples, beyond the art of Phidias and

Praxiteles—beyond the splendor of Babylon and Hekatompylos; and, 'from the anarchy of dreaming sleep,' callest into sunny light the faces of long-buried beauties, and the blessed household countenances, cleansed from the 'dishonors of the grave.' "

It might seem strange that my Victorian great-grandfather, who frowned even upon the innocent diversion of moviegoing, could admire an author who described so winningly this far more vicious pleasure. But in spite of, perhaps even because of, his upbringing, he had a nearly unlimited faith in the magic of Pharmacy. He was fond of relating horror stories of the Confederacy, of nicks and blisters turning into septic poisoning ("One bottle of rubbing alcohol!" he would say dramatically. "One bottle of rubbing alcohol could have saved hundreds of those boys!"), or of simple surgical procedures leading to shock and needless fatality because of the deadly shortage of morphine. (To this day, one of the most moving scenes for me in the film of *Gone with the Wind* is the scene at the Atlanta railroad depot, where poor Dr. Meade is surrounded by thousands of Confederate wounded: no morphine, no bandages, no chloroform, nothing.)

My great-grandfather's own mother had died, when he was a boy, a wrenching and terrible death from some illness now easily cured by penicillin; in later life, he had unwavering faith in the supernatural powers of this drug, which in the end would prove to be his undoing. Though he had been repeatedly warned not to, in the last years of his life he dosed himself almost constantly with antibiotics, whether there was anything the matter with him or not. These antibiotics were readily supplied to him—as was just about any drug in our town, to just about anybody—upon request, by local doctors and pharmacists who apparently believed that since my great-grand-father was an intelligent man, and well thought of in the community, he was therefore qualified to assume responsibility for his own medical treatment, despite his utter lack of any medical knowledge whatsoever. So he took antibiotics all the time, believing them to be a kind of healthful preventative, or nerve tonic, and over the years built up a gradual but powerful resistance, until the Easter weekend when a cold metamorphosed, unexpectedly, into pneumonia and—

the pills that would have saved his mother now powerless to help him—he died.

WHEN RELATIVES REMINISCE about my great-grandfather, they almost always precede it with some reference to his affection for me. "You were his heart's own darling," they say; and, "He thought the sun rose and set on you." This was the truth. I was the product of a skittish, immature mother—Great-grandfather's youngest granddaughter, also dearly loved—and a dashing but feckless father; my parents were neither able nor inclined to take much of an interest in my early upbringing. But my mother's family—a bevy of great-aunts and grandparents—were only too glad to rush into this breach, and I spent my days and most of my nights in the old house on Commerce Street, which had been bereft of children for nearly twenty years. Though most people in the advanced stages of life (the occupants of the Commerce Street house ranged in age from fifty to eighty) would have found the intrusion of a newborn infant unsettling, my arrival was apparently a source of excitement and much-needed diversion, and a bassinet was dragged from the attic, books were consulted, the milkman was advised to bring an extra quart or so per day. "It was," my great-aunt says happily, "like somebody just left a baby out on our doorstep." Then she goes on to tell the story that I've heard a thousand times: how, at the first, I was too small to wear regular baby clothes and had to be diapered in handkerchiefs, which had everyone in a quandary until someone hit upon the idea of doll's clothes, a small trunk of which was unearthed in some forgotten toy box. (There exists a hilarious photograph of me lying in a crib and wearing, for an infant, an oddly sophisticated career-girl outfit.)

Amidst this flurry of activity, my great-grandfather was the self-appointed arbiter of all matters relating to my care. Though he knew nothing about babies, he believed he knew everything and refused to listen to my great-grandmother's more sensible counsel. I was a healthy little girl, however, and thrived under what my great-aunts secretly thought was his nutty regime—until, to everyone's alarm, I started to become what they all called "sickly" when I was about five years old.

The problem was bad tonsils, nothing serious. But until they were removed, when I was seven, I was ill and feverish much of the time and had to stay in bed an average of about three days a week. (I came close to failing the first grade, not because of poor marks but because of a poor attendance record.) To my gloomy and sentimental great-grandfather—who was possessed of a Dickensian worldview in which rowdy children prospered while sweet little good ones were gathered swiftly to the Lord—this was nothing less than a sign that I should soon be taken from him, and he mourned for me as if I were already dead. Matters were not helped by his having had a little sister who had died at about my age. And though everyone tried to reassure him—it was the 1960s, children didn't die of trifles anymore—he refused to be comforted. Even the beacon of penicillin did not offer him much hope. While he believed implicitly in its power in all matters pertaining to himself, he did not trust it fully with the lives of his loved ones: a lucky thing, as it happened, for me, as I do not know how I would have responded to the continual and bludgeoning doses of antibiotics that he prescribed for himself.

What my great-grandfather did prescribe for me—along with whatever medicine I got from the doctor—were spoonfuls of blackstrap molasses and some horrible licorice-flavored medicine that was supposed to have vitamins in it, along with glasses of whiskey at my bedtime and regular and massive doses of some red stuff which I now know to have been codeine cough syrup. The whiskey was mixed with sugar and hot water; it was supposed to make me sleep and help me put on weight, both of which it did. The reasoning behind the cough syrup remains obscure, as a cough was not among my symptoms. Perhaps he was unaware the syrup had codeine in it; perhaps he was simply trying to make me comfortable in what he thought were my last days. But, for whatever reason, the big red bottles kept coming from the drugstore, and—between the fever and the whiskey and the codeine—I spent nearly two years of my childhood submerged in a pretty powerfully altered state of consciousness.

WHEN I REMEMBER those years, the long, drugged afternoons lying in bed, or the black winter mornings swaying dreamily at my desk (for the codeine bottle, along with the licorice medicine, accompanied me to school), I realize that I knew, even then, that the languorous undersea existence through which I drifted was peculiar to myself and understood by no one around me. Hiss of gas heater, sleepy scrape of chalk on blackboard. I saw desolate, volcanic landscapes stirring in the wood grain of the desk in front of me; a stained-glass window in the place of a taped-up sheet of construction paper. A wadded paper bag, left over from someone's lunch, would metamorphose into a drowsy brown hedgehog, snoozing sweetly by the garbage can.

My report card for the first grade stated that I was "quiet" and "cooperative." But what I really preferred was staying home sick, where I could allow my hallucinations to run free without the teacher's tedious interruptions. I would stare, sometimes for hours, at a particular View-Master reel: Peter Pan, soaring high over London, his thin, moon-cast shadow skimming over the cobblestones below. Even when unmedicated, if I stared at this particular picture long enough, I sometimes got the giddy sensation that I was flying; just as, if I closed my eyes in the backseat of my mother's Chrysler and tried hard enough, I could sometimes transform the Chrysler into an airplane. Now—to my immense satisfaction—this knack had increased itself by an almost exponential degree, to the point where the Chrysler seemed to be able to turn *itself* into a plane whenever it liked, and with no help from me whatsoever.

If Thomas De Quincey dreamed of lost Babylons, I dreamed about Neverland. I dreamed about Neverland, and Disneyland, and Oz, and other lands that had no name at all, with talking bears and swan princes. Sometimes, in the sleepy glow of the gas heater, I would catch a glimpse of Huck and Tom's campfire, out on their sandbar in the Mississippi. And sometimes at night the rattle of a truck going past would transform itself into the leaden advent of a dinosaur, its head above the telephone wires, plodding down the moonlit, empty streets. Our neighborhood was full of mimosa trees; they looked, to my eye, much like the Jurassic tree-ferns in the illustrated dinosaur book my grandmother had given me. It was not hard to imagine our yard, after dark, transforming itself into some prehistoric feeding ground; the gentle neck of a brontosaurus—mild-eyed, blinking like a tortoise—stretching to peer at me through my bedroom window.

I was spending more time at my own house now—my parents had a maid who looked after me—but it was still only around the corner from the house on Commerce Street, and my relatives there, who were mostly retired and had nothing much to do, came frequently to visit on the days I was home sick: bullying the maid, inspecting the contents of the linen closet and the refrigerator, making rueful but affectionate comments about my poor mother's lack of household-management skills. "That Baby," one of them remarked once (they all called my mother Baby, and still do, though she is now almost fifty), "isn't any better mother than a cat." This remark stuck in my mind—my mother, with her green eyes and her graceful way of sitting with her legs tucked under her, really did look like a cat—and I couldn't understand, when I repeated this to her, why she got so upset.

Feeling sick, and being warned occasionally that I might die, seemed a perfectly natural thing to me, as I had spent most of my life around old people. Though all the residents of Commerce Street possessed, in some degree or another, that affectionate, light-hearted streak which had found its culmination in my mother, they also possessed a kind of effusive, elegiac fatalism which expressed itself in long gloomy visits to the cemetery and melancholy ruminations on the vanity of human wishes, the certainty of suffering and loss. My great-grandfather liked to show me the graves of his deceased relatives ("Poor Papa," he would say with a mournful shake of the head, "that's all he's got left now") and also the spots reserved for my great-grandmother and himself. On the way to the car, he would always point out to me the tiny grave, adorned with the statue of a little girl, of some child about my age who had died nearly a hundred years before.

"I expect this is the last Christmas" (or Thanksgiving, or Easter, or whatever holiday was coming up) "that you and I are going to spend together on this old earth, darling," he would always say sorrowfully, on the way home in the old De Soto. And I would look at the side of his face and wonder: which of us was going to go first, him or me?

I WAS CONVINCED that I would die soon. This conviction, how-ever, did not cause me much alarm. I was less concerned about separa-tion from my family—a separation that, after all, would only be temporary—than I was about leaving my books and my toys and most of all my dog. In the Commerce Street theology, good dogs went to Heaven (and bad ones, presumably, to Hell), but when in Sunday school I expressed this theory as fact, I was swiftly corrected, and came home crying. My mother, my aunts, everyone tried to reassure me ("It was bad of that woman," said my great-grandfather darkly, "to tell you that"), but even so, doubt remained.

Though I disliked the idea of God and Jesus (an opinion that I, correctly, believed unwise to share with my family), everyone assured me that Heaven was a good place and I would be happy there. But I had a number of questions that no one was able to answer. Was there television? Did people exchange gifts at Christmas? Would I have to go to school? I had read in *Peter Pan* that Peter goes part of the way with dead children so they will not be frightened. Perhaps, I thought on long boring Sundays when the idea of Heaven seemed oppressive, if Peter did come to get me I could talk him into taking me not to Heaven but to wherever it was that he lived, where I could hunt pirates and swim in the lagoon with the mermaids and probably have a whole lot of fun.

I had a cigar box full of small things I loved, which I kept beneath my bed. In it were some photographs, a fossil that I'd found, a topaz ring my mother had given me, and a china dog that my great-grand-father had got in his Christmas stocking when he was a little boy. There was also a silver dollar, an ivory chess piece that had no particu-lar sentimental value but that I thought was pretty, and a lock of my great-grandmother's hair. I had some idea that I would be able to tuck this box under my arm and bring it along with me when the time came. I also kept in this box—because I had nowhere else secret enough to keep it—an old stereopticon slide that I had stolen from my uncle's house in Meridian. It depicted savages, on some horrid African veld, eating a bloody dismembered thing that I was sure was a person. In normal consciousness (and it was not a drawing, but a photograph) it frightened me so much that I wouldn't even touch it, and I kept it well hidden beneath the other photographs at the bottom of the box. But sometimes, after I had taken my medicine, I would get it out and stare at it for hours—bewitched, in a kind of abstract way, at both the horror of the scene itself and its odd lack of power to affect me.

My mother, despite the accusations leveled at her, was actually not such a bad mother as all that. She liked to play with me, listened to me as carefully as if I were an adult, and bought me Goo Goo clusters (her own favorite candy) at the little store down the street from where she worked. And though she was admittedly a bit on the childish side, this childishness enabled her to understand me better than just about anyone else. She, too, had been a dreamy little girl who sleepwalked and had imaginary playmates.

We also shared the gift—alarming to everyone else—of being able to plunge ourselves into sort of eerie, self-induced fits. I would stare fixedly at a certain object and repeat a word or phrase until it became nonsense. Then, at some subsequent point, I was never sure exactly how long, I would snap to again and have absolutely no idea who or where I was, and be unable to recognize even the members of my own family. This lasted sometimes as long as three or four minutes, during which I would be completely insensible to shakes, snapped fingers, my frantically repeated name. I was able to do this anytime I felt like it, to amuse myself when bored—the amusing thing being always those first strange minutes when I woke up and saw everything and everyone for the very first time; like a person blind from birth who has just had the bandages unwrapped after an operation restoring sight. I stumbled upon this gift quite by accident when I was four or five, while sitting in an Italian restaurant in Memphis with my parents.

On this first occasion, while my father—a black-haired, bad-tempered stranger—shook my arm and shouted an unfamiliar name in my face, my mother remained oddly calm. Later, alone, she questioned me. I explained what had happened and how I had brought it about. She then told me that she had once been able to do the exact same thing, though the knack had been lost with age. (As I grew older, my talent, too, disappeared; the last time I was ever able to successfully pull this trick was when I was a sophomore in high school, bored in the back of biology class.) We discussed it for a while, the ins and outs. Her procedure, it seemed, was slightly different from mine. And yes, she said, if you were bored, it *was* sort of an interesting thing to do, wasn't it?

It was precisely this sort of thing that made some people consider my mother an unwholesome influence. But my mother had her own ideas about what was good for me. Though she did not want to offend my great-grandfather, for instance, I knew she did not like the way he constantly dosed me with medicine. This, I think, was partly instinct and partly because she did not like me to be forced, ever, to do anything I did not want to do, even if that something—like being made to eat liver or go to bed before ten—was unquestionably good for me. (I really do not think she would have had the heart to make me go to school were it not, she explained apologetically, the law.)

Whatever the case, she never personally administered either the licorice medicine or the codeine and, left to her own devices, would have peacefully allowed the bottles to gather dust on top of the refrigerator along with the fondue pot, the mathematics flash cards somebody had given me, and various other useless and unloved articles. "Has that maid been forgetting to give this child her medicine?" my great-grandfather would sometimes say fiercely, upon noting that the levels of the bottles were suspiciously high. It was his roundabout way of accusing my mother; the maid—as he was well aware—was terrified of him and would never have skipped a dose that was to be administered while she was on duty.

"Why, no," my mother would say sweetly. "I don't think Cleo would ever forget something like that, do you?" And sometimes, if he wasn't looking, she would wink at me.

MY LONG SABBATICAL in the Land of the Poppy was by no means all pleasant. The good dreams, though sometimes effortless, usually required a bit of coaxing; when the bad ones came—as they frequently did, uninvited, like the evil fairy to the wedding feast— there was no forcing them back. I always had to sleep with a light on, and many nights woke screaming for Mother or Cleo. The worst dreams usually had to do with snakes, but the very worst dream of all still frightens me to think of, even though it is years since I last dreamed it. In it, a set of country-club types—smartly dressed, around what would have then been my parents' age—are gathered, cocktails in hand, around a barbecue grill. They are snickering with jaded amusement as one of their number—a handsome, caddish-looking fellow—holds a howling Persian cat over the barbecue, pushing its feet into the flames.

I always woke, howling myself, at this point. Though it was never quite clear exactly who these people were, it was obvious to me that what they were doing was Devil worship—which I knew all about from the maid—and that what I had glimpsed were only the more innocent, preliminary stages of the ritual. Unimaginable horrors lay beyond. Which set me thinking, as I lay back trembling in bed after Mother had come and gone, about Devils, and Hell, and all the bad things there were in the world, and what was *really* going to happen to me after I died, and I would start to scream again for Mother; and, frequently, it was lucky if anyone in the house got any sleep at all on those nights.

> *O mother, lay your hand on my brow!*
> *O, mother, mother, where am I now?*
> *Why is the room so gaunt and great?*
> *Why am I lying awake so late? . . .*
> *What have I done, and what do I fear,*
> *And why are you crying, mother dear?*

—from "The Sick Child," by Robert Louis Stevenson

The worst nights were when my fever was high, when my teeth chattered even in the summertime and the doctor had to come. I was one of those children who never told anyone when I was starting to feel bad and always crawled behind the couch or under the bed and fell asleep, to be discovered hours later, dusty and disoriented, still wrapped in the Navaho blanket I had dragged from the cupboard. (I used always to play Indian on those afternoons I was getting sick, the red Navaho blanket assisting for a while to disguise, as I crawled through the tunnel behind the sofa-back or lay in my hunter's camp beneath the table, the first creeping bone-chill of advancing fever.) So by the time they had become alarmed and begun to call through the house for me I was already pretty far gone; and when the doctor came, I sometimes had to be rubbed with alcohol or packed in ice, shot full of Compazine and God knows what.

My fever deliriums—unlike the heavy, leaden codeine hallucinations—were characterized by a whirlwind, giddy quality, a nightmarish sense of lightness. When I closed my eyes, I felt like an escaped balloon, sailing in a rapid helium rush to the ceiling; when I opened them again, I was pulled back down to my bed with a jolt, as if someone had suddenly grabbed my string and given me a sharp, fast tug to earth. The room spun like a merry-go-round; my stuffed animals, suddenly glitter-eyed and sinister, gazed hungrily at me from the mantelpiece. And my bed refused to stay still. It rocked on its moorings, pulled from beneath by some fast, spiraling undertow in the old blue carpet that threatened to break the rope entirely and sweep me, whirling bow to stern in helpless circles, out to sea.

My great-grandfather, when he came to see me on those nights, would frequently be near tears. He would sit on the bed, hold my hand, and not say much; this uncharacteristic silence disturbed me, as if he were not my great-grandfather at all but some mournful, bewitched old huntsman from a storybook, tongue-tied by the bad fairy, unable to speak. My bedroom seemed horribly elastic, as if it had somehow been pulled out of shape. And the gabble of my aunts in the background—normally the most comforting sound in the world to me—assumed a terrifying, singsong, nonsensical quality, while my mother flitted anxiously in the background, a slender ghost in her pale housecoat.

Sometimes, on the really bad nights, my great-grandfather would perform, with great seriousness, a bizarre old sickroom practice from his own boyhood that he called "fumigating." This involved lighting a rolled-up piece of newspaper on fire and walking through the house with it; it was horribly messy, since it sent black feathers of newspaper ash flying everywhere, but no one dared object because they all knew that the procedure pleased him so. It was, he said, in order to burn the germs out of the air, but it made my eyes sting and served only, in my delirium, to fan the blazes of an already raging unreality—my somber, heavy-jowled great-grandfather, gravely brandishing his flaming torch that somehow, in my mind, got all mixed up with the flames leaping from the barbecue grill in my nightmare about the Persian cat, and this in turn mingling with the madhouse babble of my aunts, until my poor balloon of a head swelled up so big that I thought it was going to explode with a bang.

I HAVE OUTLIVED my great-grandfather by a number of years. But pretty much until the day he died he was convinced, I think, that he would outlive me; and this prospect caused him terrible grief. I remember, in a faint, dreamlike way, seeing him pause in my doorway on one of the bad nights, after the lamp was out, he and my mother black silhouettes in the lighted corridor. Mournfully, mournfully, he shook his heavy old head. "I'm afraid," I heard him say to my mother, in a low but quite audible voice, "that that poor child won't live to see the morning."

"*Hush*, Granddaddy," my mother said in an agitated whisper. Then, leaning her head inside, she called to me in a bright voice: "Now, I want you to try to rest awhile, sugar. You call me if you need anything, you hear?"

The door swung shut. I was alone in the dark. The voices, now indistinct, receded along with the footsteps. And I was left, staring at the mottled shadow that the moonlit trees cast on the ceiling, waiting for that soft rap (Peter Pan? Jesus? I wasn't sure who) which I felt sooner or later was going to gently sound on my windowpane.

INTO WOODS

(APRIL 1993)

Bill Roorbach

IN A DIVE near Stockbridge in the Berkshire Hills of Massachusetts, I nearly got clobbered by a big drunk who thought he'd detected an office fairy in the midst of the wild workingman's bar. He'd heard me talking to Mary Ann, the bartender, and I didn't talk right, so by way of a joke he said loudly to himself and to a pal and to the bar in general, "Who's this little fox? From Tanglewood or something?"

I, too, was drunk and said, "I am a plumber, more or less." I was thirty years old, was neither little nor a fox, had just come to work on the restoration of an inn, and was the foreman of the crew. But that seemed like the wrong answer, and too long in any case.

He snorted and said to everyone, "A more or less plumber," then appraised me further: "I say a hairdresser."

"I say a bank teller," his pal said.

I didn't mind being called a hairdresser, but a bank teller! Oh, I was drunk and so continued the conversation, smiling just enough to take the edge off: "Ah, fuck off."

"Cursing!" my tormentor cried, making fun of me. "Do they let you say swears at the girls' school?"

"Headmaster," someone said, nodding.

"French teacher," someone else.

"*Guys* . . . ," Mary Ann said, smelling a rumble.

"Plumber," I said.

"More or less," someone added.

"How'd you get your hands so clean?" my tormentor said.

"Lily water," someone said, coining a phrase.

My hands? They hadn't looked at my hands! I was very drunk, come to think of it, and so took it all good-naturedly, just riding the wave of conversation, knowing I wouldn't get punched out if I played it right, friendly and sardonic and nasty all at once. "My hands?"

My chief interlocutor showed me his palms, right in my face. "Work," he said, meaning that's where all the calluses and blackened creases and bent fingers and scars and scabs and cracks and general blackness and grime had come from.

I flipped my palms up, too. He took my hands like a palm reader might, like your date in seventh grade might, almost tenderly, and looked closely: calluses and scabs and scars and darkened creases and an uncleanable blackness and grime. Nothing to rival his, but real.

"Hey," he said. "Buy you a beer?"

MY DAD WORKED for Mobil Oil, took the train into New York every day early-early, before we five kids were up, got home at six-thirty every evening. We had dinner with him, then maybe some roughhousing before he went to bed at eight-thirty. Most Saturdays, and most Sundays after church, he worked around the house, and I mean he worked.

And the way to be with him if you wanted to be with him at all was to work beside him. He would put on a flannel shirt and old pants, and we'd paint the house or clean the gutters or mow the lawn or build a new walk or cut trees or turn the garden under or rake the leaves or construct a cold frame or make shelves or shovel snow or wash the driveway (*we washed the fucking driveway!*) or make a new bedroom or build a stone wall or install dimmers for the den lights or move the oil tank for no good reason or wire a 220 plug for the new dryer or put a sink in the basement for Mom or make picture frames or . . . Jesus, you name it.

And my playtime was an imitation of that work. I loved tree forts, had about six around our two acres in Connecticut, one of them a major one, a two-story eyesore on the hill behind the house, built in three trees, triangular in all aspects. (When all her kids were long gone, spread all over the country, my mother had a chain-saw guy cut the whole mess down, trees and all.) I built cities in the sandbox, beautiful cities with sewers and churches and schools and houses and citizens and soldiers and *war!* And *floods!* And attacks by *giants!* I had a toolbox, too, a little red thing with kid-sized tools.

And in one of the eight or nine toolboxes I now affect there is a stubby green screwdriver that I remember clearly as being from that first red toolbox. And a miniature hacksaw (extremely handy) with "Billy" scratched on the handle, something I'd forgotten until one of my helpers on the Berkshires restoration pointed it out one day, having borrowed the little thing to reach into an impossible space in one of the eaves. Billy. Lily.

My father called me Willy when we worked, and at no other time. His hands were big and rough and wide, blue with bulgy veins. He could have been a workman easy if he'd wanted, and I knew it and told my friends so.

IN MY RICH suburban high school in Connecticut we were nearly all of us college track, which meant you could take only two shop classes in your career there. First half of freshman year you could elect Industrial Arts, which was an overview: a month of Woods, a month of Metals, a month of Technical Drawing. Second semester, if you still wanted more, you went into Woods I, Metals I, etc.

I loved Woods. I loved hanging out with some of the rougher Italian kids, Tony DiCrescenzo and Bobby LaMotta and Tony Famigliani, all of them proud and pleased to be tracked away from college. I wanted to hang out with Tommy Lincoln and Vernon Porter and Roland Fish, the three black kids in my class, all of them quietly (maybe even secretly) tracked away from college. Wood shop was first period, and it was a wild class. Mr. Schtenck, our little alcoholic teacher, made no effort to control us and often left the shop for the entire period to sit in his car.

The rough kids used the finishing room to smoke pot, the storage room to snort coke. We all made bookshelves and workbenches and record racks and knickknack shelves and lamps and tables and guitar stands and frames for photos of our girls. The year was 1968, so we also made elaborate bongs and stash boxes and chillums and hollowed-out canes and chests with secret drawers. Wood shop (and along with it the very act of working with my hands) took on a countercultural glow, the warm aura of sedition, rebellion, independence, grace.

Sophomore year I signed up for Woods II, which was the advanced course. My guidance counselor, Miss Sanderson (a nice enough lady, very well-meaning, very empathic—you could make her cry over your troubles every time if you played your cards right), thought I'd made an error on the electives form. "Only one elective a semester, William. Surely you'd like a writing course! Journalism! Or how about Occult Literature?"

"Woods II," I said, flipping my hair. I had to get parental permission to take Woods again and thought a little note with my mother's neat signature would be easy to snag, but it was not. "Why do you have to reinvent the wheel?" Mom said, one of her phrases, something of a non sequitur in this case, her meaning being *someone else will build the furniture.* Her next question was, "What kind of kids are in that class?"

Dumb kids, Mom. Mostly Italian kids and blacks and, of course, Alvin Dubronski (the class moron) and Jack Johnsen (the plumber's kid!) and me.

My dad thought it was fine, especially with the alternative being literature courses where who knew what kind of left-wing occult hippie double-talk Mrs. Morrisey would tell you!

So into the wood shop again, every day first period (if I wasn't late for school; by that time I was hitchhiking to avoid the uncool school bus). I was the only college-track kid taking Woods II, maybe the only college-track kid who had *ever* taken Woods II, though the other kids got to take it semester after semester. And I got peer-pressured into smoking pot in the finishing room and occasionally even into blowing coke in the storage room, always a sweet, nerve-jangling prelude to another round of boring college-track classes.

One day when I was in the storage room with my high-pressure peers (and the two smartest kids in Woods II, maybe in school, both destined by their blackness for bad times in Vietnam) Roland and Tommy, fat Tony Famigliani stuck his head in the door: "The Stench is coming!" But Schtenck was already there, standing in the door. I saw my college-track life pass before my eyes.

"What are you little fuckers doing?"

"We're tasting coke, sir," Tommy said, the idiot, total honesty, as we'd all learned in Boy Scouts.

Florid Schtenck raised his eyebrows clear off his face and said, "Jesus Christ, boys, put it away—you want to get me canned?"

He never looked in the storage room again.

And later that year he stumbled and cut his finger off on the band saw. For two weeks then we had a substitute who made us file all our plans and actually checked them, stood beside us as we drilled holes in our wood or turned bowls on the lathes. It seemed an eternity before Schtenck came back and we could finally fill all the bong and hash-pipe and stash-box orders we'd been sitting on. *Sedition.*

The next year I took Woods II again, having secured special permission from the principal to go along with my parents' special permission and the special permission from Miss Sanderson. Senior year I signed up for the class once more—what the hell—but I don't think I ever got to school in time to attend.

SOMEWHERE IN THERE I stopped being a willing volunteer for my father's list of chores. Now he had to *command* me to help with his corny weekend projects. I had better things to do, things in the woods with Lauren Bee or cruising-in-the-car things with some of the guys in my various garage bands—minor-league dope runs into the Village or actual gigs in actual bars in Port Chester, where the drinking age was eighteen and we could get away with it.

At home things were quiet. Except for my long hair, you wouldn't have noticed that a teen was testing his folks. I was good at talking to

my elders, and good at hooking grades without working too hard—
college track—and very, very good at staying out of trouble. I was on
the student council. I helped with the student newspaper. I went to
the homecoming rallies and proms and parades. I memorized the
headlight patterns of the town police cars (I still get nervous around
those big old Plymouth Furys), could smell a cop from miles away,
leagues away, light-years. I had a plan for every eventuality and an
escape route from every party.

Weeknights I'd turn in early, out to my room over the garage, wait
for the main house to quiet down, then slip out into the night. I was
caught only once, coming home about five in the morning with a
friend named Melanie. Someone had called me after I'd left, and Dad
couldn't find me. He was asleep in my bed when Melanie and I
walked in. I was grounded, and here was the punishment: I had to
spend the next four Saturdays and Sundays helping him build a play-
room in the basement—drilling holes in the concrete for hours to
anchor the sills for a Sheetrock wall, running cable for a hanging light
over the bumper-pool table, slamming up paneling, churlishly working side by side with my dad and his distinctive smell, Aqua Velva
mixed with cigarettes and Head & Shoulders and sweat.

THE COLLEGE TRACK barely got me to college. As part of my
desultory rebellion I put off applying until well past all the deadlines,
never lying to my folks, never lying to my guidance counselor, but
showing all of them the forms ready to go, then just plain old not mail-
ing them. My plan was to play rock and roll and maybe—if necessary—make money working as a carpenter, or maybe drilling holes in
concrete, or maybe making furniture or bongs. Then Miss Sanderson
got a list of our school's applicants from one of my supposed top
choices, and I wasn't on it. Crisis! April already, when most kids were
hearing from Colby and Yale and Michigan and the U. of Hawaii.

My trusty guidance counselor got on the phone and found some
schools that would look at a late application. She was crushed for me,
so crushed she spared my parents the full brunt of my dereliction. At
hastily arranged late interviews, admissions counselors never failed to

ask why I'd taken Woods II *six semesters straight*. Finally I was accepted by one famously lame school, to which I resigned myself; then, at the last possible minute and by great good fortune, I was put on the waiting list at Ithaca College, where, on August 21, one week before school started, I was admitted into the freshman class.

I NEVER SAW my father at work, and he never talked about his work, which I vaguely knew was Executive and had to do with Mobil Oil and was desky and involved meetings and much world travel and made us pretty rich. And because I'd never seen him at work, my natural adolescent impulse toward emulation had little to go on. What to imitate? How to surpass, destroy? What I saw of my valiant dad was his work around the house, and so, emulation gone awry, I set out to be a better home handyman than he'd ever be, the real thing, even, a tradesman.

Two dollars and fifty cents an hour was well known as great money, nearly double what I'd made stocking frozen foods at the A&P during high school. Two-fifty an hour was what truck drivers got, longshoremen, a full hundred rasbuckniks (my father's word) a week. I dropped out of Ithaca College in my junior year (just when most of my buddies were heading off for a year abroad), went back to Connecticut (not my hometown, God forbid, but one nearby), and went to work for an electrician.

Lawrence Berner was a former electrical engineer who'd thrown it all over at age sixty, a theory ace but a fairly clumsy worker, a guy who had actually tossed away everything and left the college track for good. Larry was British and Jewish and unconventional and very charming, all qualities that impressed me. Best of all, he was divorced, the first divorced person I'd ever seen up close. He was filthy of habit—decadent, disgusting (maybe not as bad as my friends at school, but Larry was *old*). He lived in his marital house, wife long gone, and had trashed the place—filled the garage with electrician junk, filled the kitchen with dirty pots and jars and cans and dishes, filled the refrigerator with his important papers (fireproof, he said), filled the bedroom with the most slathery skin magazines imaginable, filled the whole house with take-out cartons, TV-dinner tins, and his own filthy underwear. His living room seemed buried in death.

He paid me $2.50 an hour.

Working beside him (tradesmen often touch—four hands to pull the cable, four arms reaching into a small space, heads together to look into a service panel . . . *hey, hold my legs while I lean out over this here abyss*), I'd feel sometimes like I was with my dad. It was Larry's thin hair, maybe, or the Aqua Velva and cigarettes, or just regular old transference. I spent every day beside this parallel-universe effigy of my father, and I was mad at Larry almost always and desperate to impress him.

One day he said I had good hands, and that little compliment was everything—I glowed, I crowed, I told my friends, my folks. I stared at my hands late at night in bars, stared at them for hours, entranced. And my hands got callused, grotesquely callused, were always covered in cuts and scratches and dings and scabs that I hardly felt. Your knuckles never healed. And Larry mostly worked "hot," meaning with the power on, because it saved time. I got shocks and blew holes in screwdrivers. I hit my head on rafters and slammed my thumb with hammers and fell off ladders and sliced my fingers (daily) and once even poked a screwdriver hard into my eye (the blade didn't penetrate the eyeball but rolled past it and into the socket so that old Larry had to pull it out . . . and we kept on working). I drove the truck sometimes, sweet-talked the customers, ate in diners, worked squinting with a Lucky Strike in my mouth. I put in panel boxes and wired 200-amp services and installed a thousand outlets and a million switches. I drilled holes for cable, sawed rafters, snaked wire through walls. I wriggled into crawl spaces, sweated in attics, dug trenches.

I got tired of it. All that *body* work. Like every college-track kid in America, I'd been taught that someone else would do the rough stuff if I'd just use my mind. I went back to Ithaca, pleasing my parents enormously. Suddenly I was a good student—all A's, excellent attendance, papers handed in on time—fully engaged in a tough fight against the possibility of being a tradesman, the possibility of taking Woods II for *life*.

But after the college track had run its course, I needed to make money. I failed tests for newspaper jobs (*twenty minutes: neatly type a 500-word story around the following facts . . .*), gagged at the thought of ad agencies, moved around the country for a long time, worked with cattle, bartended (which left your hands clean, at least), then landed in New York, where I got the bright idea to put up posters around the Village and SoHo and be a handyman. Independence! I did every sort of odd job for every sort of odd person, moving over the months and years to larger home repairs, leaving town to restore that Berkshires inn, coming back to sub myself out to contractors. I graduated finally to a specialization in kitchen remodels and new bathrooms, getting more and more deeply into it, hiring helpers, wearing suits to estimates, taking ads in fancy magazines, cracking the codes for admittance to the wholesale supply houses, getting good at all of it, twelve years in all, Woods II, until one day I woke up and realized I was about to take out a bank loan to buy a truck and some very expensive tools, about to start looking for a storefront, about to start paying my employees *on the books.* I headed straight to graduate school.

MY WIFE AND I spent lots of our free time last summer looking for a house to buy up here in rural Maine (where I teach college), our first, an old farmhouse, we hoped. I kept telling myself that I had an advantage, which was my haphazard twenty-year fund of construction knowledge and restoration experience. I looked up at the beams and poked at the foundations and lifted the vinyl siding and pulled away carpets. I wiggled toilets and pulled on feeds and pushed on all the walls and ceilings. I got in crawl spaces and pried open hatch doors, inspected wiring, eyeballed plumbing, made the real-estate folks nervous.

And sometimes, in light of this commitment, this buying a house on a wee piece of our little planet, I thought about what would happen if the legislature shut down my branch of the University of Maine, or what would happen if I didn't get tenure, or what would happen if I just couldn't take the bureaucracy anymore and quit. Education presidents come and go, but people always need a plumber or someone to fix the roof, replace rotten sills, plaster the stairway wall. I could build furniture. Or renovate inns. I could take my clean college hands and plunge them into work, open all the old scars, stop being mincy and fastidious, once more revel in goo and slime, get into it: wrestle cable, kick at shovels, stand in the mud all day, hook my leg around ladders in the wind, lay tile, lift toilets and plunge my hand down that reeking fuzzy hole to pull the clog (poor Raggedy Andy one time, usually worse).

MY WIFE AND I found a house, bought it, moved in. And immediately my dad, now retired, came up to visit, tools in hand. The two of us got up early the first morning he was here and headed out to the garage, a forlorn little outbuilding about to fall down and stuffed to the rafters with the owner-before-last's junk (mostly pieces of Volkswagens and cans of old bolts and misshapen gaskets and used spark plugs and odd shims and clips). My plan was to leave room to park a car, sure, but to build a wood shop, a work space from which to operate while my wife and I renovate the house (a neglected nine-teenth-century quarter-cape with many additions, the newest of which is a porch built in 1953, my own year).

So for hours my dad and I worked. We cleared out and sorted all the junk, ripped down the cardboard that made the walls, stopped to stare, to think, came up with opposite plans, argued, convinced each other; then, having switched sides, we argued again. Finally we jacked up the north side of the garage, replaced the sill, dropped a corner post in cement, took the jack away, rebuilt the wall. Next we shored up the south side, then added wiring, finally installed a metal roof over the leaky old asphalt shingles. We hit our heads and cut our fingers and ripped our jackets. We peed in the woodpile. We argued, mostly about technique and a little about the Education President (who was about to go), but really, I guess, about who was in charge of the work in my garage. And even though Pop was helping me for free, even buying some of the materials, I fumed and fulminated, almost sulked: instant adolescence.

We rebuilt the barn-style sliding door and cut in a window. We ate companionably in the Farmington Diner with sawdust and plain dirt in our hair and new hammer holsters on our belts (the acerbic Down East waitress looked me over, said, "Hi, Professor," and I introduced her to my dad); we went to the dump; we gabbed at the lumber yard; we swung hammers, climbed ladders, cut wood; we gazed at our work a long time in the dark when we were done.

Pop said, "You saved that building," as if I'd done it on my own, and we went on in the house to wash up.

A Day in the Life of a Porch

(June 1992)

Reynolds Price

THE FRONT PORCH thrived in American architecture from the early eighteenth century right into the 1930s and 1940s for one main reason—throughout the young agrarian country, largely settled by families in search of a sovereign independence, a front porch served far more purposes than the obvious escape from hot interiors, stoked by the weather and kitchen fires. In the slave-owning South and the Puritan-private North, it served, for instance, as a vital transition between the uncontrollable out-of-doors and the cherished interior of the home. The master's farm business, the mistress's selections of goods and produce, the home craftsman's sales, and sundry emotional negotiations of the cooler sort (with the hired man, the foreman, the slave or house servant, the distressed or disgruntled neighbor, even with the unpredictable stranger from the muddy road) could all be conducted in the civil atmosphere offered by the shade of a prominent porch, apart from the sleeping and feeding quarters and without serious risk to the family's physical and psychic core.

A particular porch in Warren County, North Carolina, has been a vital place in my life, from birth well into manhood and now in green memory. The porch I knew ran the full width of a white-frame one-story house built by my maternal grandfather, John Egerton Rodwell, in the 1880s and lived in still, though not by my kin. My mother was born in the house in 1905, I was born there in 1933; and until my mother's sister Ida died in 1965, it remained our spiritual home and refuge. The account of a typical day in spring, summer, or fall on that porch at any point in my life, from summer visits in the late 1930s till Ida's death, will give some sense of the role and meaning of a porch in the life of a middle-class Southern family of no more than average complexity, rage, or need. I'll describe, then, an ordinary late July day in 1942, when I was nine.

THE FIRST TO wake in the still-warm house will be the bachelor great-uncle whom my mother and all her generation call Uncle Brother. Born on a family farm nearby in the early years of the Civil War, Brother's stone deaf by now and sports an ivory-yellow mustache, which I hate to kiss (as I must every visit on arriving and departing). Nearly eighty, he of course wakes early—barely after daylight. Once he's dressed—in a fresh-starched shirt with sleeve garters and a gold collar-pin—he quietly walks along the long center hall to the unlocked front door and steps out onto the porch. His unfailing first act of every day is to stand here and read the rusty thermometer nailed to the wall. He'll study it slowly, maybe tap it twice—*No doubt about it: early as it is, it's well past eighty.* He walks with unhurried ease down the steps and heads for the well to draw the first two dark-oak buckets of dazzling water for the thirsty day.

By then my Aunt Ida and Uncle Marvin are awake and up—he shaving, she washing in their separate china bowls, then carefully dressing in fresh light clothes (she's in her late fifties; he's some years older and also deaf, though not as far gone yet as Brother). The ambient air has cooled during the night, by ten degrees; but at seven, when Ida crosses the dim back hall toward the kitchen, she feels the coming heat like a meaty hand, pressing her face.

Already at the table stands Mary Lee, the black cook, in a clean white apron, cutting biscuits from a fresh spread of dough. They greet each other in quiet voices, like the seasoned colleagues they've been for decades: Ida may ask if she plans to fry apples and how is her grandson; Mary Lee says the boy's cutting eyeteeth and is in real misery.

Then Ida will head up the hall with a broom, out the front screen door to the empty porch, to sweep down last night's spiderwebs, the odd dead moth, and to straighten the chairs. She descends to the yard, finds today's newspaper flung by the carrier against the biggest oak. Not even glancing at the bold headlines—Hitler is winning ground again; the Japanese are pouring their millions at the mouths of our guns—she heads back in through the day's last cool to the warming kitchen.

Marvin is already seated with his coffee. Ida hands him the paper silently, steps back to the hall, and raises her kind voice to call me awake (I'm drowned deep still, in the far bedroom on the bed I was born in). Before I've made my way into shorts and splashed my face, Ida and Marvin and Uncle Brother are well into full plates of scrambled eggs, bacon, and fried green apples. Each of us eats with a grateful intensity, saying little; and Mary Lee works behind us quietly, ready to serve out further portions.

But even I am ready for the day, which this early on—since there are no other children nearby—means the porch again, where Marvin will read every word of his paper; and I will sit in the wide swing, six feet from him, trying again to catch his strong profile with a No. 2 pencil in my Professional Artist's Sketchbook. By half past eleven the red column in the porch thermometer moves past ninety and the air starts to sweat up close to my eyes. By then I've moved from the swing to a rocker and have been well buried for more than an hour in my library book—R. L. Stevenson's *Weir of Hermiston*. Marvin has crossed the railroad tracks for the day's first mail and sits back beside me, reading his business letters silently with moving lips.

THE PORCH BEGINS its best life, though, in late afternoon. When we've pushed back from the still-laden table at one o'clock, young as I am I'm ready for the hour's nap I take on the wide white bed in my birth-room (already the room feels mystical to me—*I landed here; here I first saw light*). Marvin declines the chance of rest; he heads out slowly in his black Chevrolet to check on Kittrel, the tenant farmer who has fallen off the wagon: Did the poor jackass get himself home alive? Is he dead in a ditch or drunk again and laid out now on his own porch floor, counting the wasp nests stuck to the raw-pine ceiling above him? Can his oldest boy take over the crop if this proves the usual ten-day drunk, once the first drink's poured?

By half past two I swim awake. I hear the porch door creak outward as Ida goes out, whistles once at the onslaught of heat, then takes her seat at the edge of the swing. The chains by which it hangs creak softly as her motion starts. I'm still a little groggy from my nap, and the hair at the back of my neck is soaked. But I move straight toward this woman I love as much as any soul on earth. First I sit beside her, and we swing a few short arcs in the air. Then I lie on my right side and lower my head to her narrow lap, gazing out at the carpenter bees (black and fat as balls of coal) that bumble at the eaves, remorselessly drilling their annual holes. Ida's hand steals onto my head and gradually her cool fingers scratch my scalp—not a word between us for maybe ten minutes. Then old black Pap rolls past in his oxcart and waves our way; even from the dirt road, heat trembles upward and blurs his hand like a drowning man's. The almost frozen lumbering stride of his ancient ox makes me want the thing Ida's taught me to love—the past, its sudden stark grief and hilarious grandeur. My head is still in the soft of her lap as I ask her to tell about when she was a girl.

"You know every bit of that already."

"But tell it again."

"Which part?" she asks, though surely she knows.

"The night when you and your best friend tied your toes together, then went to sleep and you forgot and pulled her out."

The fact that I've just told the story doesn't stop Ida. She knows that, for me, it lives in her telling; and out it comes through the next ten minutes—infinite details of kerosene lamplight, cotton nightshirts on girls age six, the icy air, the freezing china chamber pot, their yoked cold toes, the heavy quilts, their whispered secrets on into the night, then sleep till Ida wakes to pee, slides silently up, and yanks her dazed friend out on the floor.

The hours—fifty years behind us, locked in winter, though in this same house, ten yards inside—come back for me, realer than now;

and Ida and I melt down into chuckling that lasts through two or three more memories till again we calm into wide swoops against the heat, and I have spacious moments to think a sentence I very much hope is true: *I'll never be gladder than this on earth.* While I have no way at nine years old to know I'm right, I trust I am—with no doubt or fear—and fifty full years on in my life, with Ida dead near thirty years, I test the sentence and feel it again, a simple fact.

MARVIN RETURNS, STILL grim, from the farm—Kittrel's boy says he can handle the load while his dad dries out, he'll work his younger sister and brother—but when Ida tells him to sit down with us and cool before supper, he decides to obey. And till five-thirty we sit on, fanning lazy flies away and bearing the weight of a swelter that I, like children in general, ignore (though I see it burdens Ida). There'll be long stretches with no noise but crickets, distant cars on the hard-surface road to Weldon or Norfolk, and the putter of worn-out prewar jalopies on the nearer dirt road past our door; we'll wave to each, though after a few we consult one another: *Who was that? Surely not. Well, she's put on flesh, and in this weather. Lord, how does she breathe?*

I may ask Marvin to sing me a song—an awful favorite, scary each time, is "I Know an Old Woman All Skin and Bones"—and he may oblige; or he may say, "Too hot. I'll say you a poem." And he'll reel off some fifty lines of Walter Scott's *Lady of the Lake* or some war ballad he learned from his father—Caswell Drake, a Confederate major, long since gone to his rocky grave, thoroughly pickled in pure white lightning (or so my mother has laughed, many times).

Then Ida may ask a chain of calm questions about the drunk tenant—*Have they got plenty food for all those children? Did his wife look bruised? Recall how badly he beat her last time?* They'll spend twenty minutes sorting the tenant family's woes, deciding Ida will ride out tomorrow when Marvin goes back (she doesn't drive) and ask for the wife, see how she's faring. Then that sad topic will fade off, too, and the six o'clock train for Raleigh will stop, unloading two Negro boys in uniform—at 150 yards' hot distance, Ida and Marvin recognize both and say their names.

When the train slides on and only its pleasant odor survives, Ida stands and goes to lay out supper—she won't take help; other hands confuse her. In less than a minute, Marvin's head nods; and he takes at last the rest he's refused, an upright nap but all the sweeter. So I lie back full-length on the swing and taste the mulled odors of train smoke, clover, and a million green oak leaves, bitter as gall. All I have to face, between now and bed at ten o'clock, is a cool light supper of Mary Lee's leavings plus fresh-made biscuits and new iced tea.

THEN EACH ONE of us, with Brother again (in another fresh shirt, his day finally done, having said supper-grace in a helpless mumble), will move back out on the pitch-black porch and let the body heat of day leech from the house and our own bodies out onto the night, its billion singers—tree frogs, cicadas, the deathless crickets, the high whine of bats—and the hundred-odd, mostly decent neighbors circled beyond us, their own lights out in the hope of cool peace as sleep advances. Marvin and Ida and I will talk, again about not much but food and people who live within five miles of our chairs—though with glances at the two halves of the war, Europe and Asia. Brother will rock in total silence; and as the time moves on toward ten, even Marvin's deafness will still us all down—Ida and I won't raise our voices so that he can hear—and only a final brief exchange breaks the ringing silence before we all rise.

In the early dark, when we first came out, there'd been a white moon—no sign of it now. Marvin leans far forward and hunts it above—still no sign. So he turns to Brother, whom he calls Mr. Rodwell, and raises his voice to reach the old man: "Mr. Rodwell, where on earth is the moon?" It's an idle question to end the day.

But Uncle Brother takes it in earnest like everything else. He also leans and searches the patches of sky through leaves. Then he turns to Marvin—to Ida and me—and says with utter clarity, "I can't tell you, son. I'm a stranger here."

A baffled moment, then even he laughs; and we all join him, so genuinely that Buck Thompson calls from his porch to our right, "Who told the last joke?" (He's forty feet off, unseen as the moon.)

Ida nudges me. "Tell him."

I raise my voice and say, "Can't tell you, Buck. We're *strangers* here."

Buck laughs then and Anna, his pretty wife, beside him. They call "Good-night" as they hear us rise.

Family Secrets

(July 1992)

Nicholas Bromell

IN *THE TEACHINGS of Don Juan,* Carlos Castaneda learns from his Yaqui shaman that each person has his "spot" in the world, a place where the strength of the earth wells up and protects him from the demons of the psyche. But because of the work my father used to do, I come from nowhere and have no spot. Often I feel I've built my life atop an emptiness that could implode at any moment. It is, moreover, an emptiness held firm by silence, by the untellable oddity of my childhood. My wife, who rolls her eyes when my most mundane childhood stories play out in places such as Baghdad, Piraeus, Petra, or Shiraz, doesn't believe that I am awed by her childhood in a small Catholic parish on the South Side of Chicago. She can't understand that I envy her because she is a *real* American—because she experienced a childhood other Americans recognize. We all try to make sense of our lives by having stories to tell, and, like all narratives, these stories are subject to conventions. The chief of these, in this country at least, is a prohibition against the exotic. A Southern boyhood, or a prep-school boyhood, or an only-child boyhood might be interesting, but to be told, they must be grounded in the ordinary. If the prep school is in Bogotá, or if the father is a Rockefeller, the story becomes unreal and untellable. And if the father is a spy—or, as he prefers to call himself, an intelligence officer—the story becomes untellable twice over. You grow up swearing an oath of silence without knowing it and owing allegiance to an institution you will never see or know.

But now, after the demise of the Soviet Union and the war against Iraq, I have come to realize that my childhood had a certain historical specificity. It was, with more intensity than most, a Cold War childhood. Born precisely at midcentury, I was made to understand at a very young age that somewhere, or rather everywhere, an immense silent contest was being fought, that our side was locked in a struggle with another side, and that what was at stake was the very shape of the future. Of course, every American child of my generation was born into a world structured by this Manichaean paradigm—us against them, good against evil—but when your father's daily work actually contributes to the struggle, it has a different, more intimate, meaning. Not that my father was vocal about the Cold War. I never heard him say a word against the Russians. But somehow we knew (I think probably from our grandmother, his doting mother) that he did not work for money, and that his work mattered in some deeper, stronger way that could never be discussed.

When we were "home" in the United States, Dad left the house for "work" in some unspecified "office" we never saw. Overseas, however, his work was more visible, no matter how painstakingly he tried to conceal it. To me and my two brothers, the fact of what my father did was the very ground we walked on, and the élan with which he and his colleagues conducted themselves was the air we breathed. For them, World War II had never ended. They slipped out of flight jackets and fatigues and into gray suits, but their new anonymity was even more lustrous than their celebrated role as soldiers. They were an elite. They were a team. They knew one another, but no one knew them. On spring weekends we took picnics to ancient ruins in the desert; while the mothers scratched in the sand for shards and the men relaxed with cold martinis poured from my parents' thermos, my brothers and I scouted the hillocks and ravines, finally sneaking up behind the men, listening to their deep laughter, their sudden moments of seriousness, and unconsciously reproducing in our games of creeping and spying the work a number of them performed out of their embassy offices. Hearing their laughter in memory now, I feel that it perfectly expressed the double life most of them led: one day, a relaxed picnic with the family; the next, a trek in dusty Land Rovers deep into the wastes where the oil pipelines ran; where a solitary coffee-house marked the borders of Iraq, Syria, and Jordan; where Arab armies engaged in maneuvers; where bedouin chieftains beckoned them into black-cloth tents for hot, sugary tea drunk from little glasses with gold rims.

My brothers and I came to accept certain announcements as plain matters of fact. Mother: "Your father won't be home tonight." Father: "I'm expecting visitors this afternoon; I want you all to stay outside the house until after five." One morning my older brother sprang from behind a door to scare our father, who instantly spun around, fists raised to strike, and then, ashen, explained that we were never, ever to jump out and scare him. And in order to make his prohibition convincing, he had to drop a corner of the curtain he kept between us and his profession. "In my job I have to worry that someone might want to sneak up behind me like that, and I have to be ready to defend myself," he explained gently. "I might hurt you before I could stop myself." Many years later, in another country, a team of men from the embassy came to our house with suitcases of electronics equipment, tripod-mounted antennas, headphones, and other gear, and my brothers and I were old enough to realize what they were doing—debugging our house. But we were hardly surprised. Without ever knowing that we knew, we had understood for some time that our father was a spy.

The silence of this acknowledged fact was the silence that legitimat-ed many other silences within the family. "There are certain things we don't talk about," we were told. "It would be better if you didn't men-tion to your friends where we went this weekend." I realize now how often we must have been part of my father's cover. When we went as a family to visit a man somewhere, and to drink sickly sweet rose water ("Drink a little to be polite!") on the terrace while he and my father conversed inside, we made a quite different impression on the neigh-bors than my father would have made arriving and entering the house alone. We were a family of conspirators. One afternoon my best friend saw all of us piling into an army helicopter that had landed in the fields near our house. The next day he confronted me with what he had seen, and I blithely denied it. Us? Piling into a helicopter? What on earth for? And because he had no one to corroborate the outrageous thing he had seen, my friend shook his head and soon disbelieved it himself. More than most other children, I think, I grew up seeing the world double. I saw not just the doubleness of adults pretending things to children but the doubleness of adults pretending things to one another. And knowing no other world, this seemed normal to me.

The Cold War, which was not a war, or not the war it pretended to be—a war of doubleness—was thus the architecture of my family and childhood. For middle-class Americans back home, and for children my age growing up in suburban neighborhoods of bikes and lawns and newspaper routes—things I knew about only from movies and old television shows—the Cold War was at most the sound of distant thunder. It came home to them only at moments—when Francis Gary Powers was shot down, when Nikita Khrushchev famously banged his shoe on a table at the United Nations. I found, when I entered college in 1968, that my new friends were shocked by revelations about American duplicity at home and abroad. My father and his colleagues had done their work too well. All their efforts at the front lines, keeping the enemy at bay, had preserved the American delusion that the world could be seen in terms of right and wrong, Communism and democracy. That the United States had actually undermined democracies (in, for example, Iran) was incredible to my classmates. They had to rethink everything they knew, or thought they had known, about the world, about power, about history. I joined them in their expressions of outrage, I marched with them on Washington, but though I shared their disapproval of American policies I could not quite share their disgust and disappointment. I had been prepared, having known for as long as I could remember that things are seldom what they seem.

IN 1957 WE went overseas for the first time, sailing from New York on the S.S. *Excambian* and bound for Beirut. There we stayed briefly at the Hotel St. Georges, at that time the city's only luxury hotel, a faded, *fin de siècle* symbol of an era about to pass, and which my memory conflates with the "large, proud, rose colored hotel" of F. Scott Fitzgerald's *Tender Is the Night.* The St. Georges, however, had no "bright tan prayer rug of a beach." The green Mediterranean thundered onto the rocks surrounding the great railed veranda that jutted into the sea. In the morning we ate in the shade of the hotel, spearing with tiny forks the scalloped butter pats nestled in their dewy serving dish and drinking dark hot chocolate from a pewter urn. In the evening, as the sky flushed to apricot over the water, children and their nannies were given license to run, skip, hide, play over the veranda. Then night fell and waiters circulated busily, setting out tables, lighting small lanterns. Long after our bedtime we boys crouched on our balcony, peering down at the grown-ups eating their dinner, listening to the murmur of their conversation mingling with the murmur of waves in the darkness beyond the lights.

My senses—the senses of a seven-year-old—absorbed everything. I was a roll of film stretched open beneath the summer sun. Every photon that hit me sank and stayed. Even today, when I happen to get a starched white napkin at a restaurant, the smell of fresh bread issuing miraculously from the fabric strips away the years and drops me, a boy, into the morning shade of the veranda of the St. Georges. But these memories are now more than ever evanescent sensations. Whether we know it or not, in Brattleboro as much as in Beirut, history flows through childhood the way light passes through the curtains of a bedroom. I see now that the rolls and butter I consumed on the veranda of the St. Georges were not ahistorical fragments tumbling through the empty space of time but precise embodiments of French colonialism, which at that very moment was giving way to an American "presence." The St. Georges itself is just such history writ large. It was named, of course, for the warrior-saint whose lance speared the serpent of heathenism and whose emblem accompanied thousands of Christian soldiers during the Crusades. Since the time we stayed there, it metamorphosed gradually into a modern but charmless hotel in the American style. Later still, seized now by one and now by another militant faction, it crumbled under twenty years of internecine warfare to a ghostly, but miraculously functioning, ruin—like the city itself.

We flew from Beirut to Baghdad, where my father had been posted to the embassy, and stepped out of the airplane into a heat so white and thick that I gasped. Driving to what would be our house, I gazed stupidly at the tall palm trees—I had never seen palms before—beneath whose leaves hung clusters of what looked like enormous cockroaches (dates, my mother explained). The car stopped at a pair of gates set in a high mud wall. Twenty feet away, on a pile of refuse bulkier than the car, two emaciated dogs lolled motionless, not even panting. The gates swung open. This was "our" garden and that was "our" house. Inside, we found the shutters closed, the hall dark as a cave. Huge fans turned beneath immensely high ceilings. The American couple who had met us at the airport introduced us to our cook, our houseboy, our nanny, and our gardener. In low tones the American woman spoke reassuringly to our mother. Then the grown-ups moved into the "library," where the man mixed them drinks, and we boys were left alone to explore.

Looking back, I realize how young my parents were (in their early thirties) and how innocent. All of this was as new to them as it was to us. Still, I am astonished that they did not explain more to us. They had just transported their children to a place that was as different as another planet, and they simply let us loose in it. We were on our own, instructed only not to drink the water from the faucets and never to ask the servants for anything. We ambled around the shadowy house, touching, smelling, examining. In the library brown veins ran down the walls, and the books we opened had tiny sand tunnels running through them. Termites, my father explained. The kitchen cupboards were stocked with foods we had never heard of: squash (not sodas), biscuits (not crackers), sweets (not candies). Down in the basement we found the belongings, awaiting shipment, of the family we had replaced; surreptitiously, we pried into the boxes and lifted out treasures—chief among them a magnificent set of albums filled with huge, colorful stamps, most of them, if I remember correctly, from the Belgian Congo, my father's predecessor's former post.

One evening a light rain fell. We stood at an open upstairs window and looked down over the garden wall at the street. Traffic had halted and Baghdadis ran out of the shops, hands uplifted, to touch and greet the spattering drops. Soon thereafter the days grew cooler at last; we began to play in the garden. Arranging our soldiers (all of them British lead soldiers with red uniforms and black beaver hats—the only kind available in the local stores) on fortifications we had built alongside the irrigation ditches, we stayed for hours in our smaller world that we could control and understand. Like all colonial children, we discovered the mysteries of servants' quarters—a small building behind the kitchen, occupied by our cook and houseboy. We learned enough Arabic to communicate brokenly, but more often we played our spying games on them, climbing into the trees near their door and watching them move back and forth from the kitchen to their quarters, understanding almost nothing of what they said but delighting in the mere fact of being unseen, unheard, and watching.

We had just begun to explore the world beyond the garden walls—riding our bikes to the British Council library one afternoon, where we watched Laurence Olivier in the film version of *Richard III*—when the mood of the city palpably changed. Winter dust storms blew out of the desert, and coated trees and streets and cars in a fine yellow dust that penetrated doors and shutters and blurred the glossy surface of the dining-room table. But more than the weather changed. One day our cook invited us to go with him to a hanging, and when my older brother went to ask our mother for permission, she slapped him before she could think or speak. When we drove down Al-Raschid Street, we began to notice more crowds, more speeches, more banners, more soldiers. The city seemed to turn in upon itself. Then we learned the word "curfew" when the government imposed one. At dusk merchants pulled down the metal grates in front of their shops and went home. Even the tiny corner store where we bought Mars bars and firecrackers closed before dark. Because we had diplomatic plates on our car, we were allowed to drive after dusk, and the city we passed through seemed to eye us through a thousand shuttered windows.

Then it happened. The army revolted. The young king whose face was familiar to us from the stamps we collected was shot in his palace. We heard rumors that a mob chased two Americans into the Hilton Hotel, caught them in the lobby, dragged them outside, and tore them limb from limb. Tanks and armored cars squatted at the end of our street. My mother came into our room and told us to pick one book and one toy each. We were packing. We were leaving that night on a special plane. We learned two more words that day: "revolution" and "evacuation."

WHILE MY FATHER remained with a small delegation in Iraq, we flew to Rome, where we stayed for three days at the luxurious Hassler Hotel before moving to a tiny pensione in a street of perpetual shadows. Through the open bedroom window there came the sounds and smells of that great city, waking us in the morning and lulling us to sleep at night. I was eight years old—listless, restless, perhaps irked by my father's double absence. One day at lunch I watched my mother open a fresh pack of cigarettes, then I covertly pocketed the slender strip of red cellophane she discarded in the ashtray. That afternoon, during siesta, in obedience to some inarticulate inner prompting, I walked down the hall to the pensione's only bathroom, tied one end of the red strip to the bolt of the lock, closed the door, and carefully pulled the strip back through, thereby locking the door from the outside. With a swift jerk I yanked most of the strip free, leaving nothing visible. Then I returned to our bedroom and told my incredulous brothers what I had done.

We waited. At four o'clock the pensione began to stir. Pans clattered in the kitchen. The telephone rang in the vestibule. Footsteps padded by as people woke up and made their way to the bathroom. Gradually a murmur arose in the hall, and we drifted out to see what was the matter. A small crowd milled in front of the bathroom. Someone knocked, then thumped, then banged. Angry voices shouted in Italian. The proprietress emerged from the kitchen, straightened her apron, and knocked. No answer. She shouted. No answer. Finally they sent for a man who put a ladder against the wall of the building, climbed two stories, entered through the bathroom window, and opened the bathroom door to the angry, mystified crowd.

"*Ma chi è?*" cried the landlady, pouncing on a shred of the red strip dangling from the lock. At that point we thought it best to retire to our room, grateful that our father was not there to catch us in the act of imitating him.

We spent eight months in Rome without my father. Mother moved us into and out of a series of apartments with dysfunctional central heating. She found us a pretty English nanny named Nina whom I loved but who had an Italian boyfriend who was a pilot for a mercenary army fighting somewhere in Africa. Mother bought us matching flannel shorts and V-necked blue sweaters and took us out for dinner to small restaurants where the men made much of us and more of her—a beautiful young woman alone in Rome with her three boys. After the inevitable violinist had played the inevitable song that brought the inevitable tears to Mother's dark eyes, we walked home through the cobblestone streets, banging our heels on the manhole covers embossed with the letters S.P.Q.R.

S.P.Q.R.: *Senatus Populusque Romanus.* An empire once, a city now. Who can account for the influence that the vestiges of empire had on the historical consciousness of an eight-year-old American boy? At the time I understood nothing. But I absorbed, in the yellow Roman light, the knowledge that history is more than an aggregate of moments, of names of generals and dates of battles learned in school. History turns suddenly on a pivot. Whole orders of being pass away. No one tried to answer because I never asked the question that shadowed every monument and ruin we saw: what happened? But I felt that no gradual process of change could possibly connect the Arch of Constantine with the Fiats and Vespas swirling noisily beneath it. History must be dramatic, swift, inexplicable. And it is; the Cold War ended in three months, without a shot fired.

WE WERE LIVING in Maadi, a suburb of Cairo, when the Six-Day War between Israel and Egypt broke out in June of 1967. Egypt immediately severed diplomatic relations with the United States, and for the second time in my life I was evacuated, this time to Athens. Once again my father stayed behind to perform the invisible work that sustained us.

None of us really knows what he did for the next six months: he wrote one postcard, telling us that he went out a lot at night wearing the soft-soled shoes he jokingly called his "brothel creepers." Many years later, however, and after much wine, he uncharacteristically dropped the veil and let one story slip out. On the night President Gamal Abdel Nasser announced he would resign, my father had needed to go out and visit certain "people" in various quarters of Cairo. The city was in upheaval. Distraught crowds roamed the streets, carrying placards of Nasser and crying out for vengeance against Israel and its chief ally, the United States. Around midnight, in a dark street of one of the city's poorer sections, my father turned a corner and found himself twenty yards away from just such a crowd. (He is recognizably American and speaks no Arabic.) Almost before he could move, he was surrounded. A young man seized him by the arms, and instead of resisting, my father took the young man's hand and guided his fingers to the skin under his own glasses. The man paused, stepped back, then turned and quieted the crowd. When he had finished, he put his arm around my father and guided him through the mass, which parted like the waters of the Red Sea. My father continued quietly on his way.

What had happened? On seeing the crowd, my father spat on his hands and rubbed them beneath his eyes. The moisture there convinced the young man that my father, like so many Egyptians, had been weeping with sorrow at the news that Nasser planned to resign. This is what the man had explained to the crowd and why they had let my father through.

An example of quick thinking, no doubt. But more than that. My father, I know, truly was saddened by Nasser's announcement; if he were a man capable of crying easily, he might have cried that night. He wasn't just tricking the crowd; he was feeling with them. But at the same time, this moment of communion with the people of Egypt was forced to be an act of duplicity. There will always be a need for subterfuge in foreign relations and in the gathering of intelligence, but during the Cold War these necessities became enshrined as virtues. And not just overseas. For many American men of my father's generation, the Cold War paradigm of interminable struggle against an implacable foe was just the most focused articulation of a general state of being. Unlike Vietnam veterans later, many men of my father's generation who returned home from war may not have had to deal with the shock of peace. There *was* no peace. A new war was nurtured into being, providing them a field in which to go on fighting—not just abroad but at home, where the ethos of conflict made the pursuit of success a cause, not just a fate. While the idea of capitalism had to be protected by cold warriors like my father, its actual triumph could be assured only by the unremitting and self-sacrificing struggle of corporate cadres back home—a struggle that has, they claim, paid off at last.

BUT NOW WHAT? Thirty years ago, on a spring night in Washington, a man who was an intelligence officer stood with a martini in hand beside a charcoal grill, watching the coals glow. That afternoon he had left a large office building, driven home anonymously, had doffed tie and jacket and rolled up his shirtsleeves. Now his sneakers rested lightly on the brick patio of a Georgetown garden, and his gaze, when he looked up at the pale spring sky, was at once vague and vigilant. We played at his feet, and he protected us. Inside the house his wife, our mother, made potato salad and placed plastic forks and paper plates on a tray to carry out to us.

Today my own young children take root and flourish in a small town in New England. Outside, sprawled on a chaise longue and sipping wine as hamburgers cook, I protect them from nothing. Their horizon does not end at a wall topped with barbed wire but expands indefinitely. I realize now that I have tried to make my work the exact opposite of my father's. Against his commitment to silence I oppose my claims to speech—as a teacher and a writer. At the same time, though, I inevitably reproduce him—in manner, in temperament, and even in work. Closeted in my study, demanding a household of silence while I write, I may be as mysterious to my sons as my father was to his.

Constantine Cavafy's poem "Waiting for the Barbarians" asks: "And now, without the Barbarians, what is to become of us?/After all, those people were a kind of solution." The premise of the Cold War was a bipolar world, every nation allied with us or with our "enemies." For more than forty years the Cold War made this particular construction of reality more real than others. For many Americans—and I hope for my sons, whose shouts float up from the bottom of the garden—a choice has emerged: to view the world as a more complicated place, requiring subtler thinking and more varied partnerships; or to retrench behind a new polarity, peering over the battlements at the numerous, angry poor. Not, unfortunately, that these options necessarily exclude each other.

I rise to prod the hamburgers. The world is no longer two; it is many. But the boys have armed themselves anyway, I see. Hefting sticks, since we don't allow them toy guns, they stalk each other through the dusk. At their age, my brothers and I mowed down legions of Nazis and Commies. Watching my sons join the ancient hunt, I wonder: who will be designated as their enemies?

SOUTHERN WOMEN

(JULY 1982)

Shirley Abbott

LIKE ANY PROPERLY brought up Southern girl, I used to spend a lot of time in graveyards. On summer afternoons we'd pile into my mother's green Chevrolet—my Aunt Vera, her daughter June (four years my senior), and often also a massive, aged female relation. Somehow we'd fit ourselves into the front and back seats, the women in print dresses and hairnets and no stockings, we two kids in shorts, and Mother would gun on down the road at forty miles per hour with every window open.

The boredom, for my cousin June and me, was as heavy as passion. Our mothers never packed a picnic basket, or even a thermos of lemonade or any refreshments beyond a package of chewing gum, which they meted out late in the day, half a stick at a time. June was not only older than I but smarter, and we'd soon be brawling. She knew the drill: she'd tease me about my freckles or about who I "liked" ("It's that little drip Charles Lynas, ain't it?"), and like some perplexed, furious puppy, I'd attack. Since my aggression made the most racket, I got the punishment.

"Pinch a piece out of her, Vera," my mother would command— "peench" was how she said it—her hands tight on the wheel and her eyes on the dust boiling in the road. My Aunt Vera would turn and apply the thumbscrew with pleasure and efficiency. I'd weep, June would giggle. The women were contemptuous of my sorrows, their object being to keep us silent so they could talk. What they talked about, mostly, was birthdays. They'd name over all the kin who had been born in September, marvel over how many of us had arrived in November (Billie Sue and Jessie, Laura Alice and Vel), try to puzzle out why so few came in May ("Nobody but just Olive on the fourteenth and Bonnie Sue on the fifth"). The heat of August must have been what depressed the May birthrate, but nobody reasoned it out that far, least of all me.

And on we'd go, down the road, sweating thigh to thigh and mopping our necks and suffering from thirst. Our agony was immaterial. The graves had to be visited, the weeds pulled off them, the markers read aloud, the flowers renewed. It was a shame to the living if the dead lacked flowers, an almighty disgrace if the next of kin had failed to buy a headstone.

In one sun-bleached old churchyard after another, the women would read the stones and recite the names and vital dates of those neglected souls who lacked markers. One or all of them would end up sobbing before we got back into the car. Somebody had to cry or else the afternoon would have been a waste. I always looked forward to the weeping. It broke the monotony. It was passionate and mystical, and I loved it.

You cannot spend your summer afternoons in such pursuits without learning that the past matters. Southerners are famous for cherishing their fine old names, but we were not cherishing our fine old name. We were simply clinging to what had gone before with our own fierce sense of propriety. Within our family there was no such thing as a person who did not matter. Second cousins thrice removed mattered. We knew—and thriftily made use of—everybody's middle name. We knew who was buried where. We all mattered, and the dead most of all.

The South where I was born and raised was Arkansas, in a peaceable little resort town called Hot Springs. When I was a child, just before World War II began, there were two main local industries: the legal one was applying healing waters to the sick, and the illegal one was gambling. The yearly race meet—which was not only legal but operated by the sovereign state of Arkansas—also caused some cash to flow in a favorable direction, if only on a seasonal basis.

Arkansas was short on mint juleps and azalea gardens and had nothing to compare with the charms of Natchez, but it was plenty Southern. Contrary to what they showed in the movies in those days, the South didn't mean bourbon and hoop skirts, it meant red dirt and poor people, of which we had a lot. We also had our share of Southern historical monuments. Not antebellum mansions or statues of Robert E. Lee on his horse, for you could drive from Fayetteville to El Dorado and then backtrack to Texarkana without ever seeing any such thing. What you would see, though, was shanties, tar-paper houses, tumbledown barns, and chickens scratching industriously for bugs in bald front yards. In those days, if a car passed yours on the road, you'd have to roll the windows up or even pull over in the ditch and wait until the dust storm died down.

MY MOTHER AND the other women I knew as a child were farm women, one or two generations removed from the real pioneer days, gentled and domesticated by the time I came among them. But the marks were there. Their skin was leathery from working outdoors. Some of these women were serene and some hot-tempered, and in either case they brooked no transgressions of their notions of morality, and woe to anyone who spoke to these women with disrespect. They were not innocent or submissive or delicately constituted, not afraid of balky cows or chicken hawks. It took them approximately two hours to transform a live rooster into Sunday dinner. They could reason with a mule and shoot a gun. But they also knew just how to take hold of a baby and what to say to a weeping two-year-old.

I used to hang on the backs of their chairs as they peeled peaches by the bushel and talked about how to keep dill-pickle jars from exploding, and why Cousin Rosity had got the cancer she was dying from, and what effect the drought would have on cattle prices, and how the doctors had decided to cut off poor old Uncle Jules's leg ("Ought to be ashamed of themselves, him being ninety and about dead anyhow of that diabetes—but danged if the old man didn't get up off his bed

171

and run them out of his house"). Sometimes, thinking the children out of earshot, or perhaps deeming us old enough to hear, they would forget their ironclad morals and recount some scandal that was simmering in a cottage down the road a piece, or even tell a bawdy joke. Never anything explicit, merely the gropings of newlyweds, forever doomed to get the Vaseline mixed up with the glue. In later years, when I was adolescent, it shocked me to hear them laugh out loud about such things. How could they joke about anything so awesome? Had they no sense of romance?

Then, when the peaches were peeled and sliced into half a dozen enamel dishpans, they would make me stand up at a tub of scalding soapy water and wash out Kerr-Mason jars by the case. It took a child's hand for that. Theirs were too splayed. I have watched those knobby brown fingers laying French plaits into my cousin's black hair, my own being too fuzzy to braid, and I have known those women to walk five miles to spend an afternoon at a quilting frame.

Other Southern women were part of my life, too, infinitely more primitive than my own relatives, with roots farther back in time. Until I was thirteen my father had earned a living mainly as a gambler—a bookmaker, I mean, in one of the illegal Hot Springs horse books. Then an agrarian fit momentarily took hold of him, and he moved us to a forty-acre farm west of Hot Springs. But what we had was barren ground. The apple orchard that he planted in high hope never bore. The well constantly threatened to go dry. We scarcely dared flush the toilet or bathe. Urban spirit that I was, I had no more aptitude as a farmer's daughter than my father had as a farmer. I hated digging potatoes, and I hated gathering eggs. I hated the smell of chicken houses—vinegary, sweet, rotten—despised the chickens, shrank from the finger-skinning work that went on seven days a week, indoors and out. As I loaded the wire baskets, hoping not to infuriate the ill-humored old hens, I comforted myself with the thought that I had, after all, not been born for such indignities.

But there was an escape. On summer afternoons I would go across the road and visit with Grandma Lizzie Ethridge (not my grandma, of course, but the county's). We'd sit under a shade tree together, and she would try to teach me to crochet. "Make them little picots nice and even," she would command, although she called them "peekholes." I would stay and stay, laboriously chaining around my doily. At five o'clock, when I should have crossed the road again to help my parents with the chores, I would follow her on her rounds instead.

Lizzie Ethridge was scarcely five feet tall, and from planting time to harvest she never put on a shoe. Though she kept herself very clean, she always smelled faintly of sweat. She wore a sunbonnet when she walked outside, and a print housedress with a one-piece overall apron. At the neck of her dress the trimming on her homemade "princess slip" showed. This was a loose cotton garment that she never went without, even in the hottest weather. Under these various modest layers were the mighty contours of a Paleolithic stone goddess—the Venus of Willendorf—with vast breasts spreading atop a bulging belly. I would follow Granny down her rows of corn and pole beans or among her flower beds, watching as she bent over each blossom with a bucket of water and a dipper. The flowers would have made a botanist gape. They were profuse, exotic, tropical. She sent off for seeds advertised on the radio and, having no idea of the names of things, made up her own classes and genuses.

When we sat down to rest, she would tell stories, pausing now and then to pack her lower lip with snuff or spit the sickly brown liquid into a tin can. She had come into this county as a child some eighty years before, "from way over yonder," she said, waving a finger toward the eastern hills. She had helped clear a homeplace and plant a crop. She had heard mountain lions scream at night, had watched a milk snake drink from a cow's udder in the light of dawn. Had been saved by the Lord Jesus and baptized in a running stream. Had ridden home alone bareback one night from a brush-arbor tabernacle, the horse at full gallop and a puma running behind. She had married young and borne many children, some of whom died in infancy, some of whom, now old themselves, looked in on her from time to time.

SOMETIME IN THE late 1960s feminists brought forth the notion of sisterhood—of women "bonded" to women. Sisterhood was going to be "powerful," our Hanseatic League, our lobbying arm in the corridors of heightened awareness. But sisterhood was nothing new to me. It has been a zealously guarded secret among Southern women for years. Next to motherhood, sisterhood is what they value most, taking an endless pleasure in the daily, commonplace society of one another that they never experience in male company.

The most vivid memories of my childhood are long afternoons when my Aunt Vera would come to our house with her daughter June, and the four of us would form a kind of subversive cell. June and I would usually play, indoors and out, while our mothers sewed or quilted or canned. Sometimes the four of us would dress and get in the car and drive around Hot Springs, buying thread and snaps at the dry-goods store, visiting some spring or other and drinking from tin cups, or "rattling up and down," as my aunt called it, on Central Avenue. Hearing what they said on these afternoons, I gradually realized that my mother and her sister were not awed by men in the least, that they preferred each other's company to that of their respective husbands.

I also realized that these two women had unmatronly desires, usually involving beautiful dresses and travel, that otherwise went unmentioned—merely the circumspect fantasies of a pair of young housewives caught in the coils of the commonplace. And yet the sharing of these fantasies made them laugh, gave them a secret life as they bent their dark heads over the sewing machine or a "pinker" that never would pink. I could not have voiced the idea, but I knew that the part of their lives they liked most was here, with each other. Not at the supper table or at work or in bed with their husbands. My father used to be jealous of these tête-à-têtes, and he had cause.

Often I spent summer afternoons in larger groups of women, not my kin. The neighborhood beauty shop is one of the foundations of society in small Southern towns—you go there to get your hair "fixed," but that isn't the real reason, any more than men congregate at the county courthouse to transact legal business.

The beauty "operator" is invariably a middle-aged woman who found herself in need of a trade and solved the problem by getting her license and having some shampoo sinks and hair dryers installed on the glassed-in porch. All the neighborhood women would have standing appointments (as my mother did) and they'd bring their children along. It was an all-female society—no man would dare enter the place—and here, if nowhere else, women said what they thought about men. And what they thought was often fairly murderous.

Those sweet-faced wives and mothers would sit there wafting their wet, red fingernails in the air, hoping to get them dry before the comb-out was finished, saying, "Now, Maidie, spray me good, I want it to last through tomorrow. I'll sleep with my head in a bonnet," and they would gossip, of course. Every teenage romance or impending marriage, separation, illness, operation, or death got its going-over. But the leitmotif was their loyalty and fortitude in the face of male foolishness, and, as a keen obbligato, "Don't ever let them know what you really think of them. Humor them. Pretend you love them. Even love them, if you must. But play a strong card to their weak one." That was not what they said, but it was what they meant.

It was always the same, wherever I went. As they drank their Cokes, folded their stacks of fresh towels, played bridge, or sewed, they assured one another, "Men are children. Men are little boys. They can't stand pain. They never grow up. They can't face the truth." All this information was deeply buried in metaphor. "Albert got up at three o'clock to go fishing this morning. Was just going to tiptoe out, he said. Well, he couldn't find his hip boots, and I thought he would tear the house down. I finally had to get up and find them for him. It was five by the time he left." Or, "I told him if he wanted to smoke that nasty pipe he could smoke it outside. I wasn't going to have that smell in my living room." Or, "He's just like a little child. If you don't have supper on the table the minute he gets home, he gets mad. 'Course, after you feed him, you can get him to do anything."

PSYCHIATRISTS HAVE ALWAYS focused on the passion that little girls feel for their fathers—understandably, since most of them are men. Girls are all supposed to be in training from babyhood, sensing out the contours of love and loss as we fall in love with Daddy and are forced to postpone our pleasure. But I was in love with my mother too. I hated her doing housework, could not bear the sight of her in an old dress and a pair of unlaced oxfords, feeding soapy bedsheets into the wringer, scraping carrots and parsnips at the sink. But one thing she had acquired in town was the ability to be glamorous, to divorce herself, by means of paints and polishes, from that other world. I loved her glamorous aspect.

She had a marvelous drawer full of cosmetics. She had an enormous dressing table, a yellow satin-veneer piece with a kneehole and a mirrored top, and a vast standing mirror that reflected the whole bedroom. There was a little low-backed bench and four drawers; in them she kept all her wonderful implements of beauty. Not every day, but once a week, or any time she was going out shopping, she would bathe, put on her stockings and a lacy slip and high-heeled shoes, and sit down to paint. I would abandon dog, swing, book, or any other pursuit in order to watch her. I'd come indoors and post myself beside the bench.

The open drawers gave off the most ravishing smells. Down in their depths sat little white jars with pink lids, black cylinders trimmed in silver, pink glass things with tiny roses on top, high-domed boxes with face powder inside (if you opened these on your own, they'd blow dust all over the tabletop), fresh powder puffs, miniature caskets with trick openings, compacts with pearl lids that shut with a glamorous click, vials of astringent and witch hazel, red boxes with logs of mascara inside, and pencils for what Mother always called her "eyebrowls." Most seductive of all were the perfume bottles, some with glass stoppers and ribbons around the neck, one with a figurine on top.

She would take her tweezers and hand mirror, search her freckled face for any wayward sprouts, and swiftly uproot them. Anxious about a black hair or two on her upper lip, she would apply a thick paste, like a pale green caterpillar, beneath her nose. It had to set five minutes and had a loathsome vinegary stench—I smell it still. When she removed the goo, she looked exactly as she had before. But she would survey the defoliated terrain with the solemnity of a military tactician.

On those rare afternoons when she did abandon her housework

and go out, having brought her face to its state of daytime perfection, she would take up her car keys and shut the door on her immaculate house. She and I would set out for town together, and she seemed so beautiful in those moments that I knew I was in love with her. Unless we were going to the movies, "town" was a complete bust. We'd go find a parking place and go into Woolworth's for a spool of thread and a nickel's worth of candy. Maybe we'd look at a pattern book, and sometimes, to my despair, she'd bump into one of her thousands of cousins on the street and talk for half an hour. The exoticism of the afternoon would vanish sooner than the bag of candy.

Many years later, I stopped to wonder why a woman of her thoroughly practical inclinations would spend upward of an hour prettying up to go to the dime store. She certainly was not trying to attract a man—in the middle of the afternoon in Hot Springs, Arkansas, the only visible men were pumping gas in filling stations. She was not doing it for Daddy, for by the time he got home from work she'd be in a housedress again, perspiring over the kitchen range. Nor was she competing with other women. She was doing it for fun, and for a mark of her separateness, and for a way of showing herself—and me—that even so responsible a person as herself could do something that had no purpose to it. It was her one real break with her past. Maybe she wanted to let me know, in the most subtle way, that femininity was not merely the massive, serious, strenuous thing she usually made it seem to be, but occasionally a matter of pleasing yourself. And thus she delved into that dresser drawer, which is one of the most ancient sources of womanly corruption, without being corrupted by it.

NOTES FOR A LIFE NOT MY OWN

(MAY 1992)

Verlyn Klinkenborg

IN RECENT YEARS I have written several essays in which my father played a part. They were allusive, as essays tend to be, and each one seemed to catch the feeling I was after at the time I wrote it. But even good work begins to drift away the moment it is done. Sooner or later every writer reaches the point where his words feel like a shroud. He begins to wish he could brush them away and step into the present, into the open, as himself. But to write is to commit words to the past, to build with bricks that finally conceal the writer, though the wall remains for anyone to see.

MY FATHER, AT sixty-four, is still a young man in most ways. He and I use a language we have worked out for ourselves, a scientific language in which each word stands for one object. When we say "Montana" or "transmission fluid," we know what we're talking about. This tongue evolved in a disputatious time. My mother was our interpreter, and when she died we were left speechless. In the silent period that followed, I think we saw in my mother's death how much we stood to lose in each other. We have not talked about it. We have no words in our language appropriate to such feelings, though we know a thousand names for "trout lure." But this is true and I say it for myself: death makes individuals of us all. The individual it made for me was my father.

MY FATHER TELLS a story about a day in his childhood when he and his own father were making hay for neighbors in the northwest corner of Iowa. The terrain there is more exposed than the fields in Iowa's midlands. My father and his dad went home for the noon meal, and a storm blew up. When they returned to the hayfield, they found one man dead from a lightning strike and three men unconscious. They thought the four were sleeping. This is how the gods gave farmers silence.

MY FATHER TELLS another story. He and a friend had gone after whitefish in the high lakes of Colorado. The time was just before iceover, when the water turns black with cold. They were harvesting winter fish for the freezer, catching them with grubs on gold-plated hooks. As they fished, they huddled round a fire built onshore. A cowboy rode up on his horse. He dismounted, took a fishing rod from his gear, removed his boots, and wet-waded thigh-deep into the lake. He caught a short stringer of fish, waded back to shore, put on his boots, and rode away. This was one of the gods who gave farmers silence.

WHEN MY FATHER cooks, he is likely to make one of three things: oyster stew, which he saves for Christmas Eve; chicken dumpling soup, which is a Saturday noon dish; or venison chili, which is made from last year's venison burger and carried frozen into camp. The recipe for venison chili he learned in elk camp from an old man who once cooked for Teddy Roosevelt. The trick is whole cloves.

MY FATHER TELLS a harvest story from his childhood in the northwest corner of Iowa. He always carried a .410 shotgun on the tractor. When a pheasant fluttered up from the stalks ahead, he would raise the gun to his hip and fire, one hand still on the steering wheel. He is as good a shot from the hip as from the shoulder. I have never seen it proved, but I know better than to doubt it. That is not the kind of thing he exaggerates. My first shotgun was a little .410 with an old-fashioned hammer. What was missing was the tractor and the cornfield and the birds and the solitude. We moved to California in the mid-Sixties for my mother's health, but also because in Iowa the hunting had disappeared.

ONE NIGHT IN Tahoe, a famous television actress invited a stranger from the audience to join her act. That was my dad. He cut the rug, sang harmony, danced with his arm around her waist. This is a scene a writer would like to embellish, but not a son. (The crackle of her clothing, the nimbus of perfume, the sex that seemed so personal from afar but was seen onstage to be a kind of ventriloquism.) When my father left the farm, he was led away by music. He played the baritone horn, the piano, and sang. Later, he directed. Sundays I would see him, his back to the congregation, leading the choir with quick movements, the loose sleeves of the robe slipping down to his shoulders.

IN IOWA, IF the temperature fell below zero, we could eat fried corn-meal mush for breakfast. When it rose to fifty, we could wear spring jackets. Above eighty, we could swim. I love to know the temperature. I have never met farm boys who could swim well. They could strike a baseball cruelly, and they could play pinochle. Until I was fourteen, I never saw my uncles without a card table between them. Their silence was not with each other. They had their own boys. There is not a single piece of his own good work that a farmer does with his mouth. Open it and out comes the weather.

THE FIRST TIME I heard my father swear, the word was "hell." He said, "What the hell do you think you're doing?" I was playing with a friend at the high snowy bank where the railroad tracks passed the graveyard. We had sent my brother home because he was cold. We lived two blocks away, straight back the tracks, two houses in, easy, even for a kid. He had turned up frozen and had to be soaked in a lukewarm bath. My mother, too, almost froze to death as a child. She told of the sleep that nearly overcame her. As a boy I could picture the yard lights burning across the snow, too far away to reach, too far away to keep her awake.

181

THE BORDERS OF character are permeable. I distrust any man who claims to have had a continuous friendship with his father. How did he get from fourteen to twenty-six? How well does he know his father, or himself? The disputatious time for me was the late Sixties. I notice now that it was the one period of my father's life when he was cut off from the country. We lived in the suburbs of Sacramento, California. We fought over Ronald Reagan, over Janis Joplin. We lived in Iowa when the Beatles first appeared on Ed Sullivan. The whole family watched. The Beatles made a deep bow. There was John Lennon bending over his Rickenbacker guitar. I said, "He looks like Captain Kangaroo," and the whole family laughed. That laughter has burned in my ears for twenty-six years.

IN THE LATE summer of 1971 my mother died of leukemia. She was forty-three. She died after a ten-year remission, which she believed God had granted her—and who will doubt her?—so that she might raise her four children to an age of relative safety. I, the oldest, was nineteen when she died, and callow, through no fault of hers, beyond my ability to comprehend it now. My father assembled his children on a bench in the backyard and told us that our mother, his wife, had died in her hospital room earlier that afternoon. Grief scattered us. But before we began to wander wherever our feelings carried us—we would bump into each other like strangers again and again over the next few hours—I happened to look at my father's face. It was the face, as I imagine it now, of Adam as he and Eve were led away from the Garden. With this difference: that Eve was the Garden from which my father was led away alone.

WHEN WE MOVED into the Sacramento house, it had two bedrooms, one bathroom, and a lawn. When we moved out, it had five bedrooms, three bathrooms, a new hallway, a new kitchen, garden, toolshed, woodshop, patio, child's fort raised on poles, and a doughboy pool. My father had erected a portable sawmill in the driveway. There was a trailer parked under the plane tree. There were chickens in the garden. At family reunions we pour cement. We do the work ourselves. I remember how modern, how Californian I felt when my dad remarried. We saw the honeymoon couple off at the airport and then we children drove ourselves home. They were bound for Oaxaca. Soon my dad and Sally, his new wife, will have been married for as long as my mother and father were married. Sally was as sadly damaged by death as my father. It is hard to say who saved whom, but both were saved, and the children were, too.

AND YET I remember the evenings in that last long summer of my mother's life, when we had not been told what our parents knew. She and my father left the dinner table and walked out through the backyard to a bench beneath the apricot tree. Sometimes they sat and sometimes they walked among the rows of corn and beans just past the grape arbor. Their movements were graceful, slow. Soon the delta breeze carried off the heat of day. We could see them there as we cleared the table, and we did not know what we were looking at. None of us was ever again so blessed by ignorance.

NOW MY FATHER is rebuilding his childhood. He has an International Harvester tractor, fourteen acres of good pasture grown up in rye grass, a barn, and some cattle. The land is not as flat as it was in Iowa, nor as steep as it was in Colorado. I notice that I am rebuilding my father's childhood too. I have some pasture. I can see the use for some of his tools, the chain saw, the come-along, the winch. I remember the moment when I first realized that I resembled my father. Every son does. There is a spectral flash of recognition. Any woman you know sees the resemblance too plainly. I would like to be discovering now the ways I resemble my mother too.

THE BORDERS OF character are permeable. When the gods gave farmers silence, they also gave them the power to mean great things by it. Words become a frail chattering on those prairies. As a boy, my father drove a horse team. An ancient metaphor for writing is derived from the movement of a team of oxen. The farmer walks behind them, clucking and singing. Birds hop in their path. The oxen bend to the yoke and in the earth a furrow is turned. The furrow is the line of words on the page. The page is the earth. The writer turns the team homeward. The birds rise into the sky and vanish.

THE RAKE

(JUNE 1992)

David Mamet

THERE WAS THE incident of the rake and there was the incident of the school play, and it seems to me that they both took place at the round kitchen table.

The table was not in the kitchen proper but in an area called "the nook," which held its claim to that small measure of charm by dint of a waist-high wall separating it from an adjacent area known as the living room.

All family meals were eaten in the nook. There was a dining room to the right, but, as in most rooms of that name at that time and in those surroundings, it was never used.

The round table was of wrought iron and topped with glass; it was noteworthy for that glass, for it was more than once and rather more than several times, I am inclined to think, that my stepfather would grow so angry as to bring some object down on the glass top, shattering it, thus giving us to know how we had forced him out of control.

And it seems that most times when he would shatter the table, as often as that might have been, he would cut some portion of himself on the glass, or that he or his wife, our mother, would cut their hands on picking up the glass afterward, and that we children were to understand, and did understand, that these wounds were our fault.

So the table was associated in our minds with the notion of blood.

The house was in a brand-new housing development in the southern suburbs. The new community was built upon, and now bordered, the remains of what had once been a cornfield. When our new family moved in, there were but a few homes in the development completed, and a few more under construction. Most streets were mud, and boasted a house here or there, and many empty lots marked out by white stakes.

The house we lived in was the development's Model Home. The first time we had seen it, it had signs plastered on the front and throughout the interior telling of the various conveniences it contained. And it had a lawn, and was one of the only homes in the new community that did.

My stepfather was fond of the lawn, and he detailed me and my sister to care for it, and one fall afternoon we found ourselves assigned to rake the leaves.

Why this chore should have been so hated I cannot say, except that we children, and I especially, felt ourselves less than full members of this new, cobbled-together family, and disliked being assigned to the beautification of a home that we found unbeautiful in all respects, and for which we had neither natural affection nor a sense of proprietary interest.

WE WENT TO the new high school. We walked the mile down the open two-lane road on one side of which was the just-begun suburban community and on the other side of which was the cornfield.

The school was as new as the community, and still under construction for the first three years of its occupancy. One of its innovations was the notion that honesty would be engendered by the absence of security, and so the lockers were designed and built both without locks and without the possibility of attaching locks. And there was the corresponding rash of thievery and many lectures about the same from the school administration, but it was difficult to point with pride to any scholastic or community tradition supporting the suggestion that we, the students, pull together in this new, utopian way. We were, in school, in an uncompleted building in the midst of a mud field in the midst of a cornfield. Our various sports teams were called The

Spartans; and I played on those teams, which were of a wretchedness consistent with their novelty.

Meanwhile my sister interested herself in the drama society. The year after I had left the school she obtained the lead in the school play. It called for acting and singing, both of which she had talent for, and it looked to be a signal triumph for her in her otherwise unremarkable and unenjoyed school career.

On the night of the play's opening she sat down to dinner with our mother and our stepfather. It may be that they ate a trifle early to allow her to get to the school to enjoy the excitement of the opening night. But however it was, my sister had no appetite, and she nibbled a bit at her food, and then she got up from the table to carry her plate back to scrape it in the sink, when my mother suggested that she sit down, as she had not finished her food. My sister said she really had no appetite, but my mother insisted that as the meal had been prepared it would be good form to sit and eat it.

My sister sat down with the plate and pecked at her food and she tried to eat a bit, and told my mother that, no, really, she possessed no appetite whatever, and that was due, no doubt, not to the food, but to her nervousness and excitement at the prospect of opening night.

My mother, again, said that as the food had been cooked it had to be eaten, and my sister tried and said that she could not; at which my mother nodded. She then got up from the table and went to the telephone and looked the number up and called the school and got the drama teacher and identified herself and told him that her daughter wouldn't be coming to school that night, that, no, she was not ill, but that she would not be coming in. Yes, yes, she said, she knew that her daughter had the lead in the play, and, yes, she was aware that many children and teachers had worked hard for it, et cetera, and so my sister did not play the lead in her school play. But I was long gone, out of the house by that time, and well out of it. I heard that story, and others like it, at the distance of twenty-five years.

IN THE MODEL house our rooms were separated from their room, the master bedroom, by a bathroom and a study. On some weekends

I would go alone to visit my father in the city and my sister would stay and sometimes grow frightened or lonely in her part of the house. And once, in the period when my grandfather, then in his sixties, was living with us, she became alarmed at a noise she had heard in the night; or perhaps she just became lonely, and she went out of her room and down the hall, calling for my mother, or my stepfather, or my grandfather, but the house was dark, and no one answered.

And, as she went farther down the hall, toward the living room, she heard voices, and she turned the corner, and saw a light coming from under the closed door in the master bedroom, and heard my step-father crying, and the sound of my mother weeping. So my sister went up to the door, and she heard my stepfather talking to my grandfather and saying, "Jack. Say the words. Just say the words . . ." And my grandfather, in his Eastern European accent, saying, with obvious pain and difficulty, "No. No. I can't. Why are you making me do this? Why?" And the sound of my mother crying convulsively.

My sister opened the door, and she saw my grandfather sitting on the bed, and my stepfather standing by the closet and gesturing. On the floor of the closet she saw my mother, curled in a fetal position, moaning and crying and hugging herself. My stepfather was saying, "Say the words. Just say the words." And my grandfather was breath-ing fast and repeating, "I can't. She knows how I feel about her. I can't." And my stepfather said, "Say the words, Jack. Please. Just say you love her." At which my mother would moan louder. And my grandfather said, "I can't."

My sister pushed the door open farther and said—I don't know what she said, but she asked, I'm sure, for some reassurance, or some explanation, and my stepfather turned around and saw her and picked up a hairbrush from a dresser that he passed as he walked toward her, and he hit her in the face and slammed the door on her. And she con-tinued to hear "Jack, say the words."

She told me that on weekends when I was gone my stepfather ended every Sunday evening by hitting or beating her for some reason or other. He would come home from depositing his own kids back at their moth-er's house after their weekend visitation, and would settle down tired and angry, and, as a regular matter on those evenings, would find out some intolerable behavior on my sister's part and slap or hit or beat her.

Years later, at my mother's funeral, my sister spoke to our aunt, my mother's sister, who gave a footnote to this behavior. She said when they were young, my mother and my aunt, they and their parents lived in a small flat on the West Side. My grandfather was a salesman on the road from dawn on Monday until Friday night. Their family had a fiction, and that fiction, that article of faith, was that my mother was a naughty child. And each Friday, when he came home, his first question as he climbed the stairs was, "What has she done this week . . . ?" At which my grandmother would tell him the terrible things that my mother had done, after which she, my mother, was beaten.

This was general knowledge in my family. The footnote concerned my grandfather's behavior later in the night. My aunt had a room of her own, and it adjoined her parents' room. And she related that each Friday, when the house had gone to bed, she, through the thin wall, heard my grandfather pleading for sex. "Cookie, please." And my grandmother responding, "No, Jack." "Cookie, please." "No, Jack." "Cookie, please."

And once, my grandfather came home and asked, "What has she done this week?" and I do not know, but I imagine that the response was not completed, and perhaps hardly begun; in any case, he reached and grabbed my mother by the back of the neck and hurled her down the stairs.

And once, in our house in the suburbs there had been an outburst by my stepfather directed at my sister. And she had, somehow, prevailed. It was, I think, that he had the facts of the case wrong, and had accused her of the commission of something for which she had demonstrably had no opportunity, and she pointed this out to him with what I can imagine, given the circumstances, was an understandable and, given my prejudice, a commendable degree of freedom. Thinking the incident closed she went back to her room to study and, a few moments later, saw him throw open her door, bat the book out of her hands, and pick her up and throw her against the far wall, where she struck the back of her neck on a shelf.

She was told, the next morning, that her pain, real or pretended, held no weight, and that she would have to go to school. She protested that she could not walk, or, if at all, only with the greatest of difficulty and in great pain; but she was dressed and did walk to school, where she fainted, and was brought home. For years she suffered various headaches; an X ray taken twenty years later for an unrelated problem revealed that when he threw her against the shelf he had cracked her vertebrae.

WHEN WE LEFT the house we left in good spirits. When we went out to dinner, it was an adventure, which was strange to me, looking back, because many of these dinners ended with my sister or myself being banished, sullen or in tears, from the restaurant, and told to wait in the car, as we were in disgrace.

These were the excursions that had ended, due to her or my intolerable arrogance, as it was then explained to us.

The happy trips were celebrated and capped with a joke. Here is the joke: My stepfather, my mother, my sister, and I would exit the restaurant, my stepfather and mother would walk to the car, telling us that they would pick us up. We children would stand by the restaurant entrance. They would drive up in the car, open the passenger door, and wait until my sister and I had started to get in. They would then drive away.

They would drive ten or fifteen feet, and open the door again, and we would walk up again, and they would drive away again. They sometimes would drive around the block. But they would always come back, and by that time the four of us would be laughing in camaraderie and appreciation of what, I believe, was our only family joke.

WE WERE RAKING the lawn, my sister and I. I was raking, and she was stuffing the leaves into a bag. I loathed the job, and my muscles and my mind rebelled, and I was viciously angry, and my sister said something, and I turned and threw the rake at her and it hit her in the face.

The rake was split bamboo and metal, and a piece of metal caught her lip and cut her badly.

190

We were both terrified, and I was sick with guilt, and we ran into the house, my sister holding her hand to her mouth, and her mouth and her hand and the front of her dress covered in blood.

We ran into the kitchen where my mother was cooking dinner, and my mother asked what happened.

Neither of us, myself out of guilt, of course, and my sister out of a desire to avert the terrible punishment she knew I would receive, neither of us would say what occurred.

My mother pressed us, and neither of us would answer. She said that until one or the other answered, we would not go to the hospital; and so the family sat down to dinner where my sister clutched a napkin to her face and the blood soaked the napkin and ran down onto her food, which she had to eat; and I also ate my food and we cleared the table and went to the hospital.

I REMEMBER THE walks home from school in the frigid winter, along the cornfield that was, for all its proximity to the city, part of the prairie. The winters were viciously cold. From the remove of years, I can see how the area might and may have been beautiful. One could have walked in the stubble of the cornfields, or hunted birds, or enjoyed any of a number of pleasures naturally occurring.

The Children's Wing

(JULY 1986)

Joyce Johnson

THE SUMMER NICKY was so sick, I would leave work a little early and go to the Chinese takeout place on Forty-ninth Street. After a while it was my regular routine. Nicky would call me at the office and place his order. "An egg roll, of course," he'd say. "And sweet and sour shrimp. And Mom, would you bring me a Coke?" I didn't like him to have soft drinks, but he'd say, "Please, please," trying to sound pitiful, and I'd always get one for him in the end. It was hard to refuse him anything that summer. When I'd get to the hospital the other mothers would be there already with their shopping bags. Soon whole families would be gathered around the bedsides of the children, everyone eating out of foil containers or off paper plates, like an odd kind of picnic or a birthday party that had been displaced.

The children's wing was in the oldest part of the hospital, one of those gloomy gray stone buildings put up at the turn of the century. There was a marble rotunda on the ground floor. When you took the elevator up, there was no more marble, just dim green corridors and unending linoleum and muffled fake laughter from all the television sets.

I was never in the ward when the television wasn't on. The kids must have pressed the switches the moment they woke up. If you came in the afternoon, it would be soap operas or game shows; in the evening it would be reruns of *M*A*S*H* or *The Odd Couple*. There was a volunteer who called herself The Teacher and came around with little workbooks. She told me once she was going to bring Nicky some literature to explain what a biopsy was. In a stern voice I said, "I'd much rather you didn't."

I kept thinking Nicky's time in the children's ward would irrevocably change him. A shadow was falling across his vision of life and there was nothing I could do. Once I went to talk to a psychiatrist. He said, "What can I tell you? Either this will do damage to your son, or he will rise to the occasion and be a hero." This immediately comforted me, though it's hard to say why. Somehow I could accept the logic of that answer.

Nicky had seniority in Room K by August. New little boys kept coming and going, accident cases mostly. They lay beached on those high white beds, bewildered to find themselves in arrested motion. Each had been felled by some miscalculation—running out too fast in front of a car, jumping off a fence the wrong way. They'd go home with an arm or leg in a cast and sit out the summer, listening for the bell of the ice-cream truck, driving their mothers crazy. "Hey, man, what you break?" they'd ask Nicky, looking at the plaster around his torso with respect. "You break your back or something?"

He could explain his condition as if he were a junior scientist laying out an interesting problem, using the language he'd picked up from the doctors—"left lumbar vertebra . . . unknown organism." He'd say, "You see, in the X ray there's a white swelling on the left lumbar vertebra." There were men in a laboratory hunting the unknown organism. He made it sound like a movie—you could imagine the men in their white coats bent over their test tubes. All they had to do was find it, he'd say in a confident voice, and then they could cure him.

Sometimes I'd look around the room and stare at all those simple broken limbs in envy. I wondered if Nicky did that, too. Why had it been necessary for him to learn the awful possibilities, how your own body could suddenly turn against you, become the enemy?

He was the little scientist and he was the birthday boy. When the pain would come, he'd hold on to my hand the way he had at home on those nights I'd sat up with him. "Do you see that?" he'd say, pointing to the decal of a yellow duckling on the wall near his bed. "Isn't that ridiculous to have that here, that stupid duck?"

I agreed with him about the duck and Room K's other decorations—brown Disneyesque bunnies in various poses, a fat-cheeked Mary and her little lamb, all of them scratched and violently scribbled over. I could see how they threatened the dignity of a ten-year-old. The hospital would turn you into a baby if you didn't watch out.

I kept buying Nicky things; so did his father. With a sick child, you're always trying to bring different pieces of the outside in, as if to say, *That's* the reality, not this. There was a game called Boggle that he was interested in for a week, and his own tape recorder, which fell off the bed one day and broke, and incredibly intricate miniature robots from Japan. All this stuff piled up around him. The fruit my mother brought him turned brown in unopened plastic bags.

Nicky liked only one thing, really; he could have done without all the rest. A fantasy war game called D&D that was all the rage among the fifth-graders. I never even tried to understand it. I just kept buying the strange-looking dice he asked for and the small lead figures that he'd have to paint himself—dragons and wizards and goblins—and new strategy books with ever more complicated rules. "I want to live in a fantasy world," he told me. I remember it shocked me a little that he knew so explicitly what he was doing.

He refused to come back from that world very much. There were nights he'd hardly stop playing to talk to me. He'd look up only when I was leaving to tell me the colors he needed. When I'd encourage Nicky to get to know the other kids, he'd look at me wearily. "They don't have the same interests," he'd say.

"Maybe you could interest them in what you're doing."

"Mom . . . I can't. I'd have to start them from the beginning."

Still, I was grateful to the makers of D&D, grateful he had a way to lose himself. There were things happening in the children's wing I didn't want him to find out about, things I didn't want to know. If you walked those corridors you passed certain quiet, darkened rooms where there were children who weren't ever going to get well; there were parents on the elevator with swollen faces who'd never look you in the eye. A little girl in Room G died during visiting hours. I could hear her as soon as I got off on the fifth floor, a terrible high-pitched, rattling moan that I'll never forget. It went on and on and there were doctors running down the hall with machinery.

I walked into Nicky's room with my shopping bag from the Chinese takeout place. He was staring at all his figures lined up in battle formation; he didn't say hello. The other kids weren't saying much either. Their parents hadn't come yet. One little boy, looking scared, asked me, "What's that noise out there?" "Oh, someone's very sick tonight," I said, and I closed the door. I just shut the sound out. I suppose any other parent would have done the same. The strange thing was, I felt I'd done something wrong, that we all should have acknowledged it somehow, wept for the child who was dying.

I USED TO try to get Nicky out of bed for some exercise. We'd walk up and down outside his room very slowly, the IV apparatus trailing along on its clumsy, spindly stand like a dog on a leash. Some nights we'd sit on the brown plastic couch in the visitors' lounge, and Nicky would drink his Coke and go over his strategy books.

A mentally disturbed boy appeared there one night. He was tall and had a man's build already, muscled arms and shoulders, though I later found out he was only fifteen. He had a face that could have been beautiful, but you didn't want to see his eyes. They were red and inflamed, emptier than a statue's. I thought of the word "baleful" when I saw them. The boy with the baleful eyes. He was wearing dirty jeans and an old gray T-shirt. I thought he might have come in off the street.

Nicky and I were alone. This boy walked right over and stared down at us. I spoke to him softly, trying to sound calm. "Are you looking for someone?" I said.

He shook his head, grinning. "Who? Looking for Mr. Who. Have you seen Who?"

I said I hadn't seen him.

"Are you a nurse? You're not a nurse."

"The nurses are outside," I said. "Just down the hall."

He sat down next to Nicky. He rapped on Nicky's cast with his knuckles. "Hello, Mr. Who. Want a cigarette?"

Nicky was sitting very still. "No, thanks. I don't smoke," he said in a small voice.

The boy laughed and stood up. He took out a pack of cigarettes and some matches. He lit a match and held it up close to Nicky's face for a moment. Then he lit his cigarette with it and stared down at us a while longer. "My name is Joseph," he said. "Do you like me?"

"I like you very much," I said.

He studied me a long time, almost as if I were someone he remembered. Then he threw the cigarette on the floor and drifted out.

Earlier that day, a boy from Nicky's room had gone home. When we got back there, we saw that the empty bed had been taken. A small suitcase stood beside it and a nurse was tucking in the blanket, making hospital corners. A little while later an intern led Joseph in, dressed in pajamas. "Mom," Nicky whispered. "They're putting him in *here*."

"Don't worry about it, honey," I told him.

I went out to the nurse on duty at the desk and made a complaint. They had no right to put a boy like that in with sick children. The children would be frightened, they had enough to contend with.

"It's the only bed available," the nurse said. "There's no private room for him now. Try to understand—he's sick, too, he needs care. We're going to watch the situation very carefully." I told her about the cigarettes and the matches. She said, "My God. We'll take care of that."

"Where does he come from, anyway?" I asked, and she told me the name of some institution upstate.

MY TELEPHONE RANG in the middle of the night. A nurse said, "Hold on. Your son insists on speaking to you."

Nicky got on the phone, all keyed up and out of breath. "Mom, you have to give me some advice. You know that guy Joseph?"

"What's the matter, Nick?" I said.

"Well, guess who he's picked to be his friend? He keeps getting off his bed and coming over to talk to me. It's too weird. I don't know what to say to him, so I just listen."

I wanted to go straight to the hospital and bring Nicky home. I said, "I guess you're doing the right thing, honey." I asked him if he was scared.

"Not so much. But it's hard, Mom."

"The next time he bothers you, just pretend you're asleep. Maybe he'll go to sleep, too."

"Okay," Nicky said. "Can I call you again if I have to?"

I turned on the lights and sat up and read so I'd be sure to hear the phone. I called him back early in the morning. Joseph was sleeping, Nicky told me. The nurse had finally given him some kind of pill.

I WENT TO the office as usual but I couldn't get much accomplished. Around three I gave up and went to the hospital. They were mopping the corridors and a game show was on in Room K. A housewife from Baltimore had just won a walk-in refrigerator and a trip for two to Bermuda. "Yay! It's the fat lady! I knew it!" a kid was yelling. I found Nicky propped up in bed painting a dragon, making each scale of its wing a different color. I looked around for Joseph, but I didn't see him.

"I'm concentrating, Mom," Nicky said.

"Is everything okay?" I whispered.

With a sigh he put down his brush. "Joseph is taking a walk. That's what Joseph does. But don't worry—he'll be back." Then he said, "Mom, sometimes Joseph seems almost all right. I ask him questions and he tells me very sad things."

"What kinds of things?"

"Stuff about his life. He doesn't go to school, you know. He lives in a hospital with grown-ups. He thinks he's going to live there a long time—maybe always."

WHEN NICKY WAS little, I used to take him to nursery school on the way to work. It wasn't convenient, but I never minded. The place, as I recall it, was always yellow with sunlight. Green sweet potato vines climbed up the windows and there were hamsters dozing in a cage. In the morning the teacher would put up the paintings the children had done the day before. You could smell crayons, soap, chalk dust. And all the little perfect children pulling off their coats had a shine about them, a newness. I was getting my divorce then. Sometimes the thought of that bright place would get me through the day, the idea that it was there and that Nicky was in it—as if I'd been allowed a small vision of harmony.

I thought of it again that afternoon at the hospital. I couldn't get back to it; it was lost, out of reach.

IN THE INSTITUTION Joseph came from, they must have kept him very confined. In the children's wing he roamed the corridors. One day a nurse found him standing in a room he shouldn't have been in and had to bring him back to Room K. "Joseph, you stay in here," she admonished him. He walked up and down, banging his fists against the beds. He poked at little kids and chanted at the top of his voice, "Hey! Hey! What do you say today!"—which might have been a form of greeting.

He stopped by Nicky's bed and watched him paint the dragon. He pressed down on it with his thumb. "Hey, the mad monster game!"

"Wet paint, Joseph," warned Nicky.

Joseph took the dragon right off the night table. "Joseph, you creep!" Nicky yelled, his eyes filling with tears.

I went over to him and held out my hand. "I'm sorry. Nicky needs his dragon." It was odd how Joseph inspired politeness.

He stared down at my open palm as if puzzling over its significance. "That wasn't Nick's," he said.

Joseph stood by the door in the evening when the families came, when the bags of food were opened and the paper plates passed around. I went out to get Nicky a hamburger and a chocolate milkshake. When I came back, the room smelled of fried chicken and everyone was watching *The Odd Couple*. Joseph lay on his bed. He had put his arm over those red eyes, as if the light were hurting him.

Nicky tapped my arm. "Do you see that, Mom? No one came for him."

I said, "Maybe there's no one to come, Nicky."

"Someone should."

I handed him his milkshake. He peeled the paper off the straw and stuck it through the hole in the lid of the container. For a while he twirled it around. "Mom, I think you should get him something. Can you?"

I went down to the machines in the basement and got Joseph an ice-cream sandwich. I put it on his dinner tray. I said, "Joseph, this is for you." His arm stayed where it was. I touched his shoulder. "Do you like ice cream?" I said loudly.

Mrs. Rodriguez, who was sitting beside the next bed, talking to her son Emilio, whispered to me fiercely. *"Loco. Muy loco.* You understand? No good here. No good."

She wasn't wrong. I couldn't argue. The ice-cream sandwich was melting, oozing through its paper wrapping. I went back to Nicky and took him for his walk.

Later, out in the corridor, we saw Joseph. He took a swipe at Nicky's cast as we passed him and yelled after us, "Dragon Man and the Mom!" There was chocolate smeared all over his mouth.

THE NEXT DAY I bought an extra egg roll at the takeout place. It seemed I'd have to keep on with what I'd started, though I had no idea how much Joseph would remember. I kept thinking of him during visiting hours, lying there alone. What I really wanted was to walk into Room K and find him gone, some other arrangement made, so I could remove him from the list of everything that troubled me.

When I got to the hospital, some of the other parents were there, earlier than usual. They were standing in the corridor near the head nurse's desk. One of the mothers had her arm around Mrs. Rodriguez, who was wiping her eyes with some Kleenex. They gestured to me to join them. "The supervisor is coming to talk to us about our problem," someone said.

"What happened?" I asked Mrs. Rodriguez.

She blew her nose; it seemed hard for her to speak. "Joseph! Joseph! Who do you think?"

Joseph had somehow gotten hold of some cigarettes and matches. He had held a lighted match near Emilio's eyes. "To burn my son!" cried Mrs. Rodriguez. Emilio was only eight, a frail little boy with a broken collarbone.

I put down my shopping bag and waited with the others. When the supervisor came, I spoke up, too. Irresponsibility, negligence, lack of consideration—the words came so fluently, as if from the mouth of the kind of person I'd always distrusted, some person with very sure opinions about rightness and wrongness and what was good for society.

The supervisor already had his computer working on the situation. "Just give us an hour," he said.

In Room K an orderly had been posted to keep an eye on Joseph. He'd made Joseph lie down on his bed. The children were subdued; they talked in murmurs. Even the television was on low, until a parent turned up the volume. There was an effort to create the atmosphere of the usual picnic.

Nicky looked wide-eyed, pale. "Did you hear what Joseph did to Emilio?"

I leaned over him and pushed the wet hair off his forehead. "Nicky, don't worry about Joseph anymore. They're going to move him in a little while to a room by himself."

I started opening containers from the Chinese takeout place, and there was the egg roll I'd meant to give Joseph. I angled my chair so that I wouldn't have to see him. It was as though life were full of nothing but intolerable choices.

"Eat something," I said to Nicky.

In a loud, dazed voice, a kid in the room was talking on the phone. "Hey, Grandma, guess who this is? I'm gonna see you soon, you bet. I'm gonna get on a plane and fly. Yeah, I'll bring my little bathing suit. Gonna see you, Grandma. Gonna see you."

"Mom," Nicky whispered. "Can you hear him?"

WE WERE THERE when he left, everyone was there. Two nurses

came in and walked over to him. "Joseph, it's time to get moving now," one of them said. "Let's get your personal things together."

They got him out of bed very quickly. One took his suitcase; the other had him by the arm. The orderly positioned himself in front of them. Nicky turned his face into the pillow when they started walking between the rows of beds. I was holding his hand and he kept squeezing my fingers, not letting go.

As he passed by us, Joseph broke away from the nurse. For a moment he loomed over Nicky and me. He kissed me on the top of the head. Then they took him out into the long, dim corridors.

WHEN NICKY WAS thirteen, he said he couldn't remember much about his childhood. He wanted to, but he couldn't. The whole subject made him very angry. "What I remember," he said, "is Joseph."

Nicky got well but he got old.

PICKING PLUMS

(AUGUST 1992)

Bernard Cooper

IT HAS BEEN nearly a year since my father fell while picking plums. The bruises on his leg have healed, and except for a vague absence of pigmentation where the calf had blistered, his recovery is complete. Back in the habit of evening constitutionals, he navigates the neighborhood with his usual stride—"Brisk," he says, "for a man of eighty-five"—dressed in a powder blue jogging suit that bears the telltale stains of jelly doughnuts and Lipton tea, foods which my father, despite doctor's orders, hasn't the will to forsake.

He broke his glasses and his hearing aid in the fall, and when I first stepped into the hospital room for a visit, I was struck by the way my father—head cocked to hear, squinting to see—looked so much older and more remote, a prisoner of his failing senses. "Boychik?" he asked, straining his face in my general direction. He fell back into a stack of pillows, sighed a deep sigh, and without my asking described what had happened:

"There they are, all over the lawn. Purple plums, dozens of them. They look delicious. So what am I supposed to do? Let the birds eat them? Not on your life. It's my tree, right? First I fill a bucket with the ones from the ground. Then I get the ladder out of the garage. I've climbed the thing a hundred times before. I make it to the top, reach out my hand, and . . . who knows what happens. Suddenly I'm an astronaut. Up is down and vice versa. It happened so fast I didn't have time to piss in my pants. I'm flat on my back, not a breath in me. Couldn't have called for help if I tried. And the pain in my leg—you don't want to know."

"Who found you?"

"What?"

I move closer, speak louder.

"Nobody found me," he says, exasperated. "Had to wait till I could get up on my own. It seemed like hours. I'm telling you, I thought it was all over. But eventually I could breathe normal again and—don't ask me how; God only knows—I got in the car and drove here myself." My father shifted his weight and grimaced. The sheet slid off his injured leg, the calf swollen, purple as a plum, what the doctor called "an insult to the tissue."

THROUGHOUT MY BOYHOOD my father possessed a surplus of energy, or it possessed him. On weekdays he worked hard at the office, and on weekends he gardened in our yard. He was also a man given to unpredictable episodes of anger. These rages were never pre-cipitated by a crisis—in the face of illness or accident my father remained steady, methodical, even optimistic; when the chips were down he was an incorrigible joker, an inveterate backslapper, a sentry at the bedside—but something as simple as a drinking glass left out on the table could send him into a frenzy of invective. Spittle shot from his lips. Blood ruddied his face. He'd hurl the glass against the wall.

His temper rarely intimidated my mother. She'd light a Tareyton, stand aside, and watch my father flail and shout until he was purged of the last sharp word. Winded and limp, he'd flee into the living room, where he would draw the shades, sit in his wing chair, and brood for hours.

Even as a boy, I understood how my father's profession had sullied his view of the world, had made him a wary man, prone to explosions. He spent hours taking depositions from jilted wives and cuckolded husbands. He conferred with a miserable clientele: spouses who wept, who spat accusations, who pounded his desk in want of revenge. At the time, California law required that grounds for divorce be proven in court, and toward this end my father carried in his briefcase not only the usual legal tablets and manila files but bills for motel rooms, matchbooks from bars, boxer shorts blooming with lipstick stains.

After one particularly long and vindictive divorce trial, he agreed to a weekend out of town. Mother suggested Palm Springs, rhapsodized about the balmy air, the cacti lit by colored lights, the street named after Bob Hope. When it finally came time to leave, however, my mother kept thinking of things she forgot to pack. No sooner would my father begin to back the car out of the driveway than my mother would shout for him to stop, dash into the house, and retrieve what she needed. A carton of Tareytons. An aerosol can of Solarcaine. A paperback novel to read by the pool. I sat in the backseat, motionless and mute; with each of her excursions back inside, I felt my father's frustration mount. When my mother insisted she get a package of Saltine crackers in case we got hungry along the way, my father glared at her, bolted from the car, wrenched every piece of luggage from the trunk, and slammed it shut with such a vengeance the car rocked on its springs.

Through the rear window, my mother and I could see him fling two suitcases, a carryall, and a makeup case yards above his balding head. The sky was a huge and cloudless blue; gray chunks of luggage sailed through it, twisting and spinning and falling to earth like the burned-out stages of a booster rocket. When a piece of luggage crashed back to the asphalt, he'd pick it up and hurl it again. With every effort, an involuntary, animal grunt issued from the depths of his chest.

Finally, the largest suitcase came unlatched in mid-flight. Even my father was astonished when articles of his wife's wardrobe began their descent from the summer sky. A yellow scarf dazzled the air like a tangible strand of sunlight. Fuzzy slippers tumbled down. One diaphanous white slip drifted over the driveway and, as if guided by an invisible hand, draped itself across a hedge. With that, my father barreled by us, veins protruding on his temple and neck, and stomped into the house. "I'm getting tired of this," my mother grumbled.

205

Before she stooped to pick up the mess—a vast and random geography of clothes—she flicked her cigarette onto the asphalt and ground the ember out.

ONE EVENING, LONG after I'd moved away from home, I received a phone call from my father telling me that my mother had died the night before. "But I didn't know it happened," he said.

He'd awakened as usual that morning, ruminating over a case while he showered and shaved. My mother appeared to be sound asleep, one arm draped across her face, eyes sheltered beneath the crook of her elbow. When he sat on the bed to pull up his socks, he'd tried not to jar the mattress and wake her. At least he *thought* he'd tried not to wake her, but he couldn't remember, he couldn't be sure. Things looked normal, he kept protesting—the pillow, the blanket, the way she lay there. He decided to grab a doughnut downtown and left in a hurry. But that night my father returned to a house suspiciously unlived-in. The silence caused him to clench his fists, and he called for his wife—"Lillian, Lillian"—as he drifted through quiet, unlit rooms, walking slowly up the stairs.

I once saw a photograph of a woman who had jumped off the Empire State Building and landed on the roof of a parked car. What is amazing is that she appears merely to have leapt into satin sheets, to be deep in a languid and absolute sleep. Her eyes are closed, lips slightly parted, hair fanned out on a metal pillow. Nowhere is there a trace of blood, her body caught softly in its own impression.

As my father spoke into the telephone, his voice about to break—"I should have realized. I should have known"—that's the state in which I pictured my mother: a long fall of sixty years, an uncanny landing, a miraculous repose.

MY FATHER AND I had one thing in common after my mother's heart attack: we each maintained a secret life. Secret, at least, from each other.

I'd fallen for a man named Travis Mask. Travis had recently arrived in Los Angeles from Kentucky, and everything I was accustomed to—

the billboards lining the Sunset strip, the 7-Elevens open all night—stirred in him a strong allegiance; "I love this town," he'd say every day. Travis's job was to collect change from food vending machines throughout the city. During dinner he would tell me about the office lobbies and college cafeterias he had visited, the trick to opening different machines, the noisy cascade of nickles and dimes. Travis Mask was enthusiastic. Travis Mask was easy to please. In bed I called him by his full name because I found the sound of it exciting.

My father, on the other hand, had fallen for a woman whose identity he meant to keep secret. I knew of her existence only because of a dramatic change in his behavior: he would grow mysterious as quickly and inexplicably as he had once grown angry. Though I resented being barred from this central fact of my father's life, I had no intention of telling him I was gay. It had taken me thirty years to achieve even a modicum of intimacy with the man, and I didn't want to risk a setback. It wasn't as if I was keeping my sexual orientation a secret; I'd told relatives, co-workers, friends. But my father was a man who whistled at waitresses, flirted with bank tellers, his head swiveling like a radar dish toward the nearest pair of breasts and hips. Ever since I was a child my father reminded me of the wolf in cartoons whose ears shoot steam, whose eyes pop out on springs, whose tongue unfurls like a party favor whenever he sees a curvaceous dame. As far as my father was concerned, desire for women fueled the world, compelled every man without exception—his occupation testified to that—was a force as essential as gravity. I didn't want to disappoint him.

Eventually, Travis Mask was transferred to Long Beach. In his absence my nights grew long and ponderous, and I tried to spend more time with my father in the belief that sooner or later an opportunity for disclosure would present itself. We met for dinner once a month in a restaurant whose interior was dim and crimson, our interaction friendly but formal, both of us cautiously skirting the topic of our private lives; we'd become expert at the ambiguous answer, the changed subject, the half-truth. Should my father ask if I was dating, I'd tell him yes, I had been seeing someone. I'd liked them very much, I said, but they were transferred to another city. Them. They. My attempt to neuter the pronouns made it sound as if I were courting people en masse. Just when I thought this subterfuge was becoming obvious, my father began to respond in kind: "Too bad I didn't get a chance to meet them. Where did you say they went?"

Avoidance also worked in reverse: "And how about you, Dad? Are you seeing anybody?"

"Seeing? I don't know if you'd call it *seeing*. What did you order, chicken or fish?"

During one dinner we discovered that we shared a fondness for nature programs on television, and from that night on, when we'd exhausted our comments about the meal or the weather, we'd ask if the other had seen the show about the blind albino fish that live in underwater caves, or the one about the North American moose whose antlers, coated with green moss, provide camouflage in the under-brush. My father and I had adapted like those creatures to the strictures of our shared world.

And then I met her.

I looked up from a rack of stationery at the local Thrifty one after-noon and there stood my father with a willowy black woman in her early forties. As she waited for a prescription to be filled, he drew a fin-ger through her hair, nuzzled the nape of her neck, the refracted light of his lenses causing his cheeks to glow. I felt like a child who was wit-ness to something forbidden: his father's helpless, unguarded ardor for an unfamiliar woman. I didn't know whether to run or stay. Had he always been attracted to young black women? Had I ever known him well? Somehow I managed to move myself toward them and mumble hello. They turned around in unison. My father's eyes widened. He reached out and cupped my shoulder, struggled to say my name. Before he could think to introduce us, I shook the woman's hand, star-tled by its softness. "So you're the son. Where've you been hiding?" She was kind and cordial, though too preoccupied to engage in much con-versation, her handsome features furrowed by a hint of melancholy, a sadness which I sensed had little to do with my surprise appearance. Anna excused herself when the pharmacist called her name.

Hours after our encounter I could still feel the softness of Anna's hand, the softness that stirred my father's yearning. He was seventy-five years old, myopic and hard of hearing, his skin loose and liver-spotted, but one glimpse of his impulsive public affection led me to the conclusion that my father possessed, despite his age, a restless sexual energy. The meeting left me elated, expectant. My father and I had something new in common: the pursuit of our unorthodox passions. We were, perhaps, more alike than I'd realized. After years of relative estrangement, I'd been given grounds for a fresh start, a chance to establish a stronger connection.

But none of my expectations mattered. Later that week they left the country.

THE PRESCRIPTION, IT turned out, was for a psychotropic drug. Anna had battled bouts of depression since childhood. Her propensity for unhappiness gave my father a vital mission: to make her laugh, to wrest her from despair. Anna worked as an elementary-school substitute teacher and managed a few rental properties in South-Central Los Angeles, but after weeks of functioning normally, she would take to my father's bed for days on end, blank and immobile beneath the quilt she had bought to brighten up the room, unaffected by his jokes, his kisses and cajoling. These spells of depression came without warning and ended just as unexpectedly. Though they both did their best to enjoy each other during the periods of relative calm, they lived, my father later lamented, like people in a thunderstorm, never knowing when lightning would strike. Thinking that a drastic change might help Anna shed a recent depression, they pooled their money and flew to Europe.

They returned with snapshots showing the two of them against innumerable backdrops: the Tower of London, the Vatican, Versailles; monuments, obelisks, statuary. In every pose their faces were unchanged, the faces of people who want to be happy, who try to be happy, and somehow can't.

As if in defiance of all the photographic evidence against them, they were married the following month at the Church of the Holy Trinity. I was one of only two guests at the wedding. The other was an uncle of Anna's. Before the ceremony began he shot me a glance which attested, I was certain, to an incredulity as great as mine. The vaulted chapel rang with prerecorded organ music, an eerie and pious overture. Light filtered through stained-glass windows, chunks of sweet color that reminded me of Jell-O. My old Jewish father and his Episcopalian lover appeared at opposite ends of the dais, walking step by measured step toward a union in the center. The priest, swimming in white vestments, was somber and almost inaudible. Cryptic gestures, odd props; I watched with a powerful, wordless amazement. Afterward, as if the actual wedding hadn't been surreal enough, my father and Anna formed a kind of receiving line (if two people can constitute a line) in the church parking lot, where the four of us, bathed by hazy sunlight, exchanged pleasantries before the newlyweds returned home for a nap; their honeymoon in Europe, my father joked, had put the cart before the horse.

During the months after the wedding, when I called my father, he answered as though the ringing of the phone had been an affront. When I asked him what the matter was he'd bark, "What makes you think there's something the matter?" I began to suspect that my father's frustration had given rise to those ancient rages. But my father had grown too old and frail to sustain his anger for long. When we saw each other—Anna was always visiting relatives or too busy or tired to join us—he looked worn, embattled, and the pride I had in him for attempting an interracial marriage, for risking condemnation in the eyes of the world, was overwhelmed now by concern. He lost weight. His hands began to shake. I would sit across from him in the dim, red restaurant and marvel that this bewildered man had once hurled glasses against a wall and launched Samsonite into the sky.

Between courses I'd try to distract my father from his problems by pressing him to unearth tidbits of his past, as many as memory would allow. He'd often talk about Atlantic City, where his parents had owned a small grocery. Sometimes my mother turned up in the midst of his sketchy regressions. He would smooth wrinkles from the tablecloth and tell me no one could take her place. He eulogized her loyalty and patience, and I wondered whether he could see her clearly—her auburn hair and freckled hands—wondered whether he wished she were here to sweep up after his current mess. "Remember," he once asked me, without a hint of irony or regret, "what fun we had in Palm Springs?" Then he snapped back into the present and asked what was taking so long with our steaks.

THE FINAL RIFT between my father and Anna must have happened suddenly; she left behind several of her possessions, including the picture of Jesus that sat on the sideboard in the dining room next to my father's brass menorah. And along with Anna's possessions were stacks of leather-bound books, *Law of Torts, California Jurisprudence,* and *Forms of Pleading and Practice,* embossed along their spines. Too weak and distracted to practice law, my father had retired, and the house became a repository for the contents of his former office. I worried about him being alone, wandering through rooms freighted with history, crowded with the evidence of two marriages, fatherhood, and a long and harrowing career; he had nothing to do but pace and sigh and stir up dust. I encouraged him to find a therapist, but as far as my father was concerned, psychiatrists were all conniving witch doctors who fed off the misery of people like Anna.

Brian, the psychotherapist I'd been living with for three years (and live with still), was not at all fazed by my father's aversion to his profession. They'd met only rarely—once we ran into my father at a local supermarket, and twice Brian accompanied us to the restaurant—but when they were together, Brian would draw my father out, compliment him on his plaid pants, ask questions regarding the fine points of law. And when my father spoke, Brian listened intently, embraced him with his cool, blue gaze. My father relished my lover's attention; Brian's cheerfulness and steady disposition must have been refreshing in those troubled, lonely days. "How's that interesting friend of yours?" he sometimes asked. If he was suspicious that Brian and I shared the same house, he never pursued it—until he took his fall from the plum tree.

I DROVE MY father home from the hospital, trying to keep his big unwieldy car, bobbing like a boat, within the lane. I bought him a pair of seersucker shorts because long pants were too painful and constricting. I brought over groceries and my wok, and while I cooked dinner my father sat at the dinette table, leg propped on a vinyl chair, and listened to the hissing oil, happy, abstracted. I helped him up the stairs to his bedroom, where we watched *Wheel of Fortune* and *Jeopardy* on the television and where, for the first time since I was a boy, I sat at his feet and he rubbed my head. It felt so good I'd graze his good leg, contented as a cat. He welcomed my visits with an eagerness bordering on glee and didn't seem to mind being dependent on me for physical assistance; he leaned his bulk on my shoulder wholly, and I felt protective, necessary, inhaling the scents of salve and Old Spice and the base, familiar odor that was all my father's own.

"You know those hostages?" asked my father one evening. He was sitting at the dinette, dressed in the seersucker shorts, his leg propped on the chair. The bruises had faded to lavender, his calf back to its normal size.

I could barely hear him over the broccoli sizzling in the wok. "What about them?" I shouted.

"I heard on the news that some of them are seeing a psychiatrist now that they're back."

"So?"

"Why a psychiatrist?"

I stopped tossing the broccoli. "Dad," I said, "if you'd been held hostage in the Middle East, you might want to see a therapist, too."

The sky dimmed in the kitchen windows. My father's face was a silhouette, his lenses catching the last of the light. "They got their food taken care of, right? And a place to sleep. What's the big deal?"

"You're at gunpoint, for God's sake. A prisoner. I don't think it's like spending a weekend at the Hilton."

"Living alone," he said matter-of-factly, "is like being a prisoner."

I let it stand. I added the pea pods.

"Let me ask you something," said my father. "I get this feeling— I'm not sure how to say it—that something isn't right. That you're keeping something from me. We don't talk much, I grant you that. But maybe now's the time."

My heart was pounding. I'd been thoroughly disarmed by his inter-
pretation of world events, his minefield of non sequiturs, and I wasn't
prepared for a serious discussion. I switched off the gas. The red jet
sputtered. When I turned around, my father was staring at his out-
stretched leg. "So?" he said.

"You mean Brian?"

"Whatever you want to tell me, tell me."

"You like him, don't you?"

"What's not to like."

"He's been my lover for a long time. He makes me happy. We have
a home." Each declaration was a stone in my throat. "I hope you
understand. I hope this doesn't come between us."

"Look," said my father without skipping a beat, "you're lucky to
have someone. And he's lucky to have you, too. It's no one's business
anyway. What the hell else am I going to say?"

But my father thought of something else before I could speak and
express my relief. "You know," he said, "when I was a boy of maybe sixteen, my father asked me to hold a ladder while he trimmed the tree in
our backyard. So I did, see, when I suddenly remember I have a date
with this bee-yoo-tiful girl, and I'm late, and I run out of the yard. I
don't know what got into me. I'm halfway down the street when I
remember my father, and I think, 'Oh, boy. I'm in trouble now.' But
when I get back I can hear him laughing way up in the tree. I'd never
heard him laugh like that. 'You must like her a lot,' he says when I help
him down. Funny thing was, I hadn't told him where I was going."

I pictured my father's father teetering above the earth, a man hugging the trunk of a tree and watching his son run down the street in
pursuit of sweet, ineffable pleasure. While my father reminisced, night
obscured the branches of the plum tree, the driveway where my mother's clothes once floated down like enormous leaves. When my father
finished telling the story, he looked at me, then looked away. A
moment of silence lodged between us, an old and obstinate silence. I
wondered whether nothing or everything would change. I spooned
our food onto separate plates. My father carefully pressed his leg to
test the healing flesh.

BATS

(JANUARY 1993)

Bia Lowe

THE BED IS too large. The sheets extend from my feet like a lip of an iceberg. Leagues beyond the cliffs of my bed is the freezing floor, a tundra where grotesques writhe in the dark like the souls in a Bosch purgatory. One figure always emerges from that swarm and steps into the center of my room. He wants to drain my body of its life by seducing me. And I know I will be powerless to stop him, as powerless as I am to keep my body from sleep, from sex, or even someday from death. And because I am unable to control my body or my life, I am terrified.

It is 1962 and I will soon be twelve years old. Thus far I have lived in fear of little but this vampire mythology. My father drinks, my parents fight, the bleak house trembles, but I fear only Dracula. In these olden days, the story of Dracula is a bedtime waking nightmare, a drama in which I stockade myself against the dark powers of annihilation. All children are fundamentalists, and every cell in my body is zealous to win the fight against the night, my small ego trying to sustain itself against the forces I cannot name.

In 1962 my parents travel through the Mediterranean. They are in their mid-forties, and looking back on it, I'm sure they were trying to rekindle the romance in their troubled marriage. Under the lax supervision of my grandmother, I spend hours alone in the woods. One day

I explore an old shack, a derelict chicken coop. The timbers are weathered to a pewter, and lichen, as finely laced as antimacassars, have grafted themselves to the siding. At first glance there is little inside to sustain my intrigue, some ancient straw and a few daddy longlegs. Then I notice something furry in a crack near the doorjamb. I poke it with my finger but nothing happens. I poke again. This time a small claw strikes back, calling my bluff. I feel silly to be reprimanded by such a small creature, but I don't push my luck. It's the first time I've ever seen a bat. I don't remember how I know what it is, with only a claw and a patch of fur to go by, but there's no mistaking it.

The little foot shredding the air between us has permanently marred the membrane between the real and the make-believe. From that day forward I try to strike a compromise between the tiny creature in the doorjamb and the emblem of my dread.

I'M NOW IN my forties, as old as my parents were in 1962. I look at their worn passport pictures and see them both reflected in my mirror. When I was a child it took forever for their likenesses to float up to the surface of my reflection. Then I'd scour my image for their traits, hoping to recognize the hybrid confluence of genes, as if some taproot plumbed the strata of my predecessors and could ground me securely in myself. Now my face seems haunted by expressions from which I'd give anything to be cut free—mother's resignation, father's trapdoor pout.

Blessedly there is also mystery in my face, a dark physics (the closer you get the more it eludes you), a void at the gate of the pupil, a peephole to the great by-and-by. This is what keeps me glued to the mercurial glass, a hint of something other about me. The faces of bats are a little like that, a little like missing the last step of a staircase, a little (bear with me) like falling in love.

Bats' ugliness is appealing, the way a lover's least attractive feature can fill you with hopeless lust. Their nostrils blossom into radar dishes, heraldic bracts more suited to the armature of beetles. Here's a guy about the size of a hamster. His ears resemble the translucent leaves at the core of a head of romaine. He's got two little smokestacks coming out of his nostrils and a set of pearly whites as friendly as pinking shears. Another guy's got the ace of spades for a nose and a lower lip like a drip of pink frosting. Here's a face like a magnified spore, another like genitals that have been under water too long.

THERE WAS A time when all mammals shared a common face, the jittery, bug-eyed kisser of a marsupial shrew. A time before the dim winter choked the sky with dust and the last elephantine lizards grew torpid and fell. But once the cold stiffened those flat feet and the thunder through the marshlands stilled, the hirsute shrew multiplied, and the age of the warm-bloodeds began.

The waters of the New World teemed with turtles and crocodiles, the modified reptiles, but we'd be hard-pressed to spot our kin among the creatures we'd find there. Elephants looked like warthogs; dogs, arboreal weasels. We were small as lemurs, still clinging to branches, relying on our sense of smell. Bats, however, were sprinters on the evolutionary track and soon looked remarkably like themselves. While our limbs took painstaking millennia to grow beyond a childhood of rodentia, their fingers already extended, Caligari-like, to support the opened umbrella of their wings. Some varieties of bats sprouted elaborate nose florets, instruments for the broadcasting of ultrasonic signals, and fantastic ears to retrieve those signals once they'd ricocheted. These were sophisticated creatures who navigated vast distances and pollinated the new flora of the ancient world, who knew the Earth eons before we were able to snapshot it with history. They were skimming the rising mists for airborne insects, sowing seeds with their guano, leaving their fossil remains among thousands of now-outmoded species. They watched as deserts expanded, glaciers retreated, oceans swelled and shriveled.

No wonder we fear them. In the presence of bats we sense the occurrence of time before us. In their impossible faces we see a life that eludes us, centuries of caves, forests of unfamiliar trees, Edens buried under rubble. We are like Nabokov's friend, who, upon seeing a home movie made before his birth, realized to his horror that "he did not exist there at all and that nobody mourned his absence."

Bats have always done their business when we're prone, unconscious, our worlds oblivious to each other. While our hands languish and our eyes close and we fly into our dreams, their hands fan open to support the drapery of flight. A skin as thin as an eyelid is stretched across the flare of their spidery finger bones. The umbrella opens and they're airborne, departing for God knows where at dusk, returning at dawn.

What does a bat hear as it flies over my city? The sighs of the crestfallen, the rattle of dice, the chatter of countless deals? And what would music look like to them—a mirage, a distracting collection of motes, a hallucination? The basso rondos of toads, the rosin scherzo of nightingales—would the whole paean of night swirl and glow like a Turner painting? And layer onto this the polyphony that soars at a register beyond our knowing—the ultrasonic arpeggios of lovesick moths, the madrigals of countless insects—how would each sound fit into the picture?

ONE MORNING IN 1962, after my parents have returned from their trip, I enter their bedroom to have my mother sign my blue books. She's disappeared from her half of the bed, but my father, propped on his elbow, volunteers his signature. I reach across the bed and offer up my exams, which are the color of robins' eggs. And as he autographs them and I smell the spice of his skin, I notice my mother's form concealed under the covers behind him.

Later that day I'm sent home from school with my first menstrual cramps. I lie in bed and savor my morning's discovery—the only time I ever suspected my parents of having sex—and study the present they've brought me from their travels. It's a piece of rock from the crypt of a sleeping pharaoh.

The pharaoh is wrapped for the deepest slumber imaginable. Mythology says that when he finally wakes he will fly out of his stone tomb and into the night. The world will be changed by the centuries. Great rivers will be diverted. Cities will cast their own starlight. This phantom will soar long after that light is dimmed, long after the cities are buried by rubble.

RECENTLY I WAS sitting with my mother in the house she has shared for twenty years with a new husband I've come to think of as a father. We rest our feet among piles of magazines on a small wooden coffee table. It's the oldest thing in the house that bears the stamp of my history: I remember the sour taste of its varnish, how my four-year-old tongue once traced the carved bodies that ran on all sides. I'd always thought they were the bodies of flying men or dogs in capes. "Are those *bats*?" I ask her.

"Yes, it's the first piece of furniture your father and I ever bought. We were living in a little flat in Chinatown. The Chinese believe bats bring happiness."

I imagined my parents then, smooth-skinned, thinner, little to live on but love. Their room is furnished with the donations of well-wishing relatives: a hooked rug, mismatched chairs, a creaky four-poster. I can't help thinking my mother likes being on top, that in those young days their sex is playful, their smell mingling with the smoke and ginger of the street. Near the bed, at the center of their new lives, is the table, bought for hope and a toss at the future. The bats draw back the seam of night, like coverlets for my parents to fall into, and sew that seam back up at dawn, like the last good-luck kiss before rising for work. These lovers are strangers to me, unparents, animals not yet flexing around the beginning of my life. Their cells mingle hundreds of times before a fluke will yank me from the Void.

A MICKEY MANTLE KOAN

(SEPTEMBER 1992)

David James Duncan

ON APRIL 6, 1965, my brother, Nicholas John Duncan, died of what his surgeons called "complications" after three unsuccessful open-heart operations. He was seventeen at the time—four years my elder to the very day. He'd been the fastest sprinter in his high school class until the valve in his heart began to close, but he was so bonkers about baseball that he'd preferred playing a mediocre JV shortstop to starring at varsity track. As a ballplayer he was a competent fielder, had a strong and fairly accurate arm, and stole bases with ease—when he could reach them. But no matter how much he practiced or what stances, grips, or self-hypnotic tricks he tried, he lacked the hand/eye magic that consistently lays bat-fat against ball, and remained one of the weakest hitters on his team.

John lived his entire life on the outskirts of Portland, Oregon—637 miles from the nearest major league team. In franchiseless cities in the Fifties and early Sixties there were two types of fans: those who thought the Yankees stood for everything right with America, and those who thought they stood for everything wrong with it. My brother was an extreme manifestation of the former type. He conducted a one-man campaign to notify the world that Roger Maris's sixty-one homers in '61 came in three fewer at bats than Babe Ruth's sixty in '27. He maintained—all statistical evidence to the contrary—that

221

Clete Boyer was a better third baseman than his brother, Ken, simply because Clete was a Yankee. He may not have been the only kid on the block who considered Casey Stengel the greatest sage since Solomon, but I'm sure he was the only one who considered Yogi Berra the second greatest. And, of course, Mickey Mantle was his absolute hero, but his tragic hero. The Mick, my brother maintained, was the greatest raw talent of all time. He was one to whom great gifts were given, from whom great gifts had been ripped away; and the more scarred his knees became, the more frequently he fanned, the more flagrant his limp and apologetic his smile, the more John revered him. And toward this single Yankee I, too, was able to feel a touch of reverence, if only because on the subject of scars I considered my brother an unimpeachable authority: he'd worn one from the time he was eight, compliments of the Mayo Clinic, that wrapped clear around his chest in a wavy line, like stitching round a clean white baseball.

Yankees aside, John and I had more in common than a birthday. We bickered regularly with our middle brother and little sister, but almost never with each other. We were both bored, occasionally to insurrection, by schoolgoing, churchgoing, and any game or sport that didn't involve a ball. We both preferred, as a mere matter of style, Indians to cowboys, hoboes to businessmen, Buster Keaton to Charlie Chaplin, Gary Cooper to John Wayne, deadbeats to brownnosers, and even brownnosers to Elvis Presley. We shared a single cake on our joint birthday, invariably annihilating the candle flames with a tandem blowing effort, only to realize that we'd once again forgotten to make a wish. And when the parties were over or the house was stuffy, the parents cranky or the TV shows insufferably dumb, whenever we were restless, punchy, or just feeling as if there was nothing to do, catch— with a hard ball—is what John and I did.

We were not exclusive, at least not by intention: our father and middle brother and an occasional cousin or friend would join us now and then. But something in most everyone else's brain or bloodstream sent them bustling off to less contemplative endeavors before the real rhythm of the thing ever took hold. Genuine catch-playing occurs in a double limbo between busyness and idleness, and between what is imaginary and what is real. Also, as with any contemplative pursuit, it takes time, and the ability to forget time, to slip into this dual limbo and to discover (i.e., lose) oneself in the music of the game.

It helps to have a special place to play. Ours was a shaded, ninety-foot corridor between one neighbor's apple orchard and the other's stand of old-growth Douglas firs, on a stretch of lawn so lush and mossy it sucked the heat out of even the hottest grounders. I always stood in the north, John in the south. We might call balls and strikes for an imaginary inning or two, or maybe count the number of error-less catches and throws we could make (300s were common, and our record was high in the 800s). But the deep shade, the 200-foot firs, the mossy footing and fragrance of apples all made it a setting more conducive to mental vacationing than to any kind of disciplined effort. During spring-training months our catch occasionally started as a drill—a grounder, then a peg; another grounder, a peg. But as our movements became fluid and the throws brisk and accurate, the pre-tense of practice would inevitably fade, and we'd just aim for the chest and fire, *hissss pop! hissss pop!* until a meal, a duty, or total darkness forced us to recall that this was the real world in which even timeless pursuits come to an end.

Our talk must have seemed strange to eavesdroppers. We lived in our bodies during catch, and our minds and mouths, though still operative, were just along for the ride. Most of the noise I made was with the four or five pieces of Bazooka I was invariably working over, though when the gum turned bland, I'd sometimes narrate our efforts in a stream-of-doggerel play-by-play. My brother's speech was less voluminous and a bit more coherent, but of no greater didactic intent: he just poured out idle litanies of Yankee worship or even idler braggadocio à la Dizzy Dean, all of it artfully spiced with spat sunflower-seed husks.

BUT ONE DAY when we were sixteen and twelve, respectively, my big brother surprised me out there in our corridor. Snagging a low throw, he closed his mitt round the ball, stuck it under his arm, stared off into the trees, and got serious with me for a minute. All his life, he said, he'd struggled to be a shortstop and a hitter, but he was older now, and had a clearer notion of what he could and couldn't do. It was time to get practical, he said. Time to start developing obvious strengths and evading flagrant weaknesses. "So I've decided," he concluded, "to become a junk pitcher."

I didn't believe a word of it. My brother had been a "slugger worshiper" from birth. He went on embellishing his idea, though, and even made it sound rather poetic: to foil some muscle-bound fence-buster with an off-speed piece of crap that blupped off his bat like cow custard—this, he maintained, was the pluperfect pith of an attribute he called Solid Cool.

I didn't recognize until months later just how carefully considered this new junk-pitching jag had been. That John's throwing arm was better than his batting eye had always been obvious, and it made sense to exploit that. But there were other factors he didn't mention: like the sharp pains in his chest every time he took a full swing, or the new ache that half-blinded and sickened him whenever he ran full speed. Finding the high arts of slugging and base stealing physically impossible, he'd simply lowered his sights enough to keep his baseball dreams alive. No longer able to emulate his heroes, he set out to bamboozle those who thought they could. To that end he'd learned a feeble knuckler, a roundhouse curve, a submarine fastball formidable solely for its lack of accuracy, and was trashing his arm and my patience with his attempts at a screwball, when his doctors informed our family that a valve in his heart was rapidly closing. He might live as long as five years if we let it go, they said, but immediate surgery was best, since his recuperative powers were greatest now. John said nothing about any of this. He just waited until the day he was due at the hospital, snuck down to the stable where he kept his horse, saddled her up, and galloped away. He rode about twenty miles, to the farm of a friend, and stayed there in hiding for nearly two weeks. But when he snuck home one morning for clean clothes and money, my father and a neighbor caught him, and first tried to force him but finally convinced him to have the operation and be done with it.

Once in the hospital he was cooperative, cheerful, and unrelenting-ly courageous. He survived second, third, and fourth operations, several stoppings of the heart, and a nineteen-day coma. He recovered enough at one point, even after the coma, to come home for a week or so. But the overriding "complication" to which his principal surgeon kept making oblique references turned out to be a heart so ravaged by scalpel wounds that an artificial valve had nothing but shreds to be sutured to. Bleeding internally, pissing blood, John was moved into an oxygen tent in an isolated room, where he remained fully conscious, and fully determined to heal, for two months after his surgeons had abandoned him. And, against all odds, his condition stabilized, then began to improve. The doctors reappeared and began to discuss, with obvious despair, the feasibility of a fifth operation.

Then came the second "complication": staph. Overnight, we were reduced from genuine hope to awkward pleas for divine intervention. We invoked no miracles. Two weeks after contracting the infection, my brother died.

AT HIS FUNERAL, a preacher who didn't know John from Judge Kenesaw Mountain Landis eulogized him so lavishly and inaccurately that I was moved to a state of tearlessness that lasted for four years. It's an unenviable task to try to make public sense of a private catastrophe you know little about. But had I been in that preacher's shoes, I would have mentioned one or two of my brother's actual attributes, if only to reassure late-arriving mourners that they hadn't wandered into the wrong funeral. The person we were endeavoring to miss had, for instance, been a C student all his life, had smothered everything he ate with ketchup, had diligently avoided all forms of work that didn't involve horses, and had frequently gone so far as to wear sunglasses indoors in the relentless quest for Solid Cool. He'd had the disconcerting habit of sound-testing his pleasant baritone voice by bellowing *"Beeeeeee-Ooooooooooo!"* down any alley or hallway that looked like it might contain an echo. He'd had an interesting, slangy obliviousness to proportion: any altercation, from a fistfight to a world war, was "a rack"; any authority, from our mother to the head of the U.N., was "the Brass"; any pest, from the kid next door to Khrushchev, was "a buttwipe"; and any kind of ball, from a BB to the sun, was "the orb."

225

He was brave: whenever anybody his age harassed me, John warned him once and beat him up the second time, or got beat up trying. He was also unabashedly, majestically vain. He referred to his person, with obvious pride, as "the Bod." He was an immaculate dresser. And he loved to stare at himself, publicly or privately—in mirrors, windows, puddles, chrome car-fenders, upside-down in teaspoons—and to solemnly comb his long auburn hair over and over again, like his hero, Edd ("Kookie") Byrnes, on *77 Sunset Strip.*

His most astonishing attribute, to me at least, was his never-ending skein of girlfriends. He had a simple but apparently efficient rating system for all female acquaintances: he called it "percentage of Cool versus percentage of Crud." A steady girlfriend usually weighed in at around 95 percent Cool, 5 percent Crud, and if the Crud level reached 10 percent it was time to start quietly looking elsewhere. Only two girls ever made his "100 percent Cool List," and I was struck by the fact that neither was a girlfriend and one wasn't even pretty: whatever "100 percent Cool" was, it was not skin-deep. No girl ever came close to a "100 percent Crud" rating, by the way: my brother was chivalrous.

John was not religious. He believed in God, but passively, with nothing like the passion he had for the Yankees. He seemed a little more friendly with Jesus. "Christ is cool," he'd say, if forced to show his hand. But I don't recall him speaking of any sort of goings-on between them until he casually mentioned, a day or two before he died, a conversation they'd just had, there in the oxygen tent. And even then John was John: what impressed him even more than the fact of Christ's presence or the consoling words He spoke was the natty suit and tie He was wearing.

ON THE MORNING after his death, April 7, 1965, a small brown-paper package arrived at our house, special delivery from New York City, addressed to John. I brought it to my mother and leaned over her shoulder as she sat down to study it. Catching a whiff of antiseptic, I thought at first that it came from her hair: she'd spent the last four months of her life in a straight-back chair by my brother's bed, and hospital odors had permeated her. But the smell grew stronger as she began to unwrap the brown paper, until I realized it came from the object inside.

It was a small, white, cylindrical, cardboard bandage box. "Johnson & Johnson," it said in red letters. "12 inches x 10 yards," it added in blue. Strange. Then I saw it had been split in half by a knife or a scalpel and bound back together with adhesive tape: so there was another layer, something hiding inside.

My mother smiled as she began to rip the tape away. At the same time, tears were landing in her lap. Then the tape was gone, the little cylinder fell away, and inside, nested in tissue, was a baseball. Immaculate white leather. Perfect red stitching. On one cheek, in faint green ink, the signature of American League president Joseph Cronin and the trademark REACH. THE SIGN OF QUALITY. And on the opposite cheek, with bright blue ballpoint ink, a tidy but flowing hand had written, *To John—My Best Wishes. Your Pal, Mickey Mantle. April 6, 1965.*

The ball dwelt upon our fireplace mantel—an unintentional pun on my mother's part. We used half the Johnson & Johnson box as a pedestal, and for years I saved the other half, figuring that the bandage it once contained had held Mantle's storied knee together for a game.

Even after my mother explained that the ball came not out of the blue but in response to a letter, I considered it a treasure. I told all my friends about it, and invited the closest to stop by and gawk. But gradually I began to see that the public reaction to the ball was disconcertingly predictable. The first response was usually, "Wow! Mickey Mantle!" But then they'd get the full story: "Mantle signed it the day he died? Your brother never even *saw* it?" And that made them uncomfortable. This was not at all the way an autographed baseball was supposed to behave. How could an immortal call himself your "Pal," how could you be the recipient of The Mick's "Best Wishes," and still just lie back and die?

I began to share the discomfort. Over the last three of my thirteen years I'd devoured scores of baseball books, all of which agreed that a bat, program, mitt, or ball signed by a big-league hero was a sacred relic, that we *should* expect such relics to have magical properties, and that they *would* prove pivotal in a young protagonist's life. Yet here I was, the young protagonist. Here was my relic. And all the damned thing did, before long, was depress and confuse me.

I stopped showing the ball to people, tried ignoring it, found that this was impossible, tried instead to pretend that the blue ink was an illegible scribble and that the ball was just a ball. But the ink *wasn't* illegible: it never stopped saying just what it said. So finally I picked the ball up and studied it, hoping to discover exactly why I found it so troublesome. Feigning the cool rationality I wished I'd felt, I told myself that a standard sports hero had received a letter from a standard distraught mother, had signed, packaged, and mailed off the standard ingratiatingly heroic response, had failed to think that the boy he inscribed the ball to might be dead when it arrived, and so had mailed his survivors a blackly comic non sequitur. I then told myself, "That's all there is to it"—which left me no option but to pretend that I hadn't expected or wanted any more from the ball than I got, that I'd harbored no desire for any sort of sign, any imprimatur, any flicker of recognition from an Above or a Beyond. I then began falling to pieces for lack of that sign.

Eventually, I got honest about Mantle's baseball: I picked the damned thing up, read it once more, peered as far as I could inside myself, and admitted for the first time that I was *pissed*. As is always the case with arriving baseballs, timing is the key—and this cheery little orb was inscribed on the day its recipient lay dying and arrived on the day he was being embalmed! This was *not* a harmless coincidence: it was the shabbiest, most embittering joke that Providence had ever played on me. My best friend and brother was dead, dead, dead, and Mantle's damned ball and best wishes made that loss even less tolerable, and *that*, I told myself, really was all there was to it.

I hardened my heart, quit the baseball team, went out for golf, practiced like a zealot, cheated like hell, kicked my innocuous, naive little opponents all over the course. I sold the beautiful outfielder's mitt that I'd inherited from my brother for a pittance.

BUT, AS IS usual in baseball stories, that wasn't all there was to it.

I'd never heard of Zen koans at the time, and Mickey Mantle is certainly no roshi. But baseball and Zen are two pastimes that Americans and Japanese have come to revere almost equally: roshis are men famous for hitting things hard with a big wooden stick; a koan is a perfectly nonsensical or nonsequacious statement given by an old pro (roshi) to a rookie (layman or monk); and the stress of living with and meditating upon a piece of mind-numbing nonsense is said to eventually prove illuminating. So I know of no better way to describe what the message on the ball became for me than to call it a koan.

In the first place, the damned thing's batteries just wouldn't run down. For weeks, months, *years,* every time I saw those nine blithely blue-inked words they knocked me off balance like a sudden shove from behind. They were an emblem of all the false assurances of surgeons, all the futile prayers of preachers, all the hollowness of Good-Guys-Can't-Lose baseball stories I'd ever heard or read. They were a throw I'd never catch. And yet . . . REACH, the ball said. THE SIGN OF QUALITY.

So year after year I kept trying, kept hoping to somehow answer the koan.

I became an adolescent, enrolling my body in the obligatory school of pain-without-dignity called "puberty," nearly flunking, then graduating almost without noticing. I discovered in the process that some girls were nothing like 95 percent Crud. I also discovered that there was life after baseball, that America was not the Good Guys, that God was not a Christian, that I preferred myth to theology, and that, when it came to heroes, the likes of Odysseus, Rama, and Finn MacCool meant incomparably more to me than the George Washingtons, Davy Crocketts, and Babe Ruths I'd been force-fed. I discovered (sometimes prematurely or overabundantly, but never to my regret) metaphysics, wilderness, Europe, black tea, high lakes, rock, Bach, tobacco, poetry, trout streams, the Orient, the novel, my life's work, and a hundred other grown-up tools and toys. But amid these maturations and transformations there was one unwanted constant: in the presence of that confounded ball, I remained thirteen years old. One peek at the "Your Pal" koan and whatever maturity or wisdom or equanimity I possessed was repossessed, leaving me as irked as any stumped monk or slumping slugger.

IT TOOK FOUR years to solve the riddle on the ball. It was autumn when it happened—the same autumn during which I'd grown older than my brother would ever be. As often happens with koan solutions, I wasn't even thinking about the ball at the time. As is also the case with koans, I can't possibly describe in words the impact of the response, the instantaneous healing that took place, or the ensuing sense of lightness and release. But I'll say what I can.

The solution came during a fit of restlessness brought on by a warm Indian summer evening. I'd just finished watching the Miracle Mets blitz the Orioles in the World Series, and was standing alone in the living room, just staring out at the yard and the fading sunlight, feeling a little stale and fidgety, when I realized that this was *just* the sort of fidgets I'd never had to suffer when John was alive—because we'd always work our way through them with a long game of catch. With that thought, and at that moment, I simply saw my brother catch, then throw a baseball. It occurred neither in an indoors nor an outdoors. It lasted a couple of seconds, no more. But I saw him so clearly, and he then vanished so completely, that my eyes blurred, my throat and chest ached, and I didn't need to see Mantle's baseball to realize exactly what I'd wanted from it all along:

From the moment I'd first laid eyes on it, all I'd wanted was to take that immaculate ball out to our corridor on an evening just like this one, to take my place near the apples in the north, and to find my brother waiting beneath the immense firs to the south. All I'd wanted was to pluck that too-perfect ball off its pedestal and proceed, without speaking, to play catch so long and hard that the grass stains and nicks and the sweat of our palms would finally obliterate every last trace of Mantle's blue ink, until all he would have given us was a grass-green, earth-brown, beat-up old baseball. Beat-up old balls were all we'd ever had anyhow. They were all we'd ever needed. The dirtier they were, and the more frayed the skin and stitching, the louder they'd hissed and the better they'd curved. And remembering this—recovering in an instant the knowledge of how little we'd needed in order to be happy—my grief for my brother became palpable, took on shape and weight, color and texture, even an odor. The measure of my loss was precisely the difference between one of the beat-up, earth-colored, grass-scented balls that had given us such happiness and this antiseptic-smelling, sad-making, icon-ball on its bandage box pedestal. And as I felt this—as I stood there palpating my grief, shifting it around like a throwing stone in my hand—I fell through some kind of floor inside myself, landing in a deeper, brighter chamber just in time to feel something or someone tell me: *But who's to say we need even an old ball to be happy? Who's to say we couldn't do with less? Who's to say we couldn't still be happy—with no ball at all?*

And with that, the koan was solved.

I can't explain why this felt like such a complete solution. Reading the bare words, two decades later, they don't look like much of a solution. But a koan answer is not a verbal, or a literary, or even a personal experience. It's a spiritual experience. And a boy, a man, a "me," does not have spiritual experiences; only the spirit has spiritual experiences. That's why churches so soon become bandage boxes propping up antiseptic icons that lose all value the instant they are removed from the greens and browns of grass and dirt and life. It's also why a good Zen monk always states a koan solution in the barest possible terms. *"No ball at all!"* is, perhaps, all I should have written—because then no one would have an inkling of what was meant and so could form no misconceptions, and the immediacy and integrity and authority of the experience would be safely locked away.

THIS IS GETTING a bit iffy for a sports story. But jocks die, and then what? The brother I played a thousand games of catch with is dead, and so will I be, and unless you're one hell of an athlete so will you be. In the face of this fact, I find it more than a little consoling to recall how clearly and deeply it was brought home to me, that October day, that there is something in us which needs absolutely *nothing*—not even a dog-eared ball—in order to be happy. From that day forward the relic on the mantel lost its irksome overtones and became a mere autographed ball—nothing more, nothing less. It lives on my desk now, beside an old beater ball my brother and I wore out, and it gives me a satisfaction I can't explain to sit back, now and then, and compare the two—though I'd still gladly trash the white one for a good game of catch.

As for the ticklish timing of its arrival, I only recently learned a couple of facts that shed some light. First, I discovered—in a copy of the old letter my mother wrote to Mantle—that she'd made it quite clear that my brother was dying. So when The Mick wrote what he wrote, he knew perfectly well what the situation might be when the ball arrived. And second, I found out that my mother actually went ahead and showed the ball to my brother. True, what was left of him was embalmed. But what was embalmed wasn't all of him. And I've no reason to assume that the unembalmed part had changed much. It should be remembered, then, that while he lived my brother was more than a little vain, that he'd been compelled by his death to leave a handsome head of auburn hair behind, and that when my mother and the baseball arrived at the funeral parlor, that lovely hair was being prepared for an open-casket funeral by a couple of cadaverous-looking yahoos whose oily manners, hair, and clothes made it plain that they didn't know Kookie from Roger Maris or Solid Cool from Kool-Aid. What if this pair took it into their heads to spruce John up for the hereafter with a Bible camp cut? Worse yet, what if they tried to show what sensitive, accommodating artists they were and decked him out like a damned Elvis the Pelvis *greaser?* I'm not trying to be morbid here. I'm just trying to state the facts. "The Bod" my brother had very much enjoyed inhabiting was about to be seen for the last time by all his buddies, his family, and a girlfriend who was only 1.5 percent Crud, and the part of the whole ensemble he'd been most fastidious about—the coiffure—was completely out of his control! He *needed* best wishes. He needed a pal. Preferably one with a comb.

Enter my stalwart mother, who took one look at what the two rouge-and-casket wallahs were doing to the hair, said, "No, no, no!", produced a snapshot, told them, "He wants it *exactly* like this," sat down to critique their efforts, and kept on critiquing until in the end you'd have thought John had dropped in to groom himself.

Only then did she ask them to leave. Only then did she pull the autographed ball from her purse, share it with her son, read him the inscription.

As is always the case with arriving baseballs, timing is the key. Thanks to the timing that has made The Mick a legend, my brother, the last time we all saw him, looked completely himself.

I return those best wishes to my brother's pal.

About the Authors

Shirley Abbott is the author of *Womenfolks: Growing Up Down South* and *The Bookmaker's Daughter*. She is currently at work on a book about modern love.

Nicholas Bromell teaches in the English department at the University of Massachusetts at Amherst. He is the author of *By the Sweat of the Brow: Literature and Labor in Antebellum America*.

James Conaway teaches in the English department at the University of Pittsburgh. He is the author of *Napa: The Story of an American Eden* and the memoir *Memphis Afternoons*, of which "Absences" is a part.

Bernard Cooper is the author of *Maps to Anywhere* and *A Year of Rhymes*.

Bruce Duffy is the author of *The World As I Found It*. He is completing his second novel, *Memory of Our Lives Returning*.

David James Duncan is the author of two novels, *The River Why* and *The Brothers K*.

Louise Erdrich is the author of several novels, including *Tracks* and *The Beet Queen*. Her new novel, *The Bingo Palace*, is due out this year.

Richard Ford is the author of *The Sportswriter* and *Wildlife,* among other works.

Reginald Gibbons is the author of *Five Pears or Peaches,* from which "Between Father and Daughter" was excerpted, and *Maybe It Was So,* a volume of poetry. He teaches English at Northwestern University and is the editor of *TriQuarterly.* His forthcoming novel is *Sweetbitter.*

Joyce Johnson is the author of *Minor Characters: A Memoir, In the Night Café,* and *What Lisa Knew: The Truths and Lies of the Steinberg Case.* She is currently at work on a novel.

William Kittredge is the author of two collections of stories, *The Van Gogh Field* and *We Are Not in This Together.* His latest book is *Hole in the Sky: A Memoir.*

Verlyn Klinkenborg is the author of *Making Hay* and *The Last Fine Time.* "Notes for a Life Not My Own" originally appeared in *Fathers and Sons,* an anthology of essays. He is currently at work on a book about the Indian Health Service.

Bia Lowe is currently at work on *Wild Ride,* a collection of essays. "Bats," which first appeared in *The Kenyon Review,* will be included in the collection.

David Mamet is a writer, playwright, and director. His works include *American Buffalo, Glengarry Glen Ross, Speed the Plow,* and *Oleanna.*

Reynolds Price is the author of twenty-three books, including *Kate Vaiden* and *Blue Calhoun.* "A Day in the Life of a Porch" was excerpted from "The Lost Room," the introduction to *Out on the Porch: An Evocation in Words and Pictures.*

Bill Roorbach teaches in the humanities department at the University of Maine at Farmington. He is the author of *Summers with Juliet* and is currently working on a novel.

Scott Russell Sanders is the author of *Secrets of the Universe, In Limestone Country,* and *Staying Put: Making a Home in a Restless World.* He teaches in the English department at Indiana University.

Donna Tartt is the author of *The Secret History,* a novel, and is currently at work on her second novel.

Sallie Tisdale is a contributing editor at *Harper's Magazine.* Her latest work is *Stepping Westward: The Long Search for Home in the Pacific Northwest.* She is currently at work on a book about the metaphysics of sex.

ACKNOWLEDGMENTS